LIVING DETROIT

In *Living Detroit*, Brandon M. Ward argues that environmentalism in postwar Detroit responded to anxieties over the urban crisis, deindustrialization, and the fate of the city. Tying the diverse stories of environmental activism and politics together is the shared assumption environmental activism could improve their quality of life.

Detroit, Michigan, was once the capital of industrial prosperity and the beacon of the American Dream. It has since endured decades of deindustrialization, population loss, and physical decay – in short, it has become the poster child for the urban crisis. This is not a place in which one would expect to discover a history of vibrant expressions of environmentalism; however, in the post-World War II era, while suburban, middle-class homeowners organized into a potent force to protect the natural settings of their communities, in the working-class industrial cities and in the inner city, Detroiters were equally driven by the impulse to conserve their neighborhoods and create a more livable city, pushing back against the forces of deindustrialization and urban crisis. *Living Detroit* juxtaposes two vibrant and growing fields of American history which often talk past each other: environmentalism and the urban crisis. By putting the two subjects into conversation, we gain a richer understanding of the development of environmental activism and politics after World War II and its relationship to the crisis of America's cities.

This book will be of great interest to students and scholars in environmental, urban, and labor history.

Brandon M. Ward is a Lecturer in History at Perimeter College, Georgia State University, USA.

Routledge Equity, Justice, and the Sustainable City

Series editors: Julian Agyeman and Stephen Zavestoski

This series positions equity and justice as central elements of the transition toward sustainable cities. The series introduces critical perspectives and new approaches to the practice and theory of urban planning and policy that ask how the world's cities can become "greener" while becoming more fair, equitable, and just.

The *Routledge Equity Justice and the Sustainable City* series addresses sustainable city trends in the global North and South and investigates them for their potential to ensure a transition to urban sustainability that is equitable and just for all. These trends include municipal climate action plans; resource scarcity as tipping points into a vortex of urban dysfunction; inclusive urbanization; "complete streets" as a tool for realizing more "livable cities"; the use of information and analytics toward the creation of "smart cities."

The series welcomes submissions for high-level cutting-edge research books that push thinking about sustainability, cities, justice, and equity in new directions by challenging current conceptualizations and developing new ones. The series offers theoretical, methodological, and empirical advances that can be used by professionals and as supplementary reading in courses in urban geography, urban sociology, urban policy, environment and sustainability, development studies, planning, and a wide range of academic disciplines.

Living Detroit
Environmental Activism in an Age of Urban Crisis
Brandon M. Ward

The Green City and Social Injustice
21 Tales from North America and Europe
Edited by Isabelle Anguelovski and James J. T. Connolly

For more information about this series, please visit www.routledge.com/Routledge-Equity-Justice-and-the-Sustainable-City-series/book-series/EJSC

LIVING DETROIT

Environmental Activism in an
Age of Urban Crisis

Brandon M. Ward

LONDON AND NEW YORK

First published 2022
by Routledge
2 Park Square, Milton Park, Abingdon, Oxon OX14 4RN

and by Routledge
605 Third Avenue, New York, NY 10158

Routledge is an imprint of the Taylor & Francis Group, an informa business

© 2022 Brandon M. Ward

The right of Brandon M. Ward to be identified as author of this work
has been asserted by him in accordance with sections 77 and 78 of the
Copyright, Designs and Patents Act 1988.

All rights reserved. No part of this book may be reprinted or reproduced or
utilised in any form or by any electronic, mechanical, or other means, now
known or hereafter invented, including photocopying and recording, or in
any information storage or retrieval system, without permission in writing
from the publishers.

Parts of Chapter 6 appear in Brandon M. Ward, "Suburbs Against the
Region: Homeowner Environmentalism in 1970s Detroit," *Journal of
Planning History* 18 (May 2019): 83–101. Used by permission.

Trademark notice: Product or corporate names may be trademarks or
registered trademarks, and are used only for identification and explanation
without intent to infringe.

British Library Cataloguing-in-Publication Data

A catalogue record for this book is available from the British Library

Library of Congress Cataloging-in-Publication Data
A catalog record has been requested for this book

ISBN: 978-0-367-33443-7 (hbk)
ISBN: 978-0-367-33442-0 (pbk)
ISBN: 978-0-429-31991-4 (ebk)

DOI: 10.4324/9780429319914

Typeset in Bembo
by Apex CoVantage, LLC

In Memory of Kyle

CONTENTS

List of illustrations	*viii*
Acknowledgments	*x*
Archival abbreviations	*xiii*
Introduction: The many lives of Earth Day	*xvi*
1 Living just enough for Detroit	1
2 The environmental quest for a livable region	24
3 Factories, fields, and streams	47
4 The UAW confronts the urban environmental crisis	69
5 Black environmentalism in an age of urban crisis	90
6 Environmentalism in the fragmented metropolis	112
Epilogue: Age of crises	*140*
Index	*145*

ILLUSTRATIONS

Figures

0.1	Environmental Teach-In Kick-Off Rally, March 11, 1970, with a banner displaying a popular symbol of ecology.	xvii
1.1	First Lady Eleanor Roosevelt (center) with Josephine Fellows Gomon (left), Secretary of the Detroit Housing Commission, greeting reporters in Black Bottom, September 10, 1935.	2
1.2	View of Belle Isle in 1942. Belle Isle Bridge visible in lower left.	5
1.3	Map of Urban Renewal and Conservation Areas.	17
1.4	Construction of the Lodge Freeway, 1954.	18
2.1	Genevieve Gillette Portrait, Photograph by Loche Clute, Unknown year.	26
2.2	Westacres clubhouse with pond.	28
2.3	Advertisement promoting the referendum to establish the Metroparks system.	30
2.4	Walter Reuther and President Truman in Oval Office meeting, 1952.	33
3.1	A State conservation officer displays oil-sucked ducks, 1948.	57
3.2	An unidentified person scoops oil from the Detroit River, 1959.	62
4.1	Olga Madar portrait.	70
4.2	The Ford River Rouge Plant in Dearborn, Mich. When it opened in 1927, it was the largest industrial operation in the world.	75
5.1	West Central Organization members confront Mayor Cavanagh at his home.	95
6.1	Map showing the distribution of HCMA Metroparks.	119

Illustrations **ix**

| 7.1 | Conveyors at Ford River Rouge complex, with smokestacks in the background. | 141 |
| 7.2 | North Wall from Diego Rivera Murals. | 141 |

Maps

| 0.1 | Southeast Michigan counties and cities. | xv |
| 1.1 | Density of African-American population in Detroit, 1950. This map shows the latter-built Chrysler Freeway cutting through heart of black Detroit. | 9 |

ACKNOWLEDGMENTS

How does one sufficiently express gratitude to all of the people who were instrumental in seeing this book come to life after so many years of work? I can never adequately convey my appreciation, but I will try. A decade ago, this book began as a paper in a research seminar. I didn't realize I was jumping into a rabbit hole. On my first of many research trips to the Walter P. Reuther Library, I felt a strong pull to this topic and ever since I have wanted to do justice to what I still feel is the important story of ordinary people seeking to make a livable region facing difficult circumstances.

Archivists and librarians are the heroes of this book. Wayne State University and the Reuther Library have become dear places for me, providing a research home and hosting the North American Labor History conference, a most welcoming venue for a young scholar to present and develop their work. The Sam Fishman Travel Grant allowed me to spend a considerable part of one summer there, happily diving into the well-organized collections. I benefited from the help of William LeFevre, Louis Jones, and other archivists and pages. Elizabeth Clemens provided key help with book images. I was also lucky to call Bentley Historical Library at the University of Michigan a home for several research trips, thanks in part to a Mark C. Stevens Fellowship and archivist Karen Jania and Malgosia Myc. Myc provided kind help with image permissions.

At Purdue University, where I earned my doctorate, I was supported by great mentors, including Nancy Gabin, Jon Teaford, John Larson, Darren Dochuk, and Stacy Holden. To this day, whenever I need anything from Dr. Gabin, even just to catch up, she drops everything and makes it her priority. Everyone should get themselves a Dr. Gabin. But the special sauce was the community of graduate students. Well after we all went separate ways, I can still count on them for help. Mauricio Castro, Tim Lombardo, Sanket Desai, Tim Olin, Kara Kvaran, Karen Sonnelitter, Patrick Pospisek, Erica Morin, Nick Gaspar, Jeff Perry, Trevor Burrows,

Acknowledgments **xi**

Josh Jeffers, the late Chris Snively, and many others – I appreciate you all. I think often about the many conferences we traveled to as poor graduate students, and let's face it, also as supposed professionals, cramming into comically small hostels, hotel rooms, and short-term rentals from New York to Chicago to Columbia, South Carolina. An extra big shout out to Andrew McGregor, who read several versions of nearly every chapter and kept pushing me to finish the book.

I will never know the names of anonymous people who showed up to conference panels and invited talks and asked tough questions and helpful questions-which-are-really-more-of-a-comments. You all are unsung heroes. But I can thank the incisive critiques from panelists, commenters, and scholars like Richard Fry, Brittany Bayless Fremion, James Longhurst, Lisa Fine, Andrew Kahrl, Tom Klug, John Beck, Eugene Moehring, Ryan Reft, Andrew Hurley, Brinda Sarathy, and Dianne D. Glave. Josiah Rector has been a frequent collaborator on conference panels, and has provided unending encouragement and generous support from early in the project's inception.

As a contingent faculty member, my road to publishing this book has been unique. What my institution Georgia State University – Perimeter College could not give me in research support, the faculty and students there have more than made up by pushing me to be the best teacher-scholar I could possibly be. The well-kept secret of community colleges is the impressive research and writing that takes place despite challenging teaching loads. We do it because we have stories that deserve to be told, even on top of teaching six or seven classes in a semester. I'm lucky to call these colleagues my friends and inspiration: Marc Zayac, Claudette Tolson, Will Simson, George Pabis, John Mack, Otto Burianek, George Vargis, Robert Woodrum, John Farris, Lauren MacIvor Thompson, and too many others to name. Our department administrative assistant Johnetta Hawkins is a legitimate rock star.

It was a pleasure to publish with Routledge Press. I am especially grateful for acquisitions editor Rebecca Brennan believing in this project and advocating for its publication, and for Grace Harrison shepherding it through. The two editorial assistants I worked with deserve a raise: Oindrila Bose and Rosie Anderson. The anonymous reviewers were generous with their feedback and comments, and made this a better book. Every scholar should be as lucky to have anonymous reviewers as helpful as mine.

I benefited from many Detroiters who helped me better understand a city to which I was an outsider. Detroit people are deservedly skeptical of outsiders. It meant the world to me that so many unionists, environmental activists, and Detroit residents trusted me to tell the environmental story of Detroit, helping me better understand the regional dynamics, union politics, and the day-to-day life of the city. I hope I have done them justice.

My friends have provided unending patience and support as I worked on a project that consumed a decade of my life. They have given me far more love and support than I gave in return. For years of graduate school and the writing of this book, I struggled with depression and anxiety disorders that often made me a

xii Acknowledgments

miserable person to love. And yet they did so anyway. Maybe I'm not supposed to talk about this in a book, but it's important to me to let others know that they are not alone.

When I say that I've been a difficult person to love, I especially think of my partner Katie Kerr, who has stuck with me through living apart in different states during seven years of graduate school, and maybe worse, then having to live in the same apartment with me afterward. She is the most amazing person I know, and yet she somehow decides to spend her time with me. Thanks also to her wonderful family for making me one of their own. Finally, I must acknowledge the pets who accompanied me on this journey: Honey, Brown Noser, Roo, Phanton, Pickle Beans, and Buddy – you *probably* can't read this, but thanks for the companionship.

My family has been incredible. I will always be grateful for my grandparents, whose stories of the Great Depression, the Dust Bowl on the plains of Colorado and Oklahoma, World War II and beyond always thrilled me, and gave me a love of history. Mom and Dad are the most selfless people you will ever meet, and never stopped believing in me. I have been so blessed to have brilliant, empathic, hilarious, and supportive siblings. Laura visits from out of state whenever she can to pull me out of my ruts. Just before I finished my book, my younger brother Kyle died from complications due to Duchenne muscular dystrophy. I will never get over it. Kyle and I used to have telephone conversations entirely in quotes from shows like *Seinfeld*. "You don't even know what a write-off is." This book is dedicated to his memory.

ARCHIVAL ABBREVIATIONS

Bentley Historical Library, University of Michigan, Ann Arbor (BHL)

COSS	Citizens Opposed to Super Sewer Collection
DUL	Detroit Urban League Records
GG	Genevieve Gillette Papers
JL	Janet Lynn Papers
JVC	Jack Van Coevering Collection
LWV-DDH	League of Women Voters, Dearborn-Dearborn Heights Papers
MCATS	Michigan Citizens Against Toxic Chemicals Collection
MCRC	Mill Creek Research Council Collection
SCMC	Sierra Club Mackinac Chapter Collection
SEMCOG-P	Southeast Michigan Council of Governments, Publications Collection

River Rouge Public Library, Michigan (RRPL)

State Library of Michigan, Lansing (SLM)

Walter P. Reuther Library, Archives of Labor and Urban Affairs, Wayne State University, Detroit (ALUA)

DC	David Cohen Papers
DRM	Detroit Revolutionary Movement Records
DUDARP	Developing Urban Detroit Area Research Project Collection
EC	Edward Connor Collection
GE	George C. Edwards, Jr. Papers

xiv Archival abbreviations

IEB-OH	International Executive Board Oral Histories Collection
MR	Mel Ravitz Collection
MJ	Mildred Jeffrey Collection
NAACP-DB	NAACP Detroit Branch Collection
NDI	New Detroit, Inc. Collection
OM	Olga Madar Papers
RC	Roger Craig Collection
SEMCOG	Southeast Michigan Council of Governments Collection
TWS	Thomas W. Stephens Collection
UAW-CRD	United Automobile Workers – Conservation and Recreation Departments Collection
UAW-CRD-MJ	United Automobile Workers – Community Relations Department – Mildred Jeffrey Collection
UAW-HSD	United Automobile Workers – Health and Safety Department Records
UAW-PAD-RRF	United Automobile Workers – Political Action Department – Roy Reuther Files Papers
UAW-PO-WPR	United Automobile Workers – President's Office – Walter P. Reuther Collection
UAW-RD	United Automobile Workers-Recreation Department Records
UCSSR	United Community Services Studies and Reports Collection
UEC	Urban Environment Conference Collection
USCSF	United Community Services Central Files Collection
WGF	William G. Fredrick Collection

Archival abbreviations **xv**

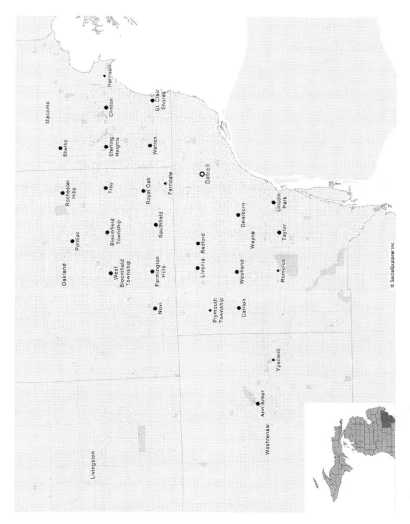

MAP 0.1 Southeast Michigan counties and cities.
Source: Created using SocialExplorer, Inc.

INTRODUCTION

The many lives of Earth Day

Detroit, Michigan, was an unlikely metropolitan region to demonstrate an outpouring of environmental activism on April 22, 1970, during the nation's first Earth Day. After all, the Motor City was the birthplace of the automotive industry, and, despite distressing evidence of deindustrialization, the region remained thoroughly identified with its factories. As in cities throughout the United States, Detroit showed that a vast, untapped support for environmental activism could be mobilized.

Earth Day festivities and protests were made possible by college students some 30 miles west of downtown, in suburban Ann Arbor at the University of Michigan. It was there that an Environmental Teach-In held one month earlier became the basis for the nation-wide activities on Earth Day. The first day of the Environmental Teach-In on March 11 featured students putting a car on trial. Detroit's identity was thoroughly implicated with the automobile and autoworkers. At the mock trial, students gave testimony, blaming the car for causing pollution, exacerbating inequality, and etching into American culture an inextricable dependency. Other advocates pressed for wilderness preservation, recycling programs, an end to the Supersonic Transport (SST) airliner, clean-up of the Huron River, and an array of other causes. Filling a 13,000-seat auditorium with an energetic crowd listening to speakers that included Michigan Governor William Milliken, Wisconsin Senator Gaylord Nelson, United Auto Workers (UAW) president Water Reuther, and the cast of the musical *Hair*, the organizers set a momentous example for activists to replicate throughout the United States as they staged Earth Day one month later.[1]

Thirty miles to the east, in the industrial communities of downriver Detroit, workers had everything to lose by confronting their employers over pollution. Factories wielded the power of "environmental blackmail" to insist that pollution regulation would come at the expense of their jobs. And yet they showed up to Earth Day events anyway – by the hundreds – at events like one held at the Great

FIGURE 0.1 Environmental Teach-In Kick-Off Rally, March 11, 1970, with a banner displaying a popular symbol of ecology.

Source: University of Michigan News and Information Services. Bentley Historical Library, University of Michigan.

Lakes Steel facility at Zug Island in the Detroit River to hold a funeral for that body of water. As a bugler played "Taps," a seven-year-old boy from the nearby working-class suburb Lincoln Park held a sign asking, "DO I HAVE TO DIE YOUNG TO LET INDUSTRIAL POLLUTION LIVE?"[2] In the nearby town of River Rouge, students at Walter White Elementary School celebrated Earth Day with a surprise visit from the musician Stevie Wonder who played two songs and delivered an inspirational message.[3]

Six miles north, at Wayne State University in Midtown Detroit, festivities took on still another tenor. As consumer advocate Ralph Nader prepared to address the Earth Day audience, protesters leaped onto the stage, dumping trash they picked up along the highway. One of the activists laid out the stakes. "Dig it. By dumping the bags of garbage on the stage where the ecology teach-in was going on, we were asking the audience to consider urban renewal in the same light as ecology." Urban renewal was not merely a destructive practice imposed on neighborhoods and disrupting housing conditions – it was an environmental crisis. "Under capitalism," Ripple argued, "urban renewal is always going to be run in the interest of the same class that polluted the environment and then tries to convince us that the problem comes from our backyard incinerators and barbeque sets rather than from their smoke stacks."[4] Here, in inner-city Detroit, activists challenged the audience to see linkages between the environmental movement and the fight against destructive urban renewal programs, which disproportionately displaced African-American residents.

xviii Introduction

The *Detroit Free Press* noted in its coverage, "Earth Day: a life and death issue for some."[5] Across the region residents sometimes expressed global environmental concerns, but more often asked how their local environments could better support a decent quality of life. Suburbanites often focused on those features of environmentalism that promoted their vision of a quality life: open space nearby, respite from pollution emanating from across town, access to outdoor recreation, and freedom from the aspects of the urban crisis that seemed antithetical to wholesome suburban living. For working-class and inner-city residents, the fight for a livable Detroit took on a different meaning. Environmental activism was often an expression of the right to healthy communities. Downriver families, like the seven-year-old Lincoln Park boy, were asking: must we continue to trade our health and lives so that factories can pollute? African Americans in Detroit wondered how the emerging environmental movement spoke to their needs, insisting that environmental activism must also defend populations most vulnerable to neglected and hazardous urban environments.

Argument

Detroit's dramatic transformation in the twentieth century created starkly contrasting environments between the inner city, industrial neighborhoods and suburbs, middle-class suburbs, and the distant and wealthy exurbs. The inequalities that characterize Southeast Michigan are manifested in the built and natural environments of Southeast Michigan communities. The overdevelopment of the suburbs and the underdevelopment of the central city created deep environmental inequalities, contributing in part to the urban crisis.[6] As evidenced by the Earth Day accounts, environmental activism differed depending on the class, race, and location of the participants. As a result, I argue in this book, there was no monolithic environmental movement in Detroit or other metropolitan areas. Instead, "metropolitan environmentalism" consisted of disjointed goals, activities, and lived experiences as individuals sought to improve their quality of life, sometimes at the expense of other groups. Metropolitan transformations led Detroiters representing diverse race and class statuses to engage in a variety of environmental practices and politics, seeking to make their communities healthier, greener, and more environmentally and economically sustainable. In short, they all sought to make Detroit a more livable place. These communities, however, met on a deeply uneven playing field, leading suburbanites to gain far greater control over their environments than inner-city and working-class residents, who faced the brunt of the environmental consequences of the urban crisis.

The built and natural environment became a key front in the battle for a livable city against a backdrop of urban crisis. Relatively wealthy white suburbanites leveraged federal policy, property rights, and the power of local sovereignty to create environments that supported leisure and sustained investments in their properties. To many white homeowners in the suburbs, environmental activism represented a defense of property rights, a form of exclusion to prevent the urban crisis – and the black people they associated with it – from spilling into their neighborhoods. Less economically secure industrial workers fought for healthier workplaces and communities, using the might of their unions to challenge factory management and promote community health. Deindustrialization and capital flight eroded the power of unions and their activism, leaving workers unable to accomplish their vision of economic and environmental sustainability. Finally, the city's black residents found it most difficult to make their communities viable and sustainable places to live, despite monumental efforts to confront the overwhelming tides of the urban crisis. For these residents, they sought to overcome decades of racist policies and practices that restricted their ability to live in healthy and thriving neighborhoods. Federal policies and local practices consistently eroded their ability to create livable communities, and the story of much of the 1970s and beyond is the black struggle to reconstruct a more humane and just city.

Living metropolitan Detroit

Detroit's suburbs expanded and new residential developments absorbed the massive exodus of white Detroiters after World War II. These residents demanded healthy, wholesome environments, close to natural amenities. The rhetoric of quality of life came to dominate the goals of suburban boosters, policymakers, planners, and others. It increasingly represented a living condition defined in opposition to the urban crisis enveloping the city. As Detroit became a blacker, bleaker, more physically and environmentally devastated place, the suburbs came to emphasize and defend quality of life as an important policy goal. Through federal, state, and local policies, the suburbs defended their quality of life by walling off, to the extent possible, the consequences of the urban crisis and the African-American residents they associated with it.

At mid-century, Detroit's city and regional planners were at their most confident. The Great Depression and World War II limited the resources of planners and policymakers to contain the environmental consequences of industrialization and physical decay of the central city. The city known as the "Arsenal of Democracy" emerged from the war boasting the fourth largest population in the nation, a prosperous industrial base, and a citizenry and political establishment certain that it could produce both industrial prosperity and a decent living environment. "Harmony" and "balance" became buzzwords for the policymakers and planners seeking to build an environmentally and economically sustainable city and region. They marshaled the significant powers of zoning, the law, regional parks development, and federal subsidies for urban and regional development to work in service of this vision, thought the benefits primarily accrued to the white residents of the suburbs.

Industrial workers were at the front lines of witnessing corporate environmental abuse. Keenly aware that their workplaces produced the pollution that followed them home, beginning during World War II workers fought back. Protecting their homes, neighborhoods, and recreational landscapes where they would hunt, fish, and boat became a key early front in the fight for a healthier Detroit during the

1940s. Their environmental efforts started from the premise the Detroit could have both industrial prosperity and a healthful living environment. The unique perspective paved a middle ground between the preservationist ethos of groups like Sierra Club and the industrial lobby, which threatened that any environmental regulation would lead to factory closures. Although industry would later effectively weaponize "environmental blackmail" to dissuade workers from making common cause with environmentalists, for more than two decades after World War II, workers remained confident that they could have industrial jobs and a livable Detroit.

Segregation and poverty trapped African Americans in unhealthy neighborhoods. Often denied the opportunity to move, whether by violence, intimidation, or policy, black Detroiters redoubled their efforts to improve the neighborhoods where they lived. Toiling against overwhelming challenges, including a built environment that sacrificed health, city planners' efforts to bulldoze their neighborhoods, and severe residential segregation, black residents nevertheless showed tremendous commitment to improving the living conditions of Detroit. Middle-class African-American-led organizations often fought to improve living conditions in Detroit, but their efforts and activism sometimes reinforced destructive urban renewal practices that uprooted African Americans and failed to restore prosperity to the central city. Urban planners pushed African Americans out of physically deteriorating neighborhoods to promote urban renewal projects. Scattering into historically white neighborhoods, white Detroiters violently pushed back. Squeezed in the middle were African Americans.

Especially after the 1967 uprising in Detroit, African Americans made significant efforts to improve the living conditions of their neighborhoods amidst white flight, abandoned neighborhoods and factories, and declining city services.[7] The urban crisis – its flames fanned by destructive policies and urban planning practices – introduced significant barriers to living in healthy, viable neighborhoods, when their homes were surrounded by vacant lots, toxic industries, and few public green spaces. They responded by building small parks, fighting blight, and cleaning up their neighborhoods and abandoned lots in the absence of effective city services. Despite the tremendous structural pressures fomenting the urban crisis, ordinary residents and community organizations kept fighting for the city. Meanwhile, wealthier suburban Detroiters engaged in environmental activism to assert local control over their communities and ensure that unwanted land uses, urban sprawl, and the urban crisis would not spill into their neighborhoods. With greater wealth, political power, and effectiveness in utilizing environmental protection laws to their advantage, they defended their environmental privilege and contributed to regional environmental inequality.[8]

Foundations

The "urban crisis" has an important environmental story, but one which has until recently been a secondary focus of modern American historians. Scholars writing about the urban crisis often speak to the degradation of the built environment, but

Introduction **xxi**

usually as a backdrop to other important action such as civil rights activism, educational inequality, policing, metropolitan busing, residential segregation, the struggle for open housing, metropolitan political fragmentation, the fate of organized labor, and other key issues in post-World War II urban history. This book asks: what does urban history look like if we move the built and natural environments to the front of the history of the urban crisis? The environment becomes a key contested site on which metropolitan residents came into conflict over distributing the benefits and hazards of a modern industrial society. Structure and agency gain new meanings on this tilted axis. The decay of the built environment is often written as though it were thrust upon urban residents – federal policies, bulldozers, urban and regional planning maps, environmental impact statements, and other depersonalized tools of environmental control forced upon hapless residents. I explore the metropolitan environment as a key site of struggle in the urban crisis.[9] The African-American residents who organized neighborhood clean-up campaigns are important actors in this story, as are the suburban homeowners who joined environmental initiatives to ensure their communities would not change in aesthetics or demographics, locking in the patterns of white hegemony in the suburbs.

Many of the first historians writing about American environmental activism argued that it resulted from the growth post-World War II prosperity, and located it firmly in the suburbs. Sure, there were predecessors, conservation organizations like the Izaak Walton League, and the nature preservationists like the Sierra Club, some argue, but it was not until Americans moved *en masse* to the suburbs that environmentalism truly coalesced. With greater financial resources and leisure time, middle-class Americans now demanded "beauty, health, and permanence." Others, including scientists and federal government officials, agonized over the tremendous destruction wrought by suburban sprawl, creating environmental catastrophes like septic system failures and drained wetlands. Still others, historians argue, were driven to environmental concern out of greater proximity to beautiful rural-like settings and access to plentiful green space they were often denied as central city residents.[10] This book builds upon the work of these scholars, finding that environmental activism in the suburbs often represented a sincere attempt to make their communities healthy and sustainable. Yet the same activism was also wielded as a method of exclusion to ensure their communities remained white and prosperous amidst a deepening urban crisis in the central city.[11] Regional institutions like planning agencies and Metroparks, I argue, were powerful agents in this process.

Several scholars have demonstrated the disparate and sometimes "hidden" origins of environmentalism in the United States, often operating alongside, or in some cases preceding, the popularity of suburban and bourgeois environmentalism. These works challenge the notion that a single narrative can explain the varieties of environmentalism produced both in the United States and globally. Historians have examined the "urban and industrial roots" of environmentalism and have shown how cities and workplaces were often key sites of environmental struggle. Their works powerfully demonstrate the numerous routes Americans took toward environmental activism.[12]

xxii Introduction

Among the most important fountains of activism were the working-class communities, unions, and their factories, many of which were located in southwest Detroit and downriver industrial communities. In the working-class communities that once had celebrated belching smokestacks as a sign of industrial prosperity, to which they owed their livelihoods, by the 1940s, workers grew empowered to resist the factories polluting their communities. They asserted that it was possible to have both industrial prosperity and healthy communities if only the factories could be pushed toward environmental responsibility. For more than three decades, industrial workers, especially represented by the United Auto Workers union in Detroit, challenged the indiscriminate polluting of their communities and homes. Workers pushed the union to leverage its power against the polluters and to support environmental legislation in the 1960s. Throughout this heyday, the United Auto Workers union labored to make its home city of Detroit a livable place. Although union environmentalism eroded in the 1970s amidst global economic recession, deindustrialization, capital flight, and declining labor power, workers offered an alternative environmental activism, sensitive to issues of class, that was often missing from middle-class, suburban environmentalism. Historian Chad Montrie has written extensively about working-class environmentalism, including UAW efforts in Detroit. This book builds on his important works to place UAW and working-class environmentalism in the larger context of metropolitan development and urban crisis in Detroit.[13]

Scholars have similarly reassessed the role of African Americans and their relationship to environmental activism. Previously restricting what we defined as an "environmental" issue proved too narrow. Social scientists and historians have urged a redefinition of what constitutes environmental care and environmental work, finding a vibrant spectrum of advocacy covering everything from hunting rights, integration of national parks, garden clubs, environmental health of inner-city homes and neighborhoods, and much more.[14] Such scholarship has demonstrated the power of shifting our perspectives. This book builds upon their insights and makes more direct connections between resistance to so-called slum clearance and the growth of neighborhood conservation as an important form of urban environmental activism. Organizing neighborhood cleanups, gardening in vacant neighborhood lots, and engaging in tenant strikes against landlords who allowed their buildings to become rat infested represent urban environmental activism that should be considered alongside the quality-of-life environmentalism of the suburbs. In the inner city, however, these efforts often constituted an assertion of a basic right to live with dignity and health.

By focusing on the metropolitan region, this book incorporates insights of the suburban-centric environmental histories with those of historians focused on working-class and urban foundations of environmentalism.[15] Placing these stories alongside each other shows the synergies, divergences, and unequal access to power that shaped activists' efforts and effectiveness.[16] Detroit is an ideal setting to explore the various expressions of environmental activism amidst a period of extraordinary change between the 1930s and 1980s. For good reason, Detroit has long captured the public imagination and led historians to give the city significant scholarly treatment. Detroit's incubation of the auto industry, home of the United Auto Workers union, its moniker as the Arsenal of Democracy in World War II, and industrial prosperity are contrasted against the dramatic emergence of the urban crisis, punctuated with urban uprisings in 1943 and 1967. Since the 1970s, Detroit has gained a reputation as a city in perpetual crisis, from deindustrialization, to the media's frenzy over the crack cocaine epidemic in the 1980s, to the more recent fiscal challenges during the Great Recession, culminating in the city's declaration of bankruptcy in 2013. Throughout, the suburbs have been deeply implicated in these crises, assiduously resisting any shared commitment to the vitality of the region or its inner-city residents.

This book could not have been written without the enormous insights of environmental justice activists and scholars. By identifying "environmental racism," social scientists opened new vistas for understanding metropolitan inequalities and delivered a toolkit to people of color to better understand why they lived and labored under oppressive environmental conditions – and how to resist. They furthermore helped to re-center the targets of environmental activism as the places where we "work, live, and play," as environmental justice activist Dana Alston urged in her 1990 speech at the first People of Color Environmental Leadership Summit.[17] These are the everyday landscapes and environs at the center of this study. From the first significant environmental justice study commissioned by the United Church of Christ, *Toxic Wastes and Race* to Robert Bullard's pioneering investigations of waste facility siting, much of the early literature established the strong relationship between racial minorities and proximity to environmental hazards. Subsequent research showed the varieties of environmental discrimination faced by indigenous, ethnic and racial minority, disabled, and working-class people. Historians followed suit, with foundational work by Sylvia Hood Washington's *Packing Them In* (1994), which explored the long history of environmental inequality in Chicago, and Andrew Hurley, whose *Environmental Inequalities* (1994) remains a powerful study of the distribution of environmental privilege and injustice in Gary, Indiana.[18]

Notably, few of the individuals examined in this book were self-described environmentalists or conservationists. Prior to the late 1960s, the term environmentalist was rarely deployed to indicate a set of politics, activism, or ideology. Indeed, the *Detroit Free Press*, one of the city's two major dailies, did not print the word until 1970.[19] More often, environmental activists called themselves conservationists, but usually the term applied to those fighting to improve outdoor recreation, efficiently manage natural resources, or preserve wild landscapes, leaving out the significant efforts to improve the built and natural environments of the inner city. Applying our contemporary terminology of environmentalism to past struggles to improve the built and natural environments therefore creates pitfalls. Although I argue that environmental activism represented a broad effort by Detroiters to improve their living conditions in a rapidly transforming region, the categories used to define such activism have traditionally been constraining rather than allowing us to see the

xxiv Introduction

connections between varying forms of politics and intervention. Instead of applying a fraught set of labels to individuals, I more often let their actions and advocacy speak for themselves.[20]

"Urban crisis" is an equally fraught term.[21] Prior to the late 1960s, the term barely appeared in print, yet since the 1930s, policymakers, planners, and urban activists collided in their approaches to the perceived blight of the city and supposed pathology of black residents. Urban crisis has proven useful to the ambitions of policymakers, planners, and real estate developers who have capitalized on its fear, so scholars must be measured in their deployment of the term. The economic and environmental calamities facing the city were real, but the fears of a metastasizing crisis animated a destructive urban renewal response in the city and protection and development of environmental amenities in the suburbs that exacerbated inequalities. The term "urban crisis" locates it as a City of Detroit problem, but this book asserts that the crisis was inherently metropolitan, and that the age of urban crisis fear forged a fragmented metropolitan environmentalism.

While working with a concept as flexible as livability, some topics we find critically important are omitted, for instance, school quality and crime, which appear on almost any metric attempting to define a city's livability. This book confines itself to how livability interacts with the environment – built and natural – of cities, and how urban environmental change from the 1930s to the 1990s affected the livability of Detroit and its suburbs. In many ways, this book employs a rather old-fashioned use of the term "environmentalism." Reformers of the Gilded Age and Progressive Era often obsessed over how the environment shaped the behavior and well-being of Americans, especially recent immigrants.[22] Reformers utilized the concept in paternalistic ways to insist that supposed criminality, laziness, and despondency of impoverished and working-class people were the result of unhealthy and damaging environments. Their crude environmental determinism should be dispensed with, but their insistence that our agency, opportunities, and destinies are often significantly shaped by our environments remains an important insight.

Sustainability, justice, and the livable city

The metropolitan dynamics of Detroit's environmental inequalities make it a compelling case study with larger applicability. Detroit possessed characteristics that made it unique among U.S. cities. Its manufacturing might during World War II powered it into the position of the fourth largest U.S. city. As the home of the Big Three automakers – Ford, General Motors, and Chrysler – it had worldwide renown as the Motor City. The United Auto Workers successfully negotiated contracts with the automakers that rippled across manufacturing in the region and delivered a reasonable standard of living to many industrial workers. Yet the industrial prosperity was not shared equally among Detroit residents, as many continued to labor and live in environmentally hazardous conditions. Deindustrialization, disinvestment, and population loss led to the sharp decline of the central city in the decades after 1950, while neighboring suburbs absorbed the wealth and resources of the region. Environmental legacies of toxic factories were embedded in the landscapes of industrial Detroit, threatening the health and livelihoods of the mostly African-American population which remained in the city. While cities in the Rust Belt of the U.S. Midwest and Northeast invite comparisons, the challenge of creating broadly shared environmental quality across urban landscapes has been faced by industrial cities like Birmingham, the UK, Toronto, Canada, and across the global north and south.[23]

Environmental quality was a contested goal across the metropolitan region. For post-World War II suburban residents, sustainability meant a home in a neighborhood zoned residential, free from industrial pollution, close to parks and green spaces, and detached from the Detroit neighborhoods becoming racially integrated places. Regional planners asserted plans to harmonize and balance industry, commerce, and residential living, but the equation was balanced on the backs of inner-city and working-class residents who continued to live in polluted, neglected environs. In many post-industrial cities, we have seen a related problem of environmental amenities and promises of sustainable urban living leading to gentrification and sharpened inequalities.[24] This highlights the need to examine in other urban contexts the regional consequences of "greening" and sustainability efforts that fail to broadly disperse the environmental benefits.

Although the term environmental justice did not become actively used until the 1980s, many of the working-class whites and inner-city African Americans of Detroit in the 1960s and 1970s articulated their struggles for a healthful living environment as a matter of justice. Despite lacking the terminology environmental justice, inner-city environmental activism began in the homes and in the neighborhoods. Residents developed creative environmental responses to sustain the livability of their neighborhoods. Recent conversations on urban sustainability in an age of climate crisis have centered building resilient communities.[25] Austerity, deindustrialization, disinvestment, and physical decay have threatened the livability of Detroit, and despite these challenges, many thriving neighborhoods have persisted. Scholars and practitioners can learn much from the resilience and practices of Detroit residents and their environmental activism in the age of urban crisis.

Today, the challenges facing Southeast Michigan, particularly in the city, often seem insurmountable. Nevertheless, for decades, Detroit citizens have made vigorous efforts to meet those challenges, often in unheralded ways. Environmental tropes have punctuated the era of urban crisis. In recent decades, artists, journalists, documentarians, and others have created images that reflect Detroit's supposed return to nature. Images of deserted neighborhood overtaken by weeds and trees. Stories of long-gone animals, like coyotes and beavers, returning to the streets and waterways of the city. Documentaries and photo exhibitions that highlight the emptiness of the city and the absence of people. Yet Detroit is more than its empty spaces. One major goal of this book is to reassert that Detroit remains a *living* city, and despite the desertion is still home to nearly 700,000 people, surrounded by a region of over 5 million. The book that follows is the story of how residents, activists, planners, and policymakers clashed in their attempts to forge a more livable Detroit metropolitan region.

xxvi Introduction

Notes

1 Doug Scott, Campaigner for America's Wilderness, Sierra Club Associate Executive Director, *Interviews Conducted by Ann Lage and Kent Gill in 1990 and 1993* (Berkeley: Regional Oral History Office, The Bancroft Library, University of California, 2013), 79–95; James Tobin, "Earth Day Eve," *Heritage Project: University of Michigan*, accessed October 24, 2019, https://heritage.umich.edu/stories/earth-day-eve/; "ENACT Teach-In Kick-Off," *Give Earth a Chance: Environmental Activism in Michigan*, accessed October 24, 2019, http://michiganintheworld.history.lsa.umich.edu/environmentalism/exhibits/show/earthday/day-one-of-enact-s-teach-in; "ENACT Huron River Walk," March 14, 1970, HS17611, University of Michigan Library Digital Collection, accessed August 4, 2020, http://quod.lib.umich.edu/b/bhl/x-hs17611/hs17611. See also Adam Rome, *The Genius of Earth Day: How a 1970 Teach-in Unexpectedly Made the First Green Generation* (New York: Hill and Wang, 2013).

2 Newspaper clipping, *Detroit News*, May 23, 1970, Folder 5, Box 2, UAW-CRD Collection, ALUA.

3 "At Walter White School," "Earth Day at Bunche School," April 29, 1970, *River Rouge Herald*, located in Volume 1970, *River Rouge Herald*, RRPL.

4 Ripple (Red), "Trashin' Wayne," *Fifth Estate*, April 16 to April 29, 1970.

5 "Don't Want to Die in Our Own Mess," *Detroit Free Press*, April 23, 1970.

6 This framework builds on the argument of Robert O. Self, *American Babylon: Race and the Struggle for Postwar Oakland* (Princeton, NJ: Princeton University Press, 2005), 1.

7 Sometimes also called the "Detroit Riot," I use "rebellion" or "uprising" throughout this book, following the preferences of black participants in the event and recent scholarship.

8 On the concept of environmental privilege, see Laura Pulido, "Rethinking Environmental Racism: White Privilege and Urban Development in Southern California," *Annals of the American Association of Geographers* 90, no. 1 (2000): 12–40; Dorceta E. Taylor, *The Environment and the People in American Cities, 1600–1900s: Disorder, Inequality, and Social Change* (Durham, NC: Duke University Press, 2009), 10–12; Dorceta E. Taylor, *The Rise of the American Conservation Movement: Power, Privilege, and Environmental Protection* (Durham, NC: Duke University Press, 2016), 9–31. David Naguib Pellow shows how black capitalists can similarly benefit from environmental privilege in *Garbage Wars: The Struggle for Environmental Justice in Chicago* (Cambridge, MA: Massachusetts Institute of Technology Press, 2002), 7.

9 Robert Gioielli has asserted the importance of centering environmental struggles of the urban crisis, from the campaign against lead paint, opposition to freeway expansion, neighborhood campaigns against pollution, and more, using a case study of three cities. By focusing on one metropolitan region's inequality and activism, I build on Gioielli's important precedent to further demonstrate how suburban environmentalism was implicated in the urban crisis and environmental inequality. See Gioielli, *Environmental Activism and the Urban Crisis: Baltimore, St. Louis, Chicago* (Philadelphia, PA: Temple University Press, 2014). Other examples of situating environmental activism within the context of urban crisis include Matthew Gandy, *Concrete and Clay: Reworking Nature in New York City* (Cambridge, MA: Massachusetts Institute of Technology Press, 2003); David Stradling, *The Nature of New York: An Environmental History of the Empire State* (Ithaca, NY: Cornell University Press, 2010); David Stradling and Richard Stradling, *Where the River Burned: Carl Stokes and the Struggle to Save Cleveland* (Ithaca, NY: Cornell University Press, 2015). Wendell E. Pritchett shows the numerous ways to define the urban crisis, obviating the need to deploy specificity in its use. Pritchett, "Which Urban Crisis? Regionalism, Race, and Urban Policy, 1960–1974," *Journal of Urban History* 34, no. 2 (January 2008): 266–86, https://doi.org/10.1177/0096144207308678. The literature on the urban crisis in a variety of American cities is vast. Some of the most important urban crisis scholarship informing this study includes Arnold R. Hirsch, *Making the Second Ghetto: Race and Housing in Chicago, 1940–1960* (New York: Cambridge University Press, 1983); Joe Darden et al., *Detroit Race and Uneven Development* (Philadelphia,

Introduction **xxvii**

PA: Temple University Press, 1990); Thomas J. Sugrue, *The Origins of the Urban Crisis: Race and Inequality in Postwar Detroit* (Princeton, NJ: Princeton University Press, 1996); Heather Ann Thompson, *Whose Detroit? Politics, Labor, and Race in a Modern American City* (Ithaca, NY: Cornell University Press, 2004); Self, *American Babylon*; Andrew R. Highsmith, *Demolition Means Progress: Flint, Michigan, and the Fate of the American Metropolis*, Historical Studies of Urban America (Chicago: University of Chicago Press, 2015); Timothy J. Lombardo, *Blue-Collar Conservatism: Frank Rizzo's Philadelphia and Populist Politics* (Philadelphia, PA: University of Pennsylvania Press, 2018).

10 Samuel P. Hays and Barbara D. Hays, *Beauty, Health, and Permanence: Environmental Politics in the United States, 1955–1985* (New York: Cambridge University Press, 1987); Adam Rome, *The Bulldozer in the Countryside: Suburban Sprawl and the Rise of American Environmentalism* (New York: Cambridge University Press, 2001); Christopher C. Sellers, *Crabgrass Crucible: Suburban Nature and the Rise of Environmentalism in Twentieth-Century America* (Chapel Hill, NC: University of North Carolina Press, 2015).

11 David M. P. Freund shows how racism in metropolitan Detroit manifested in supposedly race-neutral concepts of property rights and a defense of neighborhood character. Freund, *Colored Property: State Policy and White Racial Politics in Suburban America* (Chicago: University of Chicago Press, 2010).

12 Robert Gottlieb, *Forcing the Spring: The Transformation of the American Environmental Movement*, rev. ed. (Washington, DC: Island Press, 2005). Robert Gordon, "'Shell No!': OCAW and the Labor-Environmental Alliance," *Environmental History* 3, no. 4 (October 1998): 460, https://doi.org/10.2307/3985207; David Stradling, *Smokestacks and Progressives: Environmentalists, Engineers and Air Quality in America, 1881–1951* (Baltimore, MD: Johns Hopkins University Press, 1999); Scott Hamilton Dewey, *Don't Breathe the Air: Air Pollution and U.S. Environmental Politics, 1945–1970* (College Station, TX: Texas A&M University Press, 2000); Chad Montrie, *To Save the Land and People: A History of Opposition to Surface Coal Mining in Appalachia* (Chapel Hill, NC: University of North Carolina Press, 2003); Chad Montrie, *A People's History of Environmentalism in the United States* (New York: Continuum, 2011); Chad Montrie, *The Myth of Silent Spring: Rethinking the Origins of American Environmentalism* (Oakland, CA: University of California Press, 2018).

13 Autoworkers discussed in Chad Montrie, *Making a Living: Work and Environment in the United States* (Chapel Hill, NC: University of North Carolina Press, 2008), 1–2, 91–112; Montrie, *A People's History of Environmentalism*, 3–6, 93–95. How Michigan workers interacted with the environment through hunting and fishing, creating a unique working-class environmentalism, see especially Lisa M. Fine, "Rights of Men, Rites of Passage: Hunting and Masculinity at Reo Motors of Lansing, Michigan, 1945–1975," *Journal of Social History* 33, no. 4 (2000): 805; Lisa M. Fine, "Workers and the Land in US History: Pointe Mouillée and the Downriver Detroit Working Class in the Twentieth Century," *Labor History* 53, no. 3 (August 2012): 409–34. For superb examinations of the relationship between labor and environmental justice, see Josiah Rector, "Environmental Justice at Work: The UAW, the War on Cancer, and the Right to Equal Protection from Toxic Hazards in Postwar America," *Journal of American History* 101, no. 2 (September 1, 2014): 480–502; Josiah Rector, "Accumulating Risk: Environmental Justice and the History of Capitalism in Detroit, 1880–2015" (Ph.D. Dissertation, Wayne State University, 2017); Josiah Rector, "The Spirit of Black Lake: Full Employment, Civil Rights, and the Forgotten Early History of Environmental Justice," *Modern American History* 1, no. 1 (March 2018): 45–66.

14 Sylvia Hood Washington, *Packing Them In: An Archaeology of Environmental Racism in Chicago, 1865–1954* (Lanham, MD: Lexington Books, 1994); Dianne D. Glave and Mark Stoll, eds., *"To Love the Wind and the Rain": African Americans and Environmental History* (Pittsburgh, PA: University of Pittsburgh Press, 2006); Camille T. Dungy, ed., *Black Nature: Four Centuries of African American Nature Poetry* (Athens: University of Georgia Press, 2009); Dianne D. Glave, *Rooted in the Earth: Reclaiming the African*

xxviii Introduction

American Environmental Heritage (Chicago: Lawrence Hill Books, 2010); Carolyn Finney, *Black Faces, White Spaces: Reimagining the Relationship of African Americans to the Great Outdoors* (Chapel Hill, NC: University of North Carolina Press, 2014); Colin Fisher, *Urban Green: Nature, Recreation, and the Working Class in Industrial Chicago* (Chapel Hill, NC: University of North Carolina Press, 2015).

15 Andrew Hurley's important work *Environmental Inequalities: Class, Race, and Industrial Pollution in Gary, Indiana, 1945–1980* (Chapel Hill, NC: University of North Carolina Press, 1994), first established the significance of analyzing the post-World War II history of environmental inequality and activism using metropolitan space, race, and class as categories of analysis. This book builds on Hurley's framework. For studies on Detroit's landscape and inequalities, see Joseph Cialdella, *Motor City Green: A Century of Landscapes and Environmentalism in Detroit* (Pittsburgh, PA: University of Pittsburgh Press, 2020); Patrick D. Cooper-McCann, "The Promise of Parkland: Planning Detroit's Public Spaces, 1805–2018" (Ph.D. Dissertation, University of Michigan, 2019).

16 For studies that similarly examine the competing environmentalisms across a metropolitan region, see Gandy, *Concrete and Clay*; Jeffrey Craig Sanders, *Seattle and the Roots of Urban Sustainability* (Pittsburgh, PA: University of Pittsburgh Press, 2010); Andrew M. Busch, *City in a Garden: Environmental Transformations and Racial Justice in Twentieth-Century Austin, Texas* (Chapel Hill, NC: The University of North Carolina Press, 2017).

17 Gottlieb, *Forcing the Spring*, 31.

18 Benjamin F. Chavis, Jr., and Charles Lee, *Toxic Wastes and Race in the United States* (New York: United Church of Christ, 1987); Robert Bullard, *Dumping in Dixie: Race, Class, and Environmental Quality* (Boulder, CO: Westview Press, 1990); Washington, *Packing Them In*; Eileen McGurty, *Transforming Environmentalism: Warren County, PCBS, and the Origins of Environmental Justice*, paperback printing (New Brunswick, NJ: Rutgers University Press, 2009), 1; Bunyan I. Bryant and Elaine Hockman, *Michigan: A State of Environmental Justice?* (New York: Morgan James Pub., 2011); Carl A. Zimring, *Clean and White: A History of Environmental Racism in the United States* (New York: New York University Press, 2015).

19 Based on keyword search of *Detroit Free Press* between 1931 and 1970 at www.Newspapers.com.

20 David Stradling and Richard Stradling similarly reflect on the difficulties of labeling individuals "environmentalists" in *Where the River Burned: Carl Stokes and the Struggle to Save Cleveland* (Ithaca, NY: Cornell University Press, 2015).

21 Timothy Weaver, "Urban Crisis: The Genealogy of a Concept," *Urban Studies* 54, no. 9 (July 2017): 2039–55, https://doi.org/10.1177/0042098016640487; Rebecca J. Kinney, *Beautiful Wasteland: The Rise of Detroit as America's Postindustrial Frontier* (Minneapolis, MN: University of Minnesota Press, 2016).

22 See Sharon E. Wood, *The Freedom of the Streets: Work, Citizenship, and Sexuality in a Gilded Age City*, Gender and American Culture (Chapel Hill, NC: University of North Carolina Press, 2005), 102–31; Michael McGerr, *A Fierce Discontent: The Rise and Fall of the Progressive Movement in America, 1870–1920* (New York: Oxford University Press, 2005), 77–117; Montrie, *A People's History of Environmentalism*, 57–75.

23 Christopher A. De Sousa, "Turning Brownfields into Green Space in the City of Toronto," *Landscape and Urban Planning* 62, no. 4 (February 2003): 181–98; Corina McKendry, *Greening Post-Industrial Cities: Growth, Equity, and Environmental Governance* (New York: Routledge, 2019).

24 Susannah Bunce, *Sustainability Policy, Planning and Gentrification in Cities* (New York: Routledge, 2019).

25 Sara Meerow, Joshua P. Newell, and Melissa Stults, "Defining Urban Resilience: A Review," *Landscape and Urban Planning* 147 (March 2016): 38–49; Beth Schaefer Caniglia, Beatrice Frank, and Manuel Vallée, eds., *Resilience, Environmental Justice and the City* (New York: Routledge, 2017).

1

LIVING JUST ENOUGH FOR DETROIT

In 1935, First Lady Eleanor Roosevelt inaugurated an era of slum clearance in Detroit during a visit to a neighborhood called Black Bottom. Arriving in Detroit on September 9, along with the Secretary of the Detroit Housing Commission Josephine Fellows Gomon, she greeted a throng of city officials and residents at 651 Benton Street, several blocks north of downtown. One newspaper estimated the crowd of onlookers at 10,000 people, mostly African Americans, including "grown men hanging from nearby light poles." Roosevelt raised her hand, and at "a fluttering handkerchief," a construction truck started its engine and pulled down the first home of a $6.6 million slum clearance and public housing development program. Roosevelt told the crowd on hand that the mostly African-American neighborhood Black Bottom was a "slumlord's paradise," and an epicenter of juvenile delinquency, crime, and tuberculosis. Transforming the environment would improve the people's lives. "Better housing," Roosevelt promised, "makes for better living standards." Roosevelt's visit did more than kick off an era of slum clearance. As in numerous American cities, officials expressed a modernist faith that they could bulldoze their way to a more prosperous and healthier city.[1]

Public health and planning experts, black and white concerned citizens, and policymakers worked to create a healthier, more sustainable city between the 1930s and 1960s through slum clearance, racial segregation, pollution abatement, central business district rehabilitation, and improved urban planning practices. Efforts to create a healthier city were not always neutral endeavors, with equitable objectives and outcomes. In many cases, racist and disruptive planning practices and slum clearance schemes failed in their ambitious goals while placing the heaviest burden on African Americans. Meanwhile, reform efforts facilitated the exodus of white residents from the city, with devastating consequences for the mostly working-class and African-American residents left behind.

DOI: 10.4324/9780429319914-1

2 Living just enough for Detroit

FIGURE 1.1 First Lady Eleanor Roosevelt (center) with Josephine Fellows Gomon (left), Secretary of the Detroit Housing Commission, greeting reporters in Black Bottom, September 10, 1935.

Source: Detroit News Collection, Walter P. Reuther Library, Archives of Labor and Urban Affairs, Wayne State University.

Living in the city was a challenge for all residents, but more so for African Americans. Residents were confronted daily with environmental health problems: air and water pollution, diseases like tuberculosis, unhealthy physical dwellings, and dangerous workplaces. African Americans mounted an attack on all the obstacles to healthy living in the city, but they encountered powerful structural forces, policies, institutions, employers, and racist white residents which erected barriers to creating a more just and equitable environment. Black Detroiters' efforts to create a healthier and more sustainable city have often been neglected from the story of the urban crisis and environmental activism. Fighting to create vibrant and healthful homes and neighborhoods amidst powerful political and physical forces of urban decay represented a significant act of resistance, a determination that they too had a right to the city.

Sick in the city

Tuberculosis plagued inner-city Detroit, which, like many North American cities, struggled to control the disease. After World War I, tuberculosis control efforts in the United States and Canada centered on sanitaria – long-term tuberculosis care facilities that isolated from society patients with the disease and provided a place for recovery.[2] Public health experts, doctors, and architects aimed to manage health through building design. Medical experts worked closely with architects to develop facilities that reflected cutting-edge knowledge about tuberculosis management. With most doctors prescribing the rest cure for tuberculosis patients, maximum fresh air, sunlight, and distance from the pollution of the city were reflected in the architectural design of sanitaria. Experts recommended that facilities be developed in pleasant building sites, taking care "that any natural beauties of [the] site be preserved in laying out the building scheme, since pleasant surroundings are undoubtedly a factor in the treatment of tuberculosis patients because of its tedious nature."[3] The most important operation in Detroit was the Maybury Sanatorium, which started with 300 beds in 1921 and grew considerably in the following years.[4]

While sanitaria could contain the human vectors of tuberculosis, they could not attack the source, which public health officials increasingly identified as the overcrowded and dilapidated slums of cities like Detroit. During the 1930s, public health experts and planners began advocating slum clearance for combating tuberculosis at the supposed epicenter. The shift from sanitaria to slum clearance as a public health planning strategy emerged from the belief that tuberculosis thrived in certain environments, and changing the environment – or removing an infected person from that environment – would promote public health. Slum clearance, however, was a far more destructive public health strategy, and the support of public health officials gave that planning strategy an important credibility boost. Policymakers in other cities in the 1930s also considered tuberculosis and the spread of contagious diseases as an important motivation for slum clearance. Cities throughout the United States embarked on similar slum clearance efforts motivated by public health hysteria.[5]

Fear of disease was racialized. In Los Angeles, tuberculosis became more closely associated with people of Mexican descent while in Detroit, planners and nervous white residents pointed to African Americans as the likeliest vectors of disease. Tuberculosis became increasingly associated with African Americans during the 1930s, but World War II especially proved a pivot point. Once tuberculosis was considered primarily a working-class problem, but now planners and policymakers considered it a black disease. White residents could escape unhealthful conditions by moving into newer housing developments, but African Americans were often trapped in the inner city by residential segregation practices, where substandard housing and overcrowding were the norm.[6] In areas like Black Bottom and Paradise Valley, African Americans suffered from rates of tuberculosis up to 71.5% higher than white Detroiters.[7] Only marginal progress was made in the 1930s toward eradicating tuberculosis. Soon, a city and nation consumed by war mobilization would create new environmental health challenges.

Wartime environments

Few places were as thoroughly transformed by wartime mobilization as Detroit, as its automotive and auto parts factories retooled to build bombers and other

4 Living just enough for Detroit

war materiel to earn the moniker "Arsenal of Democracy." Much to the annoyance of industrial leaders, Water Reuther, then Director of the General Motors Department of the United Auto Workers (UAW), famously promised 500 planes per day if the factories shifted to war preparation. "The plane," Reuther argued, "from certain points of view, is only an automobile with wings."[8] Factories buzzed with new activity, creating thousands of new jobs and inviting significant migration to the city. Between 1940 and 1943, the black population of Detroit increased by approximately 50,000.[9] Overall, the population of Detroit between 1940 and 1943 increased by a half million, though housing and environmental resources like parks and recreation could not match the spectacular growth of demand.[10] A tremendous need for additional housing existed in Detroit, particularly for African Americans excluded from white neighborhoods. Crammed into places like Paradise Valley and Black Bottom, African Americans pushing the boundaries of residential segregation prompted violent retribution from white Detroiters. The development of public housing offered some hope, but even the paltry efforts to supply it, such as with the Sojourner Truth housing project, resulted in a white backlash that ensured that black Detroiters could not enjoy the opportunity to rent there. After a few black renters moved into the housing project, crowds of supporters and opponents clashed, resulting in 40 injuries and 220 arrests.[11] Only through the presence of federal troops did a few black families gain access.

Hemmed in on all sides and squeezed into a handful of neighborhoods created an untenable situation in Detroit. Frustration with wartime housing arrangements as well as working conditions lead *Life* magazine to conclude: "Detroit is dynamite. . . . Detroit can either blow up Hitler or it can blow up the U.S."[12] Just three months after its publication, deadly rioting on Detroit's streets revealed it was capable of both. The so-called Arsenal of Democracy was far better at building bombers than homes. So concerned were American customs officials about the consequences of the *Life* story that it was embargoed from shipment outside North America. The Office of Censorship found the five-page article objectionable and harmful to the war effort.[13]

The influx of migrants created clashes of culture between newly arrived black and white southerners.[14] Robert Williams, a noted civil rights and black power advocate in the 1950s and 1960s, was transformed by his wartime years in Detroit. Williams contrasted the culture of Detroit with his North Carolina upbringing, "I don't like the atmosphere of dog-eat-dog and each one is trying to survive and doesn't care how he survives and who is hurt and who is crushed."[15] On the factory floors, white workers clashed with black, with more than 240 incidents reported throughout the United States, but conflict was particularly sharp in Detroit.[16] Some white workers engaged in wildcat strikes to protest working alongside African Americans. During a so-called hate strike at a Packard plant in June 1943, one worker reportedly commented, "I'd rather see Hitler and Hirohito win than work next to a n − r."[17]

The fuse was lit

Belle Isle, an island park, sits in the middle of the Detroit River on the U.S.-Canada border, just north of downtown. Designed by Frederick Law Olmstead, of New York City's Central Park fame, its 985 acres were considered by many the "Crown Jewel" of Detroit, and one of the few major parks located close to downtown and easily accessible to inner-city residents. So many thousands of African Americans enjoyed the park, that rankled whites called it "N – r Island."[18] White and black residents sought reprieve from the summer heat and overcrowded living conditions by picnicking and playing at Belle Isle. As white and black residents came into conflict on shop floors and in the search for housing, so too did they struggle for environmental amenities. On a 91-degree Sunday afternoon of June 20, 1943, crowds of Detroiters descended on the park.[19] A fight broke out between black and white parkgoers, and as the black crowds streamed onto the bridge back to the city, white gangs blocked the egress. Robert Williams was among those trapped on Belle Isle.[20] Along with his brother and friends, Williams narrowly evaded the vicious attacks and mob violence surrounding them. The episode chased him out of Detroit and to the shipyards of San Francisco.

The metaphorical and literal dynamite exploded, as rumors swirled and fighting broke out in the city. A rumor that a black man threw a white baby off the Belle Isle bridge into the Detroit River incensed white Detroiters spoiling for a fight.[21] Detroit became a racial battlefield. The 1943 riots in Detroit revealed the devastating

FIGURE 1.2 View of Belle Isle in 1942. Belle Isle Bridge visible in lower left.

Source: Tony Spina Photo Collection. Walter P. Reuther Library, Archives of Labor and Urban Affairs, Wayne State University.

6 Living just enough for Detroit

combination of the tight wartime housing and labor market with the sharpened racism. Numerous reports in the aftermath of the riot keyed in on housing conditions and lack of recreational opportunities for African Americans. The Detroit branch of the NAACP reported: "The facilities are lacking because of racial tension, and the tension exists partly because of the lack of housing and recreation," creating a toxic cycle.[22]

The embers cooled but the overwhelming environmental challenges of inner-city living persisted, and policymakers remained alarmed that substandard housing threatened the war effort. Adequate housing was a matter of national defense importance, many policymakers agreed. Detroit's black daily newspaper the *Michigan Chronicle* argued that "unsafe, insanitary, and overcrowded dwellings" in Detroit "cripple the war effort," and reported that half of African Americans lived in substandard housing compared to 14% of whites.[23] The pitiful wartime housing stock led the *Michigan Chronicle* to lampoon the city as "The Arsenal of 'De-Mockery.'"[24] In the final year of the war, the U.S. Census Bureau found a "one percent vacancy rate for whites with no vacancies for Negroes."[25] Despite its pressing significance to the nation's war making ability, the Arsenal of Democracy never solved the problem of under-housed defense workers in the central city.

War provided convenient metaphors for the environmental problems facing Detroit. The Arsenal of Democracy turned its guns on rat infestations, a problem that had reached disturbing levels in the inner city. City leaders declared a "war on rats" and educated residents in infestation prevention. The rats posed both an economic challenge and a public health nuisance, as Detroit's health department warned in 1944 after deaths from rat bite fever and many cases of infectious jaundice spread by the rodents.[26] Food markets struggled in vain to contain the scourge, as rats found "themselves at home in a box of rolled oats or breakfast cereal" and turned loading docks into a "playground."[27] Detroit officials hoped to learn from other cities mounting offensives against the invaders. Using war rhetoric, New Orleans officials described how they used "torpedoes" of rat poison on R-Day, Rat Day, but were often outmaneuvered by clever rats that "become suspicious and avoid the bait if some of them die from it in the old districts before the bait is put out in others."[28] "News travels fast among rats," warned E.B. Carey, director of pest control in New Orleans. Despite the advanced tactical maneuvering of the rats, New Orleans reported killing two-thirds of its 2 million rat population.[29]

Demolishing disease

Like the rat infestations, tuberculosis, pneumonia, and other communicable diseases threatened the health of urban residents, and after World War II, public health experts redoubled the campaign to improve environmental health through urban planning, and in select cases, so-called slum clearance.[30] Argued public health officials in Detroit, "The optimum results in promoting health for all groups of the population cannot be expected unless the environment is healthful." They continued, "Congestion, and lack of adequate recreation facilities, general deterioration, the indiscriminate mixing of business, industrial, and residential uses requires the planning and rebuilding of certain sections for their best use."[31] This is the key to understanding why it is important to highlight the connection between public health experts and slum clearance designs: public health experts were urged to join the slum clearance crusade, and public health experts more than obliged. They lent credibility to the demolition of neighborhoods on environmental health grounds.

Researchers with various planning agencies in Detroit reinforced the premise of the public health officials. The United Community Services of Metropolitan Detroit, a significant philanthropic agency and source of demographic research in Detroit, argued that "slums are incompatible with healthful living," and suggested that "the health of people ultimately can be safeguarded, not so much by meeting problems of immediate disease as by improving all of the conditions of life which affects health."[32] They advocated an approach that would fix the root problem, in their minds the slums, rather than merely treating the infected. "So long as slums remain," researchers insisted, "their inhabitants will have an unequal chance for health, efficiency and happiness."[33] Agencies like the United Community Services collaborated with Detroit urban planners to shape the region's future, playing an important role in providing the data that planners used to determine which neighborhoods should be demolished.

Health officials highlighted the connection between disease and the built environment. Producing a remarkable series of tuberculosis maps, they correlated rent prices in different sections of the city with rates of tuberculosis deaths. Finding a relationship between rent levels and tuberculosis mortality, they discovered that the highest death rates from mortality in the city, at 64 deaths per 100,000 residents, existed in areas in which rent cost less than $30 per month.[34] For rent between $30 and $50, that rate dropped to 17 per 100,000, and in the most expensive districts, rent over $50 correlated to an average rate of 8 deaths per 100,000. Their findings also had racial implications that were clear to the researchers. Areas closer to downtown Detroit and south of downtown faced the worst tuberculosis death rates, while the northern and far western neighborhoods, areas with significant white populations, faced the lowest death rates.

Public health officials, social agencies, and public planners generally agreed that the best way to improve environmental health outcomes in the slums was to bulldoze the blighted areas. Like the maps correlating rent with tuberculosis deaths, the Council of Social Agencies of Metropolitan Detroit produced a large body of evidence to support slum clearance to improve health outcomes. Researchers James Norton and Betty Pope produced their own set of maps that demonstrated the relationship between the overcrowded and poor housing conditions of slums, and infant mortality, juvenile delinquency, and tuberculosis.[35] The researchers observed:[36]

> As a leading cause of death, tuberculosis still ranks high as a health problem. The disease is associated with environmental conditions, and a high incidence may be expected where the probability of infection is greater, such as in congested living areas.

8 Living just enough for Detroit

Such reports delivered to advocates of slum clearance a powerful justification for their strategies, even when its efficacy remained unclear.

Although efforts to connect slum clearance and tuberculosis did have national advocates, like Eleanor Roosevelt, most of the conversations and actions happened at the local levels. But by the end of the 1940s, scattered local efforts gained a prominent national spokesperson. The Surgeon General of the United States Leonard Scheele recorded his concerns in front of a congressional subcommittee in 1949, remarking that overcrowding in the slums leads to tuberculosis and other communicable diseases.[37] Said the Surgeon General, "We must work harder at creating in our communities an overall environment which is conducive to good community health, thereby leading to a populace more resistant to TB."[38] Thus, we have one of the most powerful public health voices urging slum clearance, a significant moment in the efforts to cement the relationship between tuberculosis management and the bulldozer. Soon thereafter, the advent and availability of effective drug therapies gave doctors and public health officials pharmaceutical options for managing tuberculosis, and advocacy of slum clearance as a strategy diminished.

A state of environmental inequality

Black veterans returned from the war eager to make a living and start families in Detroit. Despite their service, they found little support from white residents or their government in their quest for improved living conditions. Excluded from white neighborhoods by policy, custom, violence, and intimidation, they remained contained to unhealthy, unsanitary, and dilapidated housing and neighborhoods neglected by sanitary services. In numerous ways, federal, state, and local governments (referred to collectively as *the state*) exacerbated environmental inequalities. Despite the significant barriers to residential mobility, African Americans sought homes in ethnic white and Jewish neighborhoods on the near east side and the west side, demanding a right to live in decent housing in the city.[39]

Sanitation services often neglected black neighborhoods, contributing to poor environmental conditions and diminished property values. Many inner-city neighborhoods teemed with garbage and the rodents, which inhabited the trash heaps. Paired with the lack of adequate recreational facilities, *Michigan Chronicle* found children playing in the piles of rubbish. Detroit Public Works Commissioner Glenn Richards insisted that part of the blame belonged to African-American residents, when "thousands of people have receptacles who do not use them." Richards reflected a common refrain from City Hall and others that insisted that the blame for neglected and dilapidated neighborhoods belonged solely to African Americans. Clifford Jones, a black resident of the Elmwood neighborhood, claimed that he had not seen a garbage truck in many months. Lacking trash pickup, Jones's garbage heap in the back of his home grew, and he struggled to shovel it into piles to "make room for the next load."[40]

Preventing black residents from finding healthful housing away from the rats and garbage were racially restrictive covenants in numerous neighborhoods and

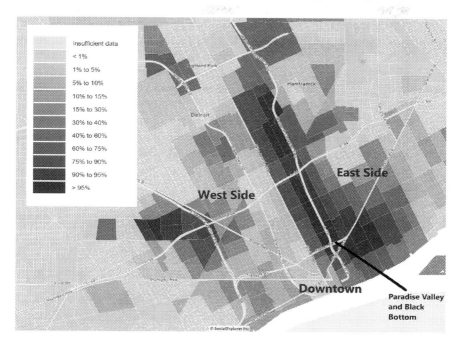

MAP 1.1 Density of African-American population in Detroit, 1950. This map shows the latter-built Chrysler Freeway cutting through heart of black Detroit.

Source: Created using SocialExplorer, Inc.

subdivisions. The *Michigan Chronicle* plainly stated, "Restrictive covenants have proved the chief obstacle in Negroes obtaining good homes in sufficient numbers in Detroit."[41] While some surely hoped that residential integration would proceed slowly and surely, the *Michigan Chronicle* pointed out that by the end of the war, the number of racially restricted covenants accelerated, increasing from just around one per year before 1940 to ten to 20 per *month* by mid-1945.[42] Significant legal disagreements played out in Michigan courts. The Housing Commission of the inner-suburb Hamtramck began building a "white project" while vaguely "promising to do the same for Negroes in the future," according to the *Michigan Chronicle*. Judge Maher held that the National Housing Authority was not obligated to ensure equal housing to African Americans because it provided subsidized monies as a lender, and could not be named as a defendant in a 14th amendment lawsuit. With the judge's ruling, the housing project could begin filling its units with whites only.

From local polities to the federal government, residential segregation was so thoroughly embedded in practices and policies that it seemed only a natural fact of urban life, obscuring the role of policies and institutions. Locally, the Detroit Housing Commission declared its unwillingness to integrate neighborhoods. "The Detroit Housing Commission," it announced, "will in no way change the racial characteristics of any neighborhood in Detroit through occupancy standards of housing projects

10 Living just enough for Detroit

under their jurisdiction."[43]The local policy merely reflected federal housing policies collectively referred to as "redlining." Beginning during the New Deal, the Federal Housing Administration (FHA) and the Home Owners' Loan Corporation established policies that assessed the racial "character" of a neighborhood to determine its suitability for underwriting home loans. Integrated blocks were denied low-interest loans to homeowners. Properties denied FHA approval faced disadvantages in the housing market. White homeowners worked hard to exclude black newcomers, creating a devastating cycle. Real estate agents employed "blockbusting" tactics, stirring rumors of impending black homeownership to scare white homeowners into selling ahead of the integration, inspiring white flight to further, often suburban, environs. Following integration, remaining homeowners had little incentive to maintain their properties, resulting in decay and abandonment. Significantly, large numbers of African Americans were denied *the* major vehicle for wealth accumulation during the postwar economic era of rapidly rising property values.[44]

Conflicts over African Americans pressing into white neighborhoods were not new to Detroit, the site of the dramatic case of Dr. Ossian Sweet. Trained at Wilberforce College, Dr. Sweet established his medical practice in 1924 in Black Bottom. On a near daily basis, the doctor witnessed the public health crisis of the crowded black neighborhood, from pneumonia to tuberculosis. His practice quickly developed, though most of his patients could little afford the treatments. Eager to move out of Black Bottom, the Sweets discovered the difficulty of finding desirable single-family housing. After a struggle to find a willing real estate agent and seller, they purchased a home in a white east side neighborhood in 1925. Quickly, neighboring homeowners organized into a mob, attacking the house with stones and threatening to murder the Sweets. The doctor and his friends fought back with guns, shooting and injuring one man and killing another. Prosecutors put Sweet on trial. The defense turned the trial on the city, implicating restrictive zoning and the white homeowners' association for fomenting the injustice and creating the inevitable reckoning. After an all-star trial featuring Clarence Darrow as a defense attorney, the all-white jury acquitted Sweet. The white racism and racist housing policies, however, remained firmly in place.[45]

Restrictive racial covenants on properties denied African Americans the opportunity to purchase homes in significant portions of the city in the late 1940s. According to one sociologist's finding, some 80% of properties outside of the inner city possessed such covenants.[46] African Americans in Detroit closely watched a restrictive covenants case as it wound its way through the courts and edged closer to the Supreme Court.[47] Attorneys argued that covenants violated plaintiff Orsel McGhee's 14th Amendment rights to equality under the law. In January 1947, the Michigan State Supreme Court upheld racially restrictive covenants, which threatened to remove McGhee from his home.[48] Along with a covenants case from St. Louis, *Shelley v. Kraemer*, the Supreme Court agreed to hear McGhee's case. Thurgood Marshall argued on behalf of the NAACP, which sought to end the covenants. In 1948, the Supreme Court unanimously agreed that racial covenants were unconstitutional, to which black Detroit rejoiced.[49]

Shelley v. Kraemer struck down a major pillar of state-supported racial inequality, but the continuation of white violence to maintain the color line indicated that the black struggle for fair housing had a long way to go. When white neighborhood residents failed to use covenants or intimidation to stop African Americans from moving in, they sometimes engaged in organized violence or destruction of property. A black family attempted to move into 2722 Vermont Avenue on the city's west side, prompting a group of white residents to destroy the property over a period of four hours (with apparently no police being called), preventing its occupation.[50] Suspicious fires burned homes of black residents in mixed neighborhoods.[51] African-American leaders excoriated neighborhood improvement associations for agitating the rabble-rousers. The *Michigan Chronicle* insisted that neighborhood councils aimed to stop "occupancy of their neighborhoods by citizens of color. This is supposed to be based on the common assumption that Negroes depreciate property."[52] African Americans struggled to overcome the stereotype that their mere presence degraded neighborhoods.

Decent, equitable public housing offered one strategy for alleviating dangerous and unhealthy living conditions. Detroit Health Commissioner Bruce Douglass lauded public housing as an important prescription for the health problems bedeviling slum residents. The housing shortage, according to Douglass, ensured that health standards could not be enforced, forcing black residents into substandard housing. Douglass hailed the Brewster Housing project as an important part of the solution. With residential segregation restricting black housing mobility atop the massive influx of war workers, some homeless African Americans took to sleeping on Belle Isle. City officials wanted to eliminate the practice, and urged an ordinance restricting the park's use from 3:00 to 6:00 A.M., but black advocates warned that this only attacked the symptom and not the disease – pitifully few housing vacancies.[53] They looked forward to several promised housing projects, like the Douglas and Jeffries projects, yet lamented that these could only put a dent in the overall shortage when a bigger public effort was needed to build and promote integrated housing.

Meanwhile, housing shortages squeezed African Americans the hardest in the immediate postwar years, ending the hope that the housing crisis was only a wartime feature, and that a large part of the defense workforce would leave Detroit after the war. A coordinated national policy was needed to address the crisis. Introduced in Congress in 1945, the Wagner-Ellender-Taft Bill promised 500,000 public housing units, reformed Federal Housing Administration insurance practices, and subsidies for builders of low-income housing, as evidence mounted that private industry was not meeting the need.[54] African-American leaders in Detroit made the case that decent housing produced good citizens. A political cartoon in the *Michigan Chronicle* showed two panels: The first showed overfilled trash cans, a building falling apart, unsupervised children, a man being frisked by police, and another being assaulted with a baton, with a caption reading: "Bad housing – poor citizens."[55] The second panel showed a handsome suburban home, with a child mowing the lawn, a couple pushing a stroller, and children playing in the yard, captioned: "Good housing – good citizens. Support the Wagner-Ellender-Taft Bill for better housing!" The cartoon complemented an editorial in the newspaper claiming, "Slums have been the breeding grounds for crime and disease for time immemorial," and urged passage of the legislation.[56]

The public health consequences of poor housing gained national attention during congressional debate. Samuel P. Hoskin and the editorial staff of *The New Jersey Afro-American* newspaper, in their comments to the congressional Joint Committee on Housing, argued that a public health crisis resulted from overcrowded and substandard housing in black neighborhoods. In Newark, they noted, "the majority of colored citizens are housed in slums."[57] With some 30% of Newark being slum housing, this resulted in widespread "crime, delinquency of juveniles, childbirth mortality, tuberculosis, and other communicable diseases . . . in the slum areas where colored people are jammed." Residents of New Jersey testified in support of the Wagner-Ellender-Taft Bill in front of the Joint Committee on Housing, providing vivid details of their living conditions. Samuel Schofield, a veteran and resident of Bergen County, described a fruitless 6-month search for housing. With his wife, he visited state veterans' housing and found a family living in the cellar.[58] To access the opening, they had to remove a board, which a woman living there explained prevented the rats from entering. When they opened another door, they found a four-year-old sleeping, with "a rat crawling across that kiddie's face." Schofield explained, "You ought to be in that position – not daring to move, not knowing what was going to happen next. That will live in my memory." Although the Wagner-Ellender-Taft Bill passed in the Senate, conservative Republicans in the House of Representatives, prodded by powerful real estate interests, ensured that the legislation did not reach a floor vote, and it subsequently died for the time being.[59]

African Americans fought back against discriminatory laws and other segregationist practices that prevented them from owning a home in certain neighborhoods unless one was "prepared to go to the Supreme Court of the United States in an effort to buy and live in it."[60] They also rejected attitudes that blamed African Americans for the poor environmental conditions of the slums. Some whites asked, "What are Negroes themselves trying to do to better their housing condition?"

> Those who have the money are trying to buy, and build better homes. Here again, however, the Negro citizen runs up against another stone wall, for practically all the land is restricted, building materials are short and, if by chance he buys an available home, it is usually on the 'wrong' side of the street and a mob forms to tell him where to go.[61]

A tremendous need for a national program to build healthful, plentiful housing existed. Even when other major liberal efforts stalled in the context of an emerging Cold War Red Scare and critiques by conservatives of the command economy and large-scale planning, quality housing also provided, it seemed, a way to avoid the red menace. Who could support communism, some asked, when well-housed, well-clothed, and well-fed?

President Truman threw his support behind a revived Taft-Ellender-Wagner Act (with the order of the names changed from the earlier legislation). Although once again nodding to an expanded public housing program, this version promised a greater assault on the blight affecting slum-dwellers' health. This time it passed in Congress to become the 1949 Federal Housing Act. The law committed the nation to "the elimination of substandard and other inadequate housing" and "a suitable living environment for every American family."[62] President Truman's signing statement promised "decent homes in wholesome surroundings for low-income families now living in the squalor of slums," through "clearing slums and rebuilding blighted areas."[63] Actual spending failed to live up to the rhetoric. By 1958, only $2.8 million was disbursed in federal grants to Detroit, but the legislation signaled a new era of concerted planning action to achieve environmental health and prosperity through the bulldozer.[64]

The City of Detroit continued its work mapping the city's blight and prepared new plans for urban renewal. Historians and other scholars have documented the significant effects of the legislation for black urbanites. The authors of the important study *Detroit: Race and Uneven Development* note the fundamental flaw of the Federal Housing Act: a law that promised a "suitable living environment" for all drove the clearance of housing stock and thrust expelled black residents into a segregated market where precious few open homes existed.[65] Although historians have made tremendous progress uncovering the devastating consequences of redlining, restrictive covenants, and other state-sanctioned inequalities, rarely are these considered environmental justice issues. It is necessary to re-assert the importance of all environments, including inner-city urban environments, to the study of environmental history. Such state-sanctioned segregationist policies ensured the unequal development of the region, leaving Detroit as a "sacrifice zone" in which the well-being of residents was almost wholly ignored outside of civil rights activists and a select few urban allies. They may not have identified as environmentalists, but black efforts to improve local environments and protect their neighborhoods from the bulldozer mirrored the suburban concern for quality of life. Where suburbanites could enjoy the environment as an *amenity*, a source of leisure and beauty, African Americans were forced to reconcile with the day-to-day struggle to survive in the challenging built environment.

Bulldozing Detroit

Some middle-class black Detroiters initially welcomed urban renewal and slum clearance programs. Two Detroit institutions in particular advocated the middle-class black viewpoint in support of slum clearance: the Detroit Urban League (DUL) and the black daily newspaper *The Michigan Chronicle*. The Detroit Urban League, established in 1916 by social workers, became an important local institution. Acting as a social agency for newly arrived African-American migrants, DUL worked with industrial employers to connect newcomers with jobs, and promoted moral values that benefited companies. Employers insisted that the DUL work to

14 Living just enough for Detroit

provide "wholesome recreation" as an antidote to the vices found in "the saloon, the cheap pool room, [and] the gambling club."[66] The Detroit Urban League played an influential role in cultivating respectability among southern African-American migrants to the city.[67] Middle-class African Americans were embarrassed of what they perceived as backward ways of the new arrivals. As historian Joseph Cialdella demonstrates, to acculturate migrants to the Detroit way, the League advocated neighborhood cleanup campaigns, high sanitary standards, clean houses and yards, and sponsored garden contests.[68]

The Michigan Chronicle teemed with articles in the late 1940s reporting residents suffering illness, injury, and sometimes death due to living in substandard housing. It featured numerous pictures of dilapidated housing, which provided "glaring evidence of the need for slum clearance in Detroit."[69] Estimates by the Detroit Housing Commission in 1949 placed the number of woefully unhealthy dwelling units at 48,000, comprising dwellings that lacked running water or possessed other serious unsanitary complications.[70] Slum clearance, the Detroit Urban League reasoned, could greatly benefit African-American health by razing many of these structures. DUL took pains to point out the health consequences of living in neglected neighborhoods and decaying housing. Yet they also demonstrated a remarkable confidence in the promises of urban renewal authorities.

Some of the most disruptive instances of slum clearance and removal of black residents took place on the city's near east side in Black Bottom. There, planners saw the opportunity to eliminate substandard housing and replace it with a modern vision of middle-class and integrated housing close to downtown in what was deemed the Detroit Plan, in 1947.[71] In the public-private cooperative effort, the city would clear an area and then sell the land to private developers for a fraction of the cost. Planners explained that eliminating dense residential housing was a priority. As attractiveness of suburban living competed for white middle-class residents, planners sought to develop attractive environmental features of suburbia like leafy neighborhoods near parks, and build an appealing waterfront close to downtown, even if that meant displacing existing black neighborhoods.[72] The city pinned its hopes on the Gratiot Redevelopment Project (later called Lafayette Gardens), on top of 43 residential blocks of African-American housing, just east of the Central Business District.[73] Clearance was necessary, according to the Detroit Housing Commission, due to the high crime rate, frequency of fires, rat bites, tuberculosis deaths, infant mortality, and other environmental health hazards. Once again, public health concerns featured prominently in planners' arguments. In 1953, the city sold the land to a private developer, which broke ground in 1956. To make way for the new development, the city removed 7,500 individuals occupying a total of 1,550 homes. Though the city accommodated 600 of 1,000 families in public housing, the rest were forced to find housing in a tight housing market, where residential segregation severely limited their options and forced black residents to pay a "race tax," the premium that residents paid for substandard housing.[74] As planning historian June Manning Thomas argues, "the Gratiot project eliminated more low-income housing than it produced, and it abused and alienated Black inner-city residents in the process."[75]

The Detroit Urban League generally supported the slum clearance practices, which greatly disrupted African-American neighborhoods. Poor housing created "human suffering and mental anguish," the League argued in 1956.[76] African Americans, their data showed, inhabited 75% of dilapidated housing units. Some 85% of residents displaced by urban renewal programs were non-white. African Americans faced long odds at securing housing in new housing developments. Resistance to public housing meant such units were practically unavailable to most displaced residents. DUL reported that the programs to re-house the displaced residents were inadequate, and yet they cheered the urban renewal agencies and responsible for thrusting black residents into an impossibly tight housing market. The director of the Community Services Department noted,

> The Detroit Urban League is both pleased and fortunate to enjoy a cooperative working relationship with responsible municipal urban renewal planning agencies and interested civic organizations which are engaged in a collective effort to cauterize this malignant growth, by clearing the slums, removing the blight and checking neighborhood deterioration under the urban renewal program of the federal government.

Black residents hoping that the Urban League would mount of a defense of their neighborhoods found little support.

Neighborhood conservation

Black Detroiters undertook enormous efforts to spare their neighborhoods from the bulldozer. While working within the system to ensure black residents could be adequately re-housed, the Urban League also promoted grassroots neighborhood improvement. Called "neighborhood conservation," these programs emerged in the 1950s as a strategy for improving the environmental quality of neighborhoods to convince renewal authorities that their homes were worthy of saving. They built on a longer legacy of Urban League efforts to improve the cleanliness, sanitation, and attractiveness of black neighborhoods. Although the initiative originated in City Hall, it was the Detroit Urban League and African-American residents who gave their labor and time to effect environmental change. Their initiative indicated the great efforts of African Americans to resist urban decay and the city's bulldozers.

Detroit's Committee for Neighborhood Conservation and Improved Housing (usually referred to as the Conservation Committee), created in 1953, spearheaded city efforts to promote a conservation-first approach to housing.[77] Officials noted that despite Detroit's reputation as the Arsenal of Democracy, and its widely admired industrial efficiency, the full might of the city had not been applied to addressing the housing crisis. Fixing "the general environment in which many of our people live" promised to reinvigorate the city.[78] The Conservation Committee

16 Living just enough for Detroit

surveyed the entirety of residential areas in the city and assigned grades that ranged from "Conservation area" to "Redevelopment area," or slum clearance.[79] Within these broad categories were further gradations. A conservation area could include

> minor improvements in the fringe areas of the city on through medium improvement areas a bit further in, to major improvement areas largely located in a belt surrounding the Grand Boulevard, to those scattered portions of the middle city that required first-aid development as an immediate treatment, but which would have to be redeveloped.

Based on the series of surveys and the maps they produced, city planners hoped to show the effects of targeted conservation action. Conservation measures included building new parks and smaller "tot-lots," improving streets, creating greenbelts, changing zoning designations, and enforcing codes. Yet without the help of neighborhood residents, the planners noted, conservation would be impossible. They made the case that residents could have "better neighborhoods without moving."

Officials chose three neighborhoods as demonstration areas for the conservation program. Representing "neither the very worst nor the very best type of conservation neighborhood," they selected neighborhoods in opposite sides of the city to get a better sense of how spatial factors affected conservation efforts.[80] One neighborhood on the east side might face different challenges than the two neighborhoods chosen on the west side, planners reasoned. Conducting a survey of 100% of the structures in the east side neighborhood, and a 20% sample of units in one of the west side neighborhoods, they sought to show the power of concerted city action and grassroots engagement. After its first year, the conservation committee reported progress in surveying, collecting data, and grading 50 conservation neighborhoods.[81] For the conservation study areas, they noted significant grassroots organizing had been accomplished. Each of the 38 blocks in conservation area #1 on the east side now had representatives for the new "Neighborhood Council." Moreover, some 600 citizens participated in a conservation conference held in 1953, representing major civic organizations and ordinary residents.[82] Securing $50,000 in funding from the city council provided essential resources to continue the program.

Supplementing the organizing work included educating the public on conservation and how residents could achieve "better neighborhoods without moving."[83] Educational materials included pleas for regular maintenance, noting, "There is no magic about protecting your investment in your home. It's a matter of regular painting and a new roof when it's needed, of replacing things that wear out before the place gets a run-down look."[84] Just as important as individual efforts, they also pitched the importance of thinking on a neighborhood level to ensure that everyone's property values could be maintained. "[T]he place to start is talking to your neighbors," they urged. Cleaning rubbish from alleyways and yards was essential to starving out rats and other unwanted visitors, but efforts by individuals were in vain if the neighbor's yard was trash-strewn. Alleys could be cleaned and turned into a

FIGURE 1.3 Map of Urban Renewal and Conservation Areas.
Source: Detroit City Plan Commission, *Detroit Urban Renewal* (1963). Hathi Digital Trust.

park-like space for neighbors to interact, but it required the cooperation of a block to make it work.[85]

In addition to the flawed relocation plans, the DUL also noted the immense pressure placed on residents to make their neighborhoods livable. As part of its demonstration project in the city's east side, the Health Department greatly ramped up code enforcements, issuing violations to 1,332 premises out of a total 1,679.[86] Only 254 avoided violations. This "broken windows" code enforcement must have terrified residents who were witnessing the slow decay of their neighborhoods by forces outside their control. Residents were being asked to spend money even as their property values plummeted. In many cases, Detroit officials argued that slums posed a public health threat to the entire community and promoted their wholesale destruction. By the end of the 1950s, the American Public Health Association also advocated a conservation first approach, "planning, code enforcement, and action by citizen groups" to salvage blocks on the verge of becoming slums.[87] Yet the burden remained on mostly African-American residents, who often had limited resources to keep up with the forces of neighborhood change. As the city's first black mayor, Coleman Young, later remembered, "Just the rumor of urban renewal was enough to ruin an area."[88] Area businesses, landlords, and residents stopped paying for the upkeep of properties, placing even greater onus on those

18 Living just enough for Detroit

who wished to remain in their homes. It amounted, Young said, to "blight by announcement."

By 1956, the Detroit Urban League began pushing back against the heavy-handed way that urban renewal was implemented but stopped short of total condemnation. Indeed, it still urged clearance of dilapidated structures. DUL instead advocated precision in clearance policies. Rather than see entire neighborhoods abolished, it pushed for finer analyses of blocks on a structure-by-structure basis. Moreover, by 1956, DUL became more insistent that re-housing plans be upfront with residents and pay fair relocation fees to those affected. William L. Price, director of the DUL Community Services Department, noted, "We realize rehousing this large percentage of minority group families is not an easy task," but insisted that relocation must not be an afterthought.[89] One solution promoted by the DUL for the inequalities in urban renewal planning was greater "non-white participation in the urban renewal areas."[90] Eighty-five percent of the Detroiters affected by clearance programs, after all, were African American.

Slowly, the DUL began to turn on the city's conservation program. By the end of 1956, DUL identified the conservation program as cover for displacing 1,100 families.[91] However noble the initial intentions might have been, the city

FIGURE 1.4 Construction of the Lodge Freeway, 1954.

Source: Tony Spina Photo Collection, Walter P. Reuther Library, Archives of Labor and Urban Affairs, Wayne State University.

was drawn back to the blunt instrument of the bulldozer to effect sweeping environmental change. Highway construction offered the twin benefit of razing slums while also supporting suburbanites' access to downtown businesses and workplaces. For those with little emotional connection to the inner-city neighborhoods, it seemed like a winning proposition. As construction began on the Hastings-Oakland Expressway (later known as the Chrsyler Freeway), DUL officials noted the segregation of the metropolitan area that limited opportunities for re-housing displaced residents. William Price pointed out that 1.76 million white residents lived in the suburbs, compared to only 60,000 African Americans.[92] Complicating the problem of displaced residents from urban renewal programs, new highway projects created thousand more refugees, yet there was little coordination of re-housing plans. Such failures reinforced the DUL's insistence on the necessity of consolidated relocation plans.

Toward black protest

Black environmentalism developed in part out of the immediate need to protect neighborhoods from the bulldozer and to create a healthier built environment for their families. Highway development in the 1950s wrecked the fabric of numerous communities throughout the United States. Accommodating the popularity of the automobile and the explosive growth of suburbs, highways promised ingress to the jobs, shopping, and entertainment of the central business district, and quick egress out of the pollution, decay, and black neighborhoods of the urban core. Unsurprisingly, the Motor City took an early lead in developing expressways even before Eisenhower's Interstate Highway System prompted a transportation revolution in 1956.[93] Detroit financed numerous roads, seeking to revitalize the central city and forestall its decentralization to the suburbs. These roads, as much as the auto factories, made Detroit a "Motor City." Though certain pain would inevitably result, historian Roger Biles notes that officials believed "expressways would actually improve the quality of life in affected residential neighborhoods," and preserve the Central Business District as the region's focal point.[94]

Urban renewal programs tore up African-American neighborhoods between the 1930s and 1960s. Lively black neighborhoods like Black Bottom and the business district Paradise Valley were bulldozed to make room for freeways like the aptly named Chrysler Freeway.[95] Devastation was severe with the John C. Lodge freeway leveling 2,200 buildings, and Edsel B. Ford Expressway demolishing 2,800 buildings, requiring removal of heavily African-American neighborhoods near downtown.[96] Black Bottom faced serious issues, including physical decay, poor property upkeep by slumlords, and high rates of tuberculosis and other diseases associated with poverty. As many African Americans later remembered it, Black Bottom meant deep community, thriving black culture, opportunity, and as future mayor Coleman Young recalled, a place "as lyrical as church chimes."[97] But to the urban planners and policymakers, it represented slums, despair, and decay, a landscape better fit for a freeway than black homes. The seeds were planted for black

20 Living just enough for Detroit

protest over destructive urban renewal and highway construction, but not until the 1960s did the scattered voices coalesce into a movement. In the meantime, highways would facilitate the exodus of white Detroiters to the suburbs, where planners, policymakers, and white residents embarked on a quest to create a high quality of life separate from the city.

Notes

1 "Detroit to Greet First Lady," *Detroit Free Press*, September 9, 1935; "Detroit Begins Clearing Slums," *Jackson Citizen Patriot*, September 10, 1935, accessed June 19, 2020, www.mlive.com/news/jackson/2016/02/peek_through_time_first_lady_e.html; "Slum Clearing Is Launched by Mrs. Roosevelt," *Detroit Free Press*, September 10, 1935; Scott Martelle, *Detroit: A Biography* (Chicago: Chicago Review Press, 2014), 133; Joe Darden et al., *Detroit Race and Uneven Development* (Philadelphia, PA: Temple University Press, 1990), 155; June Manning Thomas, *Redevelopment and Race: Planning a Finer City in Postwar Detroit* (Detroit: Wayne State University Press, 2013), 18–28.
2 Valerie Minnett, "Disease and Domesticity on Display: The Montreal Tuberculosis Exhibition, 1908," *Canadian Bulletin of Medical History* 23, no. 2 (October 2006): 381–400; Annmarie Adams, Kevin Schwartzman, and David Theodore, "Collapse and Expand: Architecture and Tuberculosis Therapy in Montreal, 1909, 1933, 1954," *Technology and Culture* 49, no. 4 (2008): 908–42.
3 Richard E. Schmidt, "Modern Hospital Design," *The Architectural Forum* 37, no. 6 (December 1922): 245–58, 247.
4 "A History of Maybury Sanatorium," accessed September 22, 2015, www.mayburysanatorium.com/#/history/4526191819.
5 Stephanie Lewthwaite, *Race, Place, and Reform in Mexican Los Angeles: A Transnational Perspective, 1890–1940* (Tucson, AZ: University of Arizona Press, 2009), 189.
6 Thomas J. Sugrue, *The Origins of the Urban Crisis: Race and Inequality in Postwar Detroit* (Princeton, NJ: Princeton University Press, 1996), 33–55.
7 Heather Ann Thompson, *Whose Detroit? Politics, Labor, and Race in a Modern American City* (Ithaca, NY: Cornell University Press, 2003), 16.
8 Nelson Lichtenstein, *Walter Reuther: The Most Dangerous Man in Detroit* (Urbana: University of Illinois Press, 1995), 154.
9 *What Caused the Detroit Riots?* (New York: National Association for the Advancement of Colored People, 1943), accessed August 18, 2017, https://archive.org/details/whatcauseddetroi00whit.
10 Johanna Russ, "The 1943 Detroit Race Riot," June 12, 2012, accessed August 2, 2017, http://reuther.wayne.edu/node/8738.
11 Sugrue, *The Origins of the Urban Crisis*, 73–75.
12 "Detroit Is Dynamite," *Life*, August 17, 1942, 15, with a retrospective in "Detroit: Six Months After," *Life*, March 1, 1943, 29.
13 "Life Banned from U.S. Mail; Export Halted," *Chicago Tribune*, August 16, 1942, 1A.
14 See, for instance, Heather Ann Thompson, "Auto Workers, Dissent, and the UAW: Detroit and Lordstown," in *Autowork*, eds. Robert Asher and Ronald Edsforth (Albany: State University of New York Press, 1995), 181–208.
15 Quoted in Timothy B. Tyson, *Radio Free Dixie: Robert F. Williams and the Roots of Black Power* (Chapel Hill, NC: University of North Carolina Press, 1999), 38.
16 Neil A. Wynn, *The African American Experience During World War II* (Lanham, Md: Rowman and Littlefield, 2010), 70.
17 Quoted in John Barnard, *The American Vanguard: The United Auto Workers During the Reuther Years, 1935–1970* (Detroit: Wayne State University, 2005), 175.
18 Tyson, *Radio Free Dixie*, 40.
19 Tyson, *Radio Free Dixie*, 41.

20 Tyson, *Radio Free Dixie*, 41–42.

21 Tyson, *Radio Free Dixie*, 42.

22 Gloster B. Current, "What's Wrong with Detroit?," Box 1, Folder: Miscellaneous Material, NAACP-DB Collection Part 1, ALUA.

23 "Officials Tackle Housing Issue," *Michigan Chronicle*, January 20, 1945.

24 "The Arsenal of 'De-Mockery'," *Michigan Chronicle*, March 17, 1945.

25 "Officials Tackle Housing Issue."

26 Undated clipping, "River Rats Make Selves at Home in Food Stores," *Detroit Free Press*, n.d. [c. 1944], Box 25, Folder 5, DUL Collection, BHL.

27 "River Rats Make Selves at Home in Food Stores."

28 Undated clipping, "New Orleans Fights Pests," *Detroit Free Press*, Box 25, Folder 5, DUL Collection.

29 Newspaper clipping, "75 Face Court for Failure to Aid Fight Against Pests," *Detroit Free Press*, September 1, 1944, Box 25, Folder 5, DUL Collection.

30 For an examination of the experience of tuberculosis in the urban environment, see René and Jean Dubos, *The White Plague: Tuberculosis, Man and Society* (Boston, MA: Little, Brown and Company, 1952); Sheila M. Rothman, *Living in the Shadow of Death: Tuberculosis and the Social Experience of Illness in American History* (Baltimore, MD: The Johns Hopkins University Press, 1995). The intersection between environmental disease, race, and public health is explored in Natalia Molina, *Fit to Be Citizens? Public Health and Race in Los Angeles, 1879–1939* (Berkeley: University of California Press, 2006).

31 Bleecker Marquette and Floyd P. Allen, M.D., "Health Report," 1948, Box 2, Folder: "Community Serrvey . . . in Wayne County," UCCSR Collection, ALUA.

32 Marquette and Allen, "Health Report."

33 Marquette and Allen, "Health Report."

34 Marquette and Allen, "Health Report."

35 James H. Norton and Betty Horning Pope, "Areas of Social Need in Detroit and Neighborhood Communities," March 1949, Box 1, Folder: "Areas of Social Need," UCSSR Collection.

36 Norton and Pope, "Areas of Social Need in Detroit."

37 "Slum Clearance: 1932–1952," in *Editorial Research Reports 1952*, Vol. II (Washington, DC: CQ Press, 1952), 801–20, accessed July 24, 2020, http://library.cqpress.com/cqresearcher/cqresrre1952112200.

38 "The Record," June 1954, Box 59, Folder 23, UCSSF Collection, ALUA.

39 Sidney Fine, *Violence in the Model City: The Cavanagh Administration, Race Relations, and the Detroit Riot of 1967* (East Lansing: Michigan State University Press, 2007), 3–4.

40 "Health Hazard Grows with Slow Garbage Disposal," *Michigan Chronicle*, April 28, 1945.

41 "Restrictive Covenants Balk Efforts to Get Better Homes," *Michigan Chronicle*, August 25, 1945.

42 "Restrictive Covenants Balk Efforts to Get Better Homes."

43 "A Negro Talks About Housing," *Michigan Chronicle*, March 24, 1945.

44 In Michigan, median home prices rose from $29,800 in 1940 to $59,100 two decades later. "Historic Census of Housing Tables," United States Census Bureau, accessed August 29, 2017, www.census.gov/hhes/www/housing/census/historic/values.html. See Highsmith, *Demolition Means Progress*, 45–53; Keeanga-Yamahtta Taylor, *Race for Profit: How Banks and the Real Estate Industry Undermined Black Homeownership* (Chapel Hill, NC: The University of North Carolina Press, 2019), 14.

45 Kevin Boyle, *Arc of Justice: A Saga of Race, Civil Rights, and Murder in the Jazz Age* (New York: Henry Holt and Company, 2004).

46 Sugrue, *The Origins of the Urban Crisis*, 44.

47 "Restrictive Covenant Question Nears Federal Supreme Court Showdown," *Michigan Chronicle*, April 19, 1947.

48 "Covenants Face Test of Constitutionality," *Michigan Chronicle*, June 28, 1947.

49 Sugrue, *The Origins of the Urban Crisis*, 181–82.

22 Living just enough for Detroit

50 "Vandalism," *Michigan Chronicle*, September 15, 1945.
51 "No Motive in Burning of 3 Homes, Garages," *Michigan Chronicle*, September 15, 1945.
52 "Improvement Groups Encourage Restrictive Covenants," *Michigan Chronicle*, September 8, 1945.
53 "The Vanishing House," *Michigan Chronicle*, September 1, 1945.
54 Roger Biles, *The Fate of Cities: Urban America and the Federal Government, 1945–2000* (Lawrence: University Press of Kansas, 2011), 20–21; "'The Ruins of the Postwar Dream Homes': Housing Reform Advocates Testify Before Congress," accessed July 18, 2016, http://historymatters.gmu.edu/d/6907/; "Wagner-Ellender-Taft Housing Bill," in *CQ Almanac 1946* (Washington, DC: Congressional Quarterly, 1947), 2nd ed., 4–456, accessed August 10, 2020, http://library.cqpress.com/cqalmanac/cqal46-1410466; Jon C. Teaford, *The Rough Road to Renaissance: Urban Revitalization in America, 1940–1985* (Baltimore, MD: Johns Hopkins University Press, 1990), 107–8.
55 *Michigan Chronicle*, March 22, 1947.
56 "Housing Again," *Michigan Chronicle*, March 22, 1947.
57 "'The Right to Housing Is a Civil Right Due Without Restriction': Racial Bias in Public and Private Housing," accessed July 18, 2016, http://historymatters.gmu.edu/d/6900.
58 "'A Decent Home . . . for Every American Family': Postwar Housing Shortage Victims Testify Before Congress," accessed July 18, 2016, http://historymatters.gmu.edu/d/6908.
59 Biles, *Fate of Cities*, 21.
60 "Home Sweet Home," *Michigan Chronicle*, September 6, 1947.
61 "Home Sweet Home."
62 "42 U.S. Code § 1441 – Congressional Declaration of National Housing Policy," accessed October 4, 2017, www.law.cornell.edu/uscode/text/42/1441.
63 Harry S. Truman, "Statement by the President Upon Signing the Housing Act of 1949," *The American Presidency Project*, July 15, 1949, accessed October 4, 2017, www.presidency.ucsb.edu/ws/?pid=13246.
64 Teaford, *The Rough Road to Renaissance*, 107.
65 Joe Darden, Richard Child Hill, June Thomas, and Richard Thomas, *Detroit Race and Uneven Development* (Philadelphia, PA: Temple University Press, 1990), 158–67.
66 Njeru Murage, "Making Migrants an Asset: The Detroit Urban League-Employers Alliance in Wartime Detroit, 1916 to 1919," *The Michigan Historical Review* 26, no. 1 (2000): 66–104, quote on 73.
67 On respectability politics in the interwar era, see Victoria W. Wolcott, *Remaking Respectability: African American Women in Interwar Detroit*, Gender and American Culture (Chapel Hill, NC: University of North Carolina Press, 2001); Leslie Brown, *Upbuilding Black Durham: Gender, Class, and Black Community Development in the Jim Crow South* (Chapel Hill, NC: University of North Carolina Press, 2008). On the post–World War II widening of African American class distinctions, see Sugrue, *The Origins of the Urban Crisis*, 197–207.
68 Joseph Cialdella, *Motor City Green: A Century of Landscapes and Environmentalism in Detroit* (Pittsburgh, PA: University of Pittsburgh Press, 2020), 45–74.
69 "Glaring Evidence of the Need for Slum Clearance in Detroit," *Michigan Chronicle*, May 22, 1948.
70 "Some Facts About the Housing Situation in Detroit," Detroit Housing Commission, April 1949, Box 43, Folder A7–6, DUL Collection.
71 Thomas, *Redevelopment and Race*, 48–51, 56–65.
72 "Proposed Generalized Land Use Plan," May 1947, Box 8, Folder 10, DUDARP Collection, ALUA; Detroit Master Plan 1951, Box 8, Folder 4, DUDARP Collection; "Proposed Plan for Redevelopment of the Riverfront," May 1946, Box 1, Folder: "Citizens Housing and Planning Council of Detroit," UAW-RD Collection, ALUA.
73 "Gratiot Redevelopment Project," Detroit Housing Commission, June 30, 1964, Box 8, Folder 21, DUDARP Collection.
74 Figures from Thomas, *Redevelopment and Race*, 56. On the race tax, see Taylor, *Race for Profit*, 51–53.

75 Thomas, *Redevelopment and Race*, 56.

76 "The Detroit Urban League's Brief on Urban Renewal Activity in the City of Detroit," November 29, 1956, Box 44, Folder A8–28, DUL Collection.

77 "Summary Progress Report," June 17, 1955, Box 41, Folder A5–15, DUL Collection.

78 Committee for Neighborhood Conservation and Improved Housing memo, June 28, 1954, Box 41, Folder A5–15, DUL Collection.

79 "Summary Progress Report of Detroit's Neighborhood Conservation and Improvement Program," June 1954, Box 41, Folder A5–15, DUL Collection.

80 "Summary Progress Report of the Committee for Neighborhood Conservation and Improved Housing," Box 41, Folder A5–15, DUL Collection. Conservation area #1 was "bounded by Mack, Concord, Gratiot, Warren, and Van Dyke"; conservation area #2 was "bounded by Joy Road, Dexter, Elmhurst, Livernois, and Grand River"; and conservation area #3 was "bounded by Warren, West Grand Boulevard, Tireman, and Epworth."

81 "Summary Progress Report," June 29, 1954, Box 41, Folder A5–14, DUL Collection.

82 "Summary Progress Report," June 29, 1954.

83 "Summary Progress Report," June 17, 1955.

84 Bulletin, "What Is Neighborhood Conservation," Box 41, Folder A5–15, DUL Collection.

85 Bulletin, "Alleys," Box 41, Folder A5-15, DUL Collection.

86 Meeting Minutes, "Committee for Neighborhood Conservation and Improved Housing," October 16, 1956, Box 41, Folder A5–16, DUL Collection.

87 Editorial, "Housing Conversation and Urban Renewal," *Journal of Public Health* (October 1958): 1403–4.

88 Coleman A. Young and Lonnie Wheeler, *Hard Stuff: The Autobiography of Coleman Young* (New York: Viking, 1994), 146.

89 Newspaper article transcription, *Detroit News*, December 1, 1956, Box 44, Folder A8–28, DUL Collection.

90 "The Detroit Urban League's Brief on Urban Renewal Activity in the City of Detroit," November 29, 1956, Box 44, Folder A8–28, DUL Collection.

91 "The Detroit Urban League's Brief on Urban Renewal Activity in the City of Detroit," November 29, 1956, Box 44, Folder A8–28, DUL Collection.

92 Newspaper article transcription, *Detroit News*, December 1, 1956, Box 44, Folder A8–28, DUL Collection.

93 Roger Biles, "Expressways Before the Interstates: The Case of Detroit, 1945–1956," *Journal of Urban History* 40, no. 5 (2014): 843–54.

94 Biles, "Expressways Before the Interstates," quote on 849–50.

95 Bill McGraw, "Bringing Detroit's Black Bottom Back to (Virtual) Life," *Detroit Free Press*, February 27, 2017.

96 Biles, "Expressways Before the Intestates," 850.

97 Young and Wheeler, *Hard Stuff*, 1.

2

THE ENVIRONMENTAL QUEST FOR A LIVABLE REGION

Few individuals transformed the landscape of Michigan as vigorously as Genevieve Gillette, the "very determined woman," who drove the creation of the Michigan parks system and sought, through much of her work, to use natural settings to bring balance to modern, urban life.[1] The *Detroit Free Press*, in its featured obituary of Gillette, described her as "the one-woman force behind natural preservation and conservation in Michigan for more than 60 years," who pursued the conservation of natural beauty with evangelical zeal.[2] Her efforts in the Detroit area resulted in a Metroparks system preserving a ribbon of green draping the suburban fringe and today enjoyed by millions of visitors each year. Gillette's activism demonstrated one aspect of metropolitan environmentalism between the 1930s and 1960s, as she and a variety of urban and regional planners, policymakers, and engaged citizens attempted to re-make the built and natural environments of Southeast Michigan into a harmonious whole. They sought to balance a region overwhelmed by industrial growth and overcrowded housing conditions by providing access to natural beauty. Policymakers and planners like Gillette brandished an attractive, if incomplete, salve for the emerging urban crisis: bringing more green space and nature to the metropolitan area. In seeking to develop a sustainable, harmonious region, Gillette, like most other planners, policymakers, and activists, failed to witness her own role in overdeveloping environmental amenities in the suburbs while neglecting the inner city.

Gillette's path to conservation champion was an unlikely and winding journey, for she had no other examples to follow. Born in 1898 in Lansing, Michigan, Gillette grew up on her family's farm which abutted the Grand River. Occupying prime recreational land, Gillette recalled the several strangers each week who knocked on their door asking to picnic on the property.[3] In an age in which state parks did not exist, "and nobody else had ever heard of a state park," she boasted, "at that time we practically ran one for free." Her family laid the responsibility on

DOI: 10.4324/9780429319914-2

The environmental quest for a livable region **25**

her feet for ensuring picnickers closed the gate behind them to prevent livestock escapes, which, she laughed, made her Michigan's first Park Ranger.[4] The wistful memories contrasted against the darker episode in which Consumer's Power company bullied and cajoled the family into selling the forestland lining the Grand River for an impoundment that would supply hydroelectric power. The Gillette family felled the trees and sold the lumber, at which point "nobody even came after that to have a picnic in the place and it went to mullens and has looked like a no-mans [*sic*] land ever since." After witnessing the desolation of her beloved woods, the company abandoned constructing the impoundment. The experience no doubt convinced her that recreational resources were subject to the whims of corporate power, and common folks needed the force of the state to protect select landscapes from development.

But that still lay ahead. She spent her days exploring the land around her farm, often coming home covered in mud, to the chagrin of a mother who wished she would act more "girlish."[5] Witnessing the slow rhythms of nature shaped the rest of her life – the wildflowers emerging in spring, the killdeer building nests, the weeds competing with the corn crop, and the verdant summer scenery turning kaleidoscopic in the autumn. The environmental historian William Thomas Okie writes of an aesthetic environmentalism, in which engaging with all the senses in our environments can be a path to environmental care, and so it was with Gillette.[6] Like Rachel Carson and Aldo Leopold, both careful students of nature from a young age, Gillette found her path to conservation through nature study.[7] She filled notebooks with pressed flowers and plant clippings, drawing the natural scenery and gaining hard-earned firsthand knowledge of the ecology of their small world on the farm. From this modest start, she acquired the aesthetic sensibilities and knowledge of Michigan ecology that shaped her into a budding landscape architect and champion for public parks.

Gillette graduated high school zealous to be something more than a housewife. She recalled entering Michigan Agricultural College (precursor to Michigan State University) in 1916, enrolling in what was called "dumb sci," which she expected was a Latin term for some scientific field, but in fact was domestic science, an affront to her intelligence.[8] Exasperated by exercises like learning how to fry an egg in cooking class, she approached the president of the college, who sent her to science classes to pursue plant pathology. She remembered excelling in the science classes, particularly in the botany classes, where her experience picking the flowers and plants of the farm surely helped. Her professor witnessed Gillette's exceptional drawings and knowledge of plants and nudged her toward becoming a landscape architect. Go see Jens Jensen in Chicago, the professor insisted.

In 1920, Gillette arrived in the North Lakeshore of Chicago at the office of Jens Jensen asking for a job.[9] Jensen had grown famous as a sort of landscape architecture counterpart to his contemporary Frank Lloyd Wright, pioneer of the prairie style of architecture. Similarly, Jensen developed a practice dependent on utilizing native plants, in contrast to adopting the taste and non-native plants of the English landscapes. His establishment of the Friends of the Native Landscape

26 The environmental quest for a livable region

FIGURE 2.1 Genevieve Gillette Portrait, Photograph by Loche Clute, Unknown year.

Source: Genevieve Gillette Papers, Bentley Historical Library, University of Michigan.

organization transformed professional practice into public outreach inspiring conservation efforts. From this perch, Gillette became an ambassador for Jensen and the Friends of the Native Landscape, spreading the good news of landscape conservation and helping groups acquire parklands.[10] She likely heard Jensen describe parks as "breathing spaces" for the city, and his wisdom that "there should be a park area within walking distance of every city resident," as his democratic view of park space influenced Gillette.[11] After two years working in Chicago, Jensen insisted that Gillette "go home and make parks."[12]

From her conservation efforts, Gillette developed a reputation that led her to reconnect with an old acquaintance, P.J. Hoffmaster, a long-serving Michigan Director of Conservation. Along with Gillette, the pair successfully lobbied the Michigan legislature to develop a state park system. Hoffmaster would long reap the credit, despite the extensive lobbying and organizing work of Gillette. As wealthy Detroiters began contemplating a regional park system, they consulted Gillette, now living in Ann Arbor. With the same "evangelical zeal" that made possible the state parks system, Gillette worked to develop the Huron-Clinton Metropolitan Authority, a park system that remains focused on Metropark development on the suburban fringe.

Region of suburbs

The two-plus decades after World War II witnessed two significant trajectories. The City of Detroit reached its population and manufacturing peak before beginning a harrowing downward slide in population, manufacturing, and taxable wealth. Meanwhile, Southeast Michigan grew from an area with Detroit as its center of gravity, to a vibrant and sprawling six-county region of thriving, wealthy, and desirable suburbs, some of which acted as satellite downtowns, or what journalist Joel Garreau calls "edge cities," by the 1960s.[13] The federal government significantly aided the development of a high quality of life in the suburbs, while policies simultaneously stripped African Americans in the segregated central city of the same opportunities to build housing wealth.[14] Suburban overdevelopment and urban underdevelopment, one of the key stories of the twentieth century, was the result.[15] This chapter focuses on the parks, houses, highways, and zoning policies that attempted to bring balance and a high quality of life to the Southeast Michigan region, but which often exacerbated metropolitan environmental inequality.

The pattern of metropolitan inequality repeated throughout the United States in this era, leading to urban cores and inner suburbs in the throes of urban crisis while concentric rings of suburbs generally prospered with greater incomes accruing to those in the outer rings. Policy, intimidation, and violence trapped African Americans and other people of color in the urban core while white residents in many suburbs erected barriers to prevent the erosion of their privileged and racially homogeneous communities. In Detroit, suburbs represented numerous orientations, including manufacturing, blue-collar workers, African Americans, and at times attempts at racially integrated suburbanization.[16] Two unique manufacturing suburbs, Highland Park (birthplace of Ford's assembly line) and Hamtramck, were not on the periphery, but were in fact encircled by the City of Detroit. In each case, however, the suburbs defined themselves as places apart from the central city, promising a quality of life different from Detroit, whether in terms of the economic opportunities of the manufacturing suburbs or the racial homogeneity of a lily-white place like mid-century Dearborn.

As Michiganders grew more prosperous in the post-World War II era, they demanded greater access to natural settings and places to spend their leisure time. Gillette helped to re-shape a landscape in Southeast Michigan and beyond to accommodate the rising demands in the suburbs for a better way of living and proximity to nature. The suburban planners and policymakers who re-shaped the landscape to match their middle-class tastes contributed to increasing inequality in the region. Failing to recognize any similar claims to environmental quality in the inner city, they insisted on destructive urban renewal, highway development, and industrial land uses for central city residents, contributing to the creation of a landscape of urban crisis in Detroit. Promoting a rural character for the suburbs, they helped to ensure that unwanted land uses remained concentrated in the urban core.

Greener living during the Great Depression

The federal blessing for a new age of suburban housing took shape in Detroit and elsewhere during the Franklin Roosevelt presidency. New Deal agencies promoted exciting projects promising to revolutionize communities. Genevieve Gillette worked as the landscape architect for one of the celebrated Greenbelt Towns promoted by the Federal Emergency Relief Administration (FERA) and Resettlement Administration.[17] In Oakland County, 25 miles from downtown Detroit, the Westacres development combined features of urban living with a rural sensibility of large spaces, "country living," and subsistence gardening. Established in 1935, the 874 acres were subdivided to provide 150 homes on one-acre lots affordable to industrial workers who often faced seasonal unemployment.[18] The community leased houses to workers earning $1200-$1800 per year deemed "to have good character and credit rating and have shown some interest in gardening." The community delayed evictions in cases they deemed legitimate hardships, though it exercised rights to evict when a "family evidences a general shiftlessness and lack of thrift." At the end of the lease term, those workers judged good candidates were offered a contract to purchase the home at a cost of $4,400.

From its inception, the Resettlement Administration branded Greenbelt Towns as a "demonstration in suburban planning" and an escape for families from "badly crowded cities."[19] Michigan Senator James Couzens gifted the land to FERA and

FIGURE 2.2 Westacres clubhouse with pond.

Source: Genevieve Gillette Papers, Bentley Historical Library, University of Michigan.

The environmental quest for a livable region **29**

planners began with thrift in mind to develop a site emphasizing community, "rural economy," and a natural setting surrounded by a green belt.[20] In her eight years working at Westacres, Gillette worked within severe cost restrains that intended to keep the homes affordable for industrial workers.[21] The community maintained the environmental amenities of the site, including lakefront, which abutted Middle Straits Lake and some 55 acres of forest. The lots were sized large enough for families to supplement their incomes by gardening vegetables, raising poultry, and growing fruit trees.

The "union of town and country" reflected the regional planning ideals promoted by the famed architectural critic Lewis Mumford.[22] The theme of achieving industrial and environmental "balance" in metropolitan regions ran throughout many of Mumford's writings, and for planners and policymakers offered an attractive alternative to the rapid industrialization and urbanization of places like Detroit. Greenbelt Towns promised an industrial worker could have "healthful country surroundings . . . within easy reach of his job."[23] Planners spent little effort wondering if the approach could accommodate more than a tiny percentage of the nation's urban residents jammed into "decaying residential districts," nor whether they offered any lessons for planning more humane and healthful city centers. Tight finances and a backlash from the private sector and conservative congressional representatives ensured that the ultimate impact of the Greenbelt Towns would remain limited.

The dynamic region

On the eve of World War II, the U.S. census reported Detroit's population at 1.6 million, making it the nation's fourth largest city, with a total of 2.2 million residents living in the three-county metropolitan region.[24] Detroit expanded at an alarming rate during World War II, and authorities and planners fought to manage the urban change in ways that would not impede the war effort. World War II introduced environmental pressures that led planners and policymakers to widen the scope of their imaginations to consider how the city and suburbs operated as a metropolitan whole.

As Chapter 1 describes, Detroit exploded in a dramatic fashion in June 1943. The metropolitan ripples would be enormous. Reacting in part to the riot, the Citizens' Housing and Planning Council (CHPC), an organization led by elite Detroiters and pushing urban planning, urged fellow Detroiters to stop sweeping urban problems under the rug, using vivid metaphors. "What are we waiting for?," the citizen planners asked in 1944, in the midst of the wartime housing crisis.[25] "Detroit is a sick city," they warned. "Its circulation is clogged, it is vermin-infested, it is down at the heel, its complexion is grey, it tries to hide its sickness under a blanket of soot." Connecting disease and social dysfunction to the environmental conditions of the slums, they lamented "the distress in family life where mothers and children must fight rats and other vermin, dodge fallen plaster and dripping rain water and sewage, [and] must struggle against disease in damp cellars and dark

30 The environmental quest for a livable region

living quarters." While seeking to call attention to the grim challenges facing planners and policymakers, they were simultaneously making a case for Detroiters to abandon the city and remake their lives in the suburbs.

The racial violence that erupted on Belle Isle in June 1943 highlighted the need for desirable recreational spaces for industrial workers in a city growing ever more crowded.[26] For planners who saw the suburbs as a pressure relief valve from the over-crowding and racial tensions of the city, the lands outside city boundaries offered attractive development opportunities. The push for regional parks preceded the war, but despite war rationing delaying nonessential construction, many planners and policymakers continued to push for parks and recreation as an essential balancing force against the rapid industrialization and urbanization of wartime Detroit. Planning officials increasingly looked to the newly formed Huron-Clinton Metropolitan Authority (HCMA) to assume responsibility for the region's recreational needs.

Genevieve Gillette provided important early support for the development of HCMA. The Michigan legislature passed Act 147 in 1939, a law which enabled the formation of an agency comprising the five-county region of Wayne, Washtenaw, Livingston, Oakland, and Macomb to provide parks and connecting roads, and to collect a quarter-percent mill levy among member counties.[27] First, the new agency required a public vote among residents of the five counties. Wayne

FIGURE 2.3 Advertisement promoting the referendum to establish the Metroparks system.

Source: Harlow Olin Whittlemore Papers, Bentley Historical Library, University of Michigan.

County's Board of Supervisors expressed strong reservations due to the inequitable funding arrangements that saw its residents supplying 88% of the funding while only holding one of the five seats on the HCMA Board of Commissioners.[28] The public, however, overwhelmingly approved the ballot measure by a 2.5-to-1 margin. As soon as the agency formed in 1941, Wayne County challenged the legality of the enabling act in a case that wended its way to the state Supreme Court.[29] In January 1942, the Michigan Supreme Court affirmed the legality of the HCMA and its taxing authority.[30] This was the beginning of an often-contentious relationship between Wayne County and the HCMA, as we shall see in a later chapter.

War mobilization accelerated environmental change in Detroit, casting the region into disarray. HCMA officials decried the "transition from 'The Beautiful' to 'The Dynamic'," as pollution and sprawl resulted from the industrial dynamism.[31] Parks offered the promise of "health and morale" to workers living in industrial environs, and officials insisted that a "mother will have more peace of mind knowing her children are engaged in clean healthful sport . . . rather than risking their lives in dangerous and polluted waters or playing on the streets in congested areas."[32] Fuel and tire rations placed demands on local parks, as a trip to a nearby park could be celebrated as a patriotic decision when weighed against a car ride to Upper Michigan or farther afield. Years of planning went into the first parks, as officials awaited the end of the war and rationing to unleash their potential on the region.[33]

Postwar dreams

Among the biggest questions facing Detroiters at the end of the war was how to put their energies into making a more balanced, humane city. It seemed clear to nearly everyone that that Detroit's wartime development had created a deeply unsustainable city. With the wartime emergency behind them – along with the rationing, manpower disruptions, and other sacrifices – planners and policymakers believed a balanced Detroit and thriving suburbs were achievable goals. As Detroit Common Council President George Edwards put it in 1946:

> Here are two general important ideas: Detroit, a place where its people find a home, and live with all the satisfaction and joys which home life in a modern community should mean; and Detroit, an industrial area, the center of industrial development capable of producing goods not just for our community but for our nation and for the world. . . . Can you have an industrial community and at the same time have a city beautiful? Can you have an arsenal of democracy and can you have at the same time a city or an area which boasts that in its homes are located in a place where life is worth living?[34]

Quality housing, plentiful parks and recreation, effective zoning, and convenient highways all factored into policymakers' visions of a sustainable thriving region. Planners in the suburbs and the city each worked to make their environments

32 The environmental quest for a livable region

attractive, yet the suburbs, working on a relatively blank slate and with significant federal support, found it far easier to create the quiet, green, and healthful living conditions that postwar Americans demanded.

The rapid development of the region during World War II created a constellation of city and suburban governments with little coordination in planning. The Detroit Metropolitan Area Regional Planning Commission (DRPC) was created by the state legislature in 1947 to provide a more orderly system of cooperation between local governments and planning agencies. As the DRPC pointed out in an early report, agencies representing the ports, expressways, and parks, several counties, 60 planning commissions, and approximately 75 zoning ordinances created a complicated patchwork.[35] Initially, the agency represented Wayne, Oakland, and Macomb Counties, with Monroe and Washtenaw Counties joining later.[36] The objectives of the newly formed planning agency included "good living and business conditions."[37] Eyeing the vast and haphazard transformations to the region, the DRPC noted the difficult corrective work that lay ahead. "We have accumulated our good and our bad points for over a hundred years," they warned. "They are made of steel and concrete. They are nailed down by laws; they are sanctified by tradition and habit."

Planners insisted that the days of factories, working class bungalows, and ill-defined land uses intermixing would no longer do. Planning powers cooperated to redefine the Southeast Michigan landscape into one with suburban homeowners living close to parks and natural settings. For those whose jobs remained in the city, new highways promised to deliver them to and from their jobs at high speeds, and without immersing in the slums they feared were overtaking the city. The good life, these planners, real estate investors, and suburban civic leaders insisted, was in the suburbs. Utopianism suffused the visions of these planners, whose glossy brochures in the 1950s smoothed over the rough edges of implementation and neglected to include African Americans in their plans. So all-encompassing was the suburban vision for Southeast Michigan that much of the region's political power organized to support suburbanization. Principal among these was the United Auto Workers (UAW) Union, which shifted its focus from supporting wartime mobilization to promoting suburbs as an answer for the ill-housed workers who had struggled to find accommodations in wartime Detroit.

As one of the most important institutions in the Detroit region, the UAW made the living conditions of its members a high priority. Not content to merely focus on bread-and-butter issues like wages and working conditions, the union created a holistic program in which historian Sarah Jo Peterson writes of the wartime era, "housing was the UAW's most conspicuous social campaign."[38] The union's focus on housing remained after the war, as wartime workers often remained in the city, and returning servicepersons drove high demand for limited jobs and housing. At the union's national convention in 1946, outgoing union president R. J. Thomas reported: "With the end of the war, the nation was once again able to turn to the task of improving the living standards of its people."[39] Yet, progress in this area stalled significantly, and newspaper reports teemed with examples of skyrocketing rents, poor environmental conditions, and sluggish private construction.[40] The promise of "good shelter for every family" could only be accomplished through the "complete reconstruction and decentralization of our great metropolitan areas . . . for healthy, happy and safe living."[41] The union cast its lot with the planners and policymakers promising a suburban future for Detroit.

The housing shortage after World War II presented an opportunity for the federal government to promote and extend the promises of New Deal liberalism to the postwar era. President Harry Truman's Fair Deal program included a significant focus on housing and the built environment. The landmark Housing Act of 1949, notable for its emphasis on slum clearance and greater construction, contained language promising "a decent home and suitable living environment for every American family."[42] There were many reasons to be optimistic about a vigorous federal program to meet the housing shortage. The housing shortage gave liberals ample evidence that private construction alone could not meet the nation's needs, either in the short term or in the long term. Turning over responsibility to private housing companies, they argued, meant abandoning hope for well-planned communities on the urban fringe in favor of haphazard development that lacked a focus on community and environmental amenities. What the nation needed, the UAW's indomitable president Walter Reuther remarked in 1949, is "not dwelling space alone, but living space that meets up-to-date standards of health, recreation, efficiency."[43] Such an important charge could not be left in the hands of private developers seeking the quickest buck.

FIGURE 2.4 Walter Reuther and President Truman in Oval Office meeting, 1952.
Source: National Archives and Records Administration. Identifier No. 200406.

34 The environmental quest for a livable region

Reuther insisted that the union could push the federal government to provide the kind of housing developments desperately needed by an under-housed nation. But just as Detroit did retool successfully to provide war material, earning Detroit the moniker "Arsenal of Democracy," Reuther believed that the same industrial might could fight the war on housing through mass production of prefabricated homes while at the same time promoting the union's dream of a political economy based on full employment.[44] Capitalizing on abundant land, affordable housing construction, and federal highway development, suburbanization became a key element of the UAW's postwar vision for a livable and prosperous city. Addressing the postwar housing crisis would come before the union made any effort to address widespread residential segregation. By the time the union made institutional efforts to support integration of neighborhoods, the patterns were too well entrenched and policies too hardened to effectively disrupt. Even when the union leadership could make overtures at supporting residential integration, those people at the front lines, the rank-and-file white union members, overwhelmingly rejected black equality either on the shop floor or in the neighborhoods.[45] In an effort to reduce the inner-city tensions over limited housing and economic resources revealed during World War II in places like Detroit, the UAW advocated policies meant to facilitate suburbanization, but lacked the power – and the will – to enforce housing equality, with dramatic effects on the environmental inequality of the region. In its vision of suburban utopias, African Americans were neglected.

Breathing room

The Huron–Clinton Metropolitan Authority became a powerful ally in the push to beautify and preserve land on the metropolitan fringe. At the end of 1945, the HCMA announced, "Now that the war is over and materials and manpower are becoming available, the Huron–Clinton Metropolitan Authority is going beyond the planning phase of its work, and has entered upon a program of actual construction."[46] HCMA saw its postwar burden as providing a greenbelt around the city, developing massive parks with diverse recreational amenities that could provide families with a day of leisure. Early park leaders defended their attempt to save for the people park lands, which would otherwise be privately developed.[47] Funding came from a mill levy paid by residents of the district, who all then theoretically enjoyed access to the superparks.[48] Pooling resources created a recreational economy of scale. By purchasing massive tracts of land on Detroit's periphery, HCMA and its supporters reasoned, they could create more acreage per capita, serving current parks needs while also preparing for the future, before suburban developers swallowed affordable land.[49] The park system, as intended in the original design, would provide a greenbelt around industrial Detroit, saving prime natural areas from industry and residential development.[50]

The HCMA promised regional parks for day use, a place to take the family when few such places existed in the towns sprouting on the suburban fringe. The eight-year-old park and parkway agency announced itself as the "solution offered by the three million residents of the Detroit Metropolitan Region to a serious lack of park and recreational facilities within a reasonable driving distance of their homes."[51] The agency believed that its role was to provide recreation for people whose local government could not or would not do so, leaving Detroit's residents outside this definition. Though they belonged to the region and paid into the Metropark system, HCMA argued that they were in the business of providing parks for those who did not belong to a well-organized political unit. The metropolitan system allowed suburbanites to leverage the authority and taxes of the five counties to deliver amenities that they otherwise could not afford.

By the early 1950s, the HCMA narrowed its vision for the park system. Where earlier plans by the HCMA promised to distribute parks across the region, by 1952, the HCMA indicated that its master plan was to "preserve and develop the scenic and recreational facilities and possibilities in the valleys of the Huron and Clinton rivers . . . and to make them available to the public by means of Parkways and Connecting drives."[52] Two features of the plans stand out: the Clinton River valley flowed north of the City of Detroit and the Huron River valley was entirely south of the city, leaving Detroit proper out of the HCMA's master plan. "True to its symbol [of a man holding buildings in one hand and a tree in the other], the Authority is preserving for all time the scenic possibilities in the 'green belt' surrounding the Metropolitan district as provided by the valleys of the Huron and Clinton Rivers."[53] At the same time, the HCMA indicated that it aimed to provide parkways and drives to connect the system, though it would later abandon that approach and allow the growing highway system to fulfill that purpose. The HCMA from its inception designed the Metroparks as dependent on the automobile – it was necessary for most residents to drive considerable distances to the parks, to get from one side of a massive park to the other, or to travel between the parks. In part, the automobile-centered design was based on Robert Moses's park development philosophies made famous in New York City.[54] The Metroparks fit comfortably in the car-centered culture of Detroit, one that constantly quashed efforts to develop effective mass transit.[55]

Recreational planners in Detroit faced challenges associated with a rapidly expanding metropolitan area and a culture that valued leisure in the outdoors. By the mid-1950s, these challenges generated tremendous discussion within planning agencies and among union representatives. DRPC executive Robert Carpenter discussed with his agency some of the questions they would confront in the coming years. Staying ahead of the population trends posed numerous difficulties, requiring planners to predict decades in advance when making parks provisioning decisions. Failure to acquire land in a quickly developing area could prove extremely costly as, they noted, "competition for land and for water is increasing every year."[56] Yet more than just population trends entered the planning equation. Predicting family trends, the popularity of certain leisure activities like boating and fishing, and income levels all required calculation.[57] "The trend of a shortened work week from 40 hours to 32 hours is noted," argued Carpenter.

36 The environmental quest for a livable region

"The recreation people assume that the total eight hours thus added to leisure time will be devoted to recreation."[58] Because autoworkers now increasingly lived in the suburbs, planners suggested, delivering better recreational facilities to these residents would be a key responsibility of their agencies.

The rapid urbanization of Detroit and its suburbs in World War II and the following two decades threatened to destroy the rural scenery surrounding the city. Land was in great demand everywhere, warned Carpenter. More land for highways, bigger lots for houses, industry which required sites "four to eight times" bigger than before.[59] All this indicated that waiting was no option. Land must be acquired immediately, while it was still available close to Detroit. In 1956, Carpenter warned that the region was falling behind as its population increased and failed to create the parks to accommodate the newcomers. The biggest challenge: "Municipal inertia and backsliding."[60] Planners blamed communities for failing to do enough to provide parks for their residents, instead leaving the job to the regional planners. Parks helped lead the way to greater regional consolidation in the late 1950s, since many local communities were unwilling to pay for parks, and park development had few opponents. Regional planners took seriously the need to get parks right, finding it to be "an integral step in . . . a comprehensive plan for the orderly development of the region."[61]

Recreation opportunities were one criterion used to judge the quality of Detroit's neighborhoods, among a number of indicators that planners used to assess which areas should be targeted for slum clearance.[62] Regional planners recognized that the central city had long since been left behind in parks and recreational planning, but only exhibited an interest in providing improved environmental amenities on the suburban fringe, places that rarely needed environmental amenities as much as the central city. Planners blamed the City of Detroit for not providing enough parks and recreation, though tax levies imposed on city residents funded the accounts of the Huron-Clinton Metropolitan Authority while it provided no parks within the City of Detroit, and only one on the southwestern edge of Wayne County. The inequalities in park provisioning between Detroit and the suburbs would become a major target of inner-city residents and some suburbanites, a conflict explored in Chapter 6.

By 1957, the HCMA faced enough criticism that it felt compelled to respond to "John Q. Public." "[W]hen the whispers are of recession and taxes, public debt and welfare loads, reduction in taxes or more government spending, 'John Q.' wants to know 'What am I getting?' and 'What has it cost me?'"[63] The HCMA indicated that over the 16 years of its existence, the "average family man" had only paid $20.50.[64]

> The Authority is always on the lookout for new park sites particularly to preserve the native areas along the Huron and Clinton Rivers as a 'Green Belt' in the Metropolitan District. For its major parks, the site must be of regional size with capacity to sustain visitors in the thousands, and its terrain must be interesting as an attraction by itself.[65]

The environmental quest for a livable region **37**

Although the agency recognized the inadequacy of open space in the central city, like other planning agencies, it tried to solve central city problems with suburban solutions.

> Our metropolitan area, like most centers of population, finds itself out of balance – particularly in the recreation and transportation fields. Inadequate open space within the cities and the destruction of natural elements in the environs present the number one problem – the preservation of open space in public ownership. Striving to do its part in the solution of this problem the Authority has embarked on a land acquisition program within the framework of a metropolitan plan.[66]

Above all, the agency sought to provide the experience of "open country" when it was quickly disappearing in Southeastern Michigan. Rather than providing neighborhood-level recreation, which the HCMA saw as a local problem, the agency developed amenities for the fragmented suburban governments, which could not provide big facilities without cooperating with others. "Huron-Clinton parks are designed – not for an hour's use as a neighborhood unit – but for a full day away from the worries of our everyday existence," the agency insisted. "If our site planners can entice man to recreation – to the re-creation of mind and body – the relaxation from everyday worry – then we will consider that we have accomplished our purpose."[67]

Parks and recreation were essential to making the good life in the suburbs. Freed from the constraints of space, the automobile-ready Detroiter demanded parks to spend the day with their families. As DRPC lead planner Robert Carpenter noted in 1956, "Our people are more mobile. They are able to get into the family car and travel to more distant open spaces for place, quicker and with greater frequency than ever before."[68] In that spirit, the recreation-conscious leaders of Southeast Michigan sought to preserve massive parks that could host a wide variety of activities, from boating to picnicking to conservation education. Policymakers locally and nationally by the late 1950s shared the conviction that recreation was essential to everything from property values and neighborhood stability, to good public health, morals, and mental and physical fitness of children.[69] Planners and policymakers leaned on parks and recreation to provide more than just leisure. As Carpenter put it in 1956, "We have attributed to recreation, qualities which improve physical and mental health and moral values."[70] President of Sylvania Electric further revealed how recreational provision was also labor control: "Employees, we feel, should have wholesome recreation available for their leisure time. . . . The more they can enjoy at a cost they can afford, the less time will they spend in undesirable places."[71] Regional parks, then, represented far more than just a day of carefree leisure for Detroiters. Planners, employers, and policymakers considered them a means of social control.

Balancing the region

Planners and policymakers in the city asserted that competing with the suburban quality of life necessitated interventions in zoning and land use planning to ensure desirable places remained in the city. In 1947, the City Plan Commission revealed an

38 The environmental quest for a livable region

anxious city witnessing the startling growth of suburban communities pulling residents and tax dollars away from the central city, yet they projected a confidence that determined planning actions could address the impending crisis. Land use planning represented "an attempt to bring about a measure of balance and harmony among the various land uses."[72] Urban resilience was achievable if the right balance of industry, commerce, recreation, transportation, and housing could be achieved. Tools like zoning were nearly always insufficient to addressing the structural challenges facing the city, and even more so when they consistently misdiagnosed why residents were leaving the city for the suburbs. Federal support for suburbanization, freeways, and the racial homogeneity of the suburbs added up to an attractive package, and all these factors were beyond the power of planners to meaningfully change.

In the mid-1950s, planners still wrestled with the environmental challenges of creating a healthy equilibrium between housing and industrial land uses. City planners promoted greenbelts as a mechanism to help zone neighborhoods and improve the environmental health of residents in proximity to industrial land uses.[73] As with other aspects of urban planning, the city urged residents to propose greenbelts. Once ten neighborhood residents signed a petition, the process was set in motion for the city to study the desired greenbelt location. "The City Plan Commission believes that many neighborhoods in Detroit have land alongside them that should be used for greenbelts," one pamphlet alerted residents. "Those vacant lots make a no-man's land between homes and industry. They can be turned to their greatest use by protecting existing property values."[74] With targeted planning action, they hoped, economic and environmental sustainability could be mutually reinforcing. It is unclear how many, if any, greenbelts were initiated by neighborhood residents, though the city went to extensive effort to produce handsome brochures and distribute them through civic groups like the Detroit Urban League.

Planners anticipated continued migration of central-city dwellers to the suburbs, but they badly missed the mark in their calculation that urban renewal and slum clearance would attract back into the central city some of these residents. In one report, a Columbia University political scientist argued that central cities were being "reclaimed . . . faster than the slum dwellers can move to the suburbs."[75] University of Michigan political scientist William Gable suggested to the Detroit Regional Planning Commission that increasing commitment to regional solutions would be sought by a divided populace, which could not do many of the functions at that level on their own, such as in the areas of "health, welfare, and related services" as well as public works and highway design. It seemed to Gable obvious that some problems exceeded the capacity of local governments, as localities would assert their autonomy where possible, but "intimate planning relationships" would nevertheless rise to meet "those metropolitan-wide programs which require participation by the local units."[76] Regional planners were still bullish in 1958. The optimism would diminish over the course of the 1960s, as growing urban crisis in Detroit alarmed suburbanites, who sought to reassert their independence from Detroit and refused responsibility for any of the challenges associated with the central city.

Growing pains

Southeast Michigan experienced rapid urbanization during the 1950s, even as the population of Detroit proper dropped. The city of Detroit lost 9.7% of its population during the 1950s, while the six-county metropolitan area grew by 890,000 between 1950 and 1958.[77] Optimistic planners expected as many as 2.5 million more people in the region by 1980. Suburban governments and regional planners struggled to strategize how to manage the change and create a livable region. Building effective environmental services for the bourgeoning communities represented an ongoing hurdle.

Water and sewer service posed a significant challenge. In suburban Detroit, like many major cities, septic tanks facilitated the quick construction of neighborhoods in areas where sewer systems had not been extended. As Adam Rome revealed in his landmark study *The Bulldozer in the Countryside*, the haphazard and ill-controlled nature of much suburban sprawl alarmed local and federal officials throughout the United States. County administrators in the mid-1950s struggled to stop the "large-scale housing developments" installing home septic systems, and in Wayne County, these were referred to the Health Department for certification to ensure that the land was suitable for these purposes.[78] Outside Wayne County, which had a well-established health administration, enforcement was much more haphazard. Yet developers could respond that connecting to county drain facilities was unlikely, when Wayne County claimed a three-year backlog for constructing sewerage facilities.[79] Without centralized sewer lines extending into the far reaches of the suburbs, many of the out-suburbs failed to effectively manage their own sewage treatment, and polluted the waterways of Southeast Michigan. Birmingham, Bloomfield Hills, and Bloomfield Township faced a lawsuit over their inaction in 1955, leading a judge to impose a deadline for these governments to combine their sewage by December 31, 1957.[80] The Supervisors Inter-County Committee admitted that as late as 1960, it and other regional agencies had not prioritized water and sewage planning to the same extent as land use, highways, and recreation.[81]

Detroit Water and Sewerage Department (DWSD) became the bogeyman in Southeast Michigan upon which suburbanites could attach their fears of the central city. It was the issue around which much political maneuvering occurred, as suburban polities sought – desperately at times – to avoid DWSD services. In 1959, Detroit and Wayne County agreed that the county would construct a new water intake site and all the related pumping, filtration, and storage functions at a cost of $50 million.[82] The city would lease those facilities through 1991, under the direction of a Board comprised mostly of city residents appointed by the Mayor. One report in the mid-1960s claimed that some detractors harbored "suspicion of the motives of the city as a purveyor of water," yet the 1959 contract forestalled any serious prospect that a competitor could break up the Detroit monopoly. With Wayne County and Detroit linking through the contract, they held most of the cards.

40 The environmental quest for a livable region

Driving all of this conflict was the spectacular growth of the suburbs made possible by a car-dependent citizenry.[83] Detroit lived and died by the automobile. The same internal combustion that powered the creation of Detroit likewise made possible the spectacular success of the suburbs. It also, in no small part, contributed to regional inequality. The automobile blessed suburban residents with mobility and cursed city planners and regional policymakers which struggled to tame the beast. In the mid-1960s, close to 40% of suburban household possessed two or more automobiles, while city residents had an ownership rate half of that.[84] Though writing about the city of Portland, Oregon, historian Carl Abbott could easily be summing up the situation in Detroit: "Whether the concern was explicit or implicit, most planning issues have centered on the automobile."[85] Planners were thoroughly implicated in – and reacting to – the problem of automobility.

Lewis Mumford described his deep suspicion of the automobile's deleterious effects on regional sustainability. In 1958, he wrote, "Highway planners have to realize that these arteries must not be thrust into the delicate tissue of our cities; the blood they circulate must rather enter through an elaborate network of minor blood vessels and capillaries."[86] The blunt instruments of highway development in lieu of careful urban and regional planning, Mumford warned, created a "bulldozing habit of mind," and engineering habits which "lay waste [to] woods, streams, parks, and human neighborhood. . . ." Not until the mid-1960s did Detroit residents mount a sustained revolt against freeways, long after much of the damage had been wrought.

The city built on the automobile inevitably reaped the rewards and challenges of mobility. Allowing residents to enjoy the advantages of the suburban lifestyle simultaneously produced an array of challenges for the city and region. Detroit's urban crisis, in no small part, resulted from the automobile – from the manufacturing, the pollution from factories (the auto plants and suppliers), vehicle emissions, and the out-migration of the city's homeowners and taxpayers. "The city that created the automobile age created for itself the problems of a complex era," one landmark land use study summarized, including, "congestion and obsolescence at the regional core, the need and means to escape, and blight that emerged from these conditions."[87] For most Americans, the automobile seemed central to the good life. For those trapped in the urban crisis of its making, the automobile had created a slow disaster.[88]

Toward "Pure" Michigan

After working for decades on parks as an antidote to runaway industrialization and urbanization, Genevieve Gillette set her sights on one last campaign to make Detroit a more livable city. She significantly contributed to beautification campaigns focused on improving Detroit through citizen action. The beautification campaigns offered one route through which a diverse group of Detroiters could engage in environmental activism.

Gillette participated in the Lyndon Johnson administration's White House National Conference on Beauty and was subsequently invited to join the board of the Citizens Advisory Committee on Natural Beauty and Recreation in 1966. Lady Bird Johnson and many emerging environmentalists recognized highways as a serious detriment to the aesthetics of both countryside and city and critiqued their detrimental effects on quality of life. Yet they narrowly missed an obvious critique that, in spite of all the trash, billboards, and unsightly landscaping these roads produced, their impacts on inner-city quality of life were much graver. Highway construction destroyed neighborhood, increased noise pollution, added vehicle emissions to residential neighborhoods, threatening basic life necessities for many residents. The committee debated the assault of highways on the environment, with the Chair Laurance Rockefeller arguing that "outdoor recreation, esthetic, natural beauty and environmental quality values are not being taken into account sufficiently in selecting the proper routes."[89] No member raised the possibility of city residents being disproportionately burdened by the environmental hazards associated with highways and their development.

Although the committee developed out of Lady Bird Johnson's beautification crusade, the members pushed in new directions to encompass the "total environment."[90] The committee grappled with environmental inequalities and inner-city beautification. One handbook by the Citizens Advisory Committee envisioned the urban and suburban cooperation that could take place in schools. The authors lamented "the dreary facts of life in these United States in 1965. . . that the vast majority of boys and girls existing in Great Cities will spend their days and nights in 'Black Asphalt Jungles' and not the verdant green parks accessible to only a few of us affluent citizens."[91] The authors demanded that "national energies for conservation should be poured into Great Cities, not just Great Open Spaces." In the state of Michigan, they argued, while the tax dollars from the major cities supported vast numbers of conservationists, recreation specialists, and other public servants, they had neglected the "daily lives of children bound in by black, dirty, city sidewalks." A true urban renewal was possible, the authors argued, if America set its sights on providing "Green Islands" for city children. The school handbook and publications by the Citizens Advisory Committee offered the possibility of achieving integration through conservation, providing equitable green spaces for inner-city and suburban children alike.

Locally, the Beautification Council of Southeastern Michigan developed to coordinate the energies of garden clubs, conservationists, city planners, unions, and 58 member communities to fight the war on litter.[92] While BCSM had developed in 1963, it had grown substantially by 1966, reflecting publicity from Lady Bird Johnson's beautification crusade as well as growing environmental activism across the region. Gillette helped to facilitate the group's development, and her participation, as a member of the Johnson advisory committee, lent prestige to the young coalition. Groups like the Beautification Council created a bridge for many suburban and urban residents to greater environmental consciousness, seeking to bring a higher quality of life to their communities through environmental activism. Their activism, however, often neglected to critique the region's industrial polluters or the neglect of inner-city neighborhoods by city sanitation services.

42 The environmental quest for a livable region

Beautification provided a non-threatening entry point for many residents new to environmental causes.

A capstone to Gillette's career was the dedication in 1976 of the Gillette Nature Center in P.J. Hoffmaster State Park in the shores of Lake Michigan. Gillette's career reflected many of the trends in environmental politics in Southeast Michigan in the mid-twentieth century. From lobbying for the establishment of a leading state park system in the nation, to advocating for environmental amenities for the expanding suburban population of Detroit, to incorporating many of the new challenges and opportunities of the emerging modern environmental movement of the postwar period into environmental politics, Gillette helped to propel many of the new causes and issues forward. Although Gillette was often sensitive to the racial and class inequalities of environmental politics, she was part of a system that created and reinforced spatial inequality in Southeast Michigan, which she, along with a significant movement of activists, attempted to rectify beginning in the late 1960s. Many of those activists worked in the factories of Detroit, a space that exposed them to in-plant pollution, and put them on the front lines of witnessing environmental abuses in their communities. Workers fought for healthful natural opportunities close to home and in wilderness areas throughout Michigan. Far from being merely a quality-of-life issue, environmentalism represented a defense of the health and well-being of workers, their families, and their neighborhoods. It is them to whom we turn in the next chapter.

Notes

1 "'Mother of Michigan's Park System'," *Ann Arbor News*, May 27, 1986.
2 "Parks: Miss Gillette Was a Saving Angel," *Detroit Free Press*, May 29, 1986.
3 Biographical details from Patricia M. Frank, "An Oral History Project of Genevieve Gillette," 1973, in Box 1, Folder "Personal – Oral History," GG Papers, BHL.
4 Frank, "An Oral History Project of Genevieve Gillette."
5 Frank, "An Oral History Project of Genevieve Gillette," 16.
6 William Thomas Okie, "Beauty and Habitation: Fredrika Bremer and the Aesthetic Imperative of Environmental History," *Environmental History* 24, no. 2 (April 2019): 258–81.
7 Kevin C. Armitage, *The Nature Study Movement: The Forgotten Popularizer of America's Conservation Ethic* (Lawrence: University Press of Kansas, 2009).
8 Frank, "An Oral History Project of Genevieve Gillette," 14.
9 Frank, "An Oral History Project of Genevieve Gillette."
10 Jens Jensen to Genevieve Gillette, June 4, 1928, Gillette Papers, Box 2, Folder "Correspondence. 1928–1950," GG Papers.
11 Nature Bulletin No. 608, September 10, 1960, Box 6, Folder "Jensen and 'The Clearing' (1)," GG Papers.
12 Dave Dempsey, *Ruin and Recovery: Michigan's Rise as a Conservation Leader* (Ann Arbor: University of Michigan Press, 2001), 94.
13 Joel Garreau, *Edge City: Life on the New Frontier* (New York: Anchor Book, 1991); Dolores Hayden, *Building Suburbia: Green Fields and Urban Growth, 1820–2000* (New York: Vintage Books, 2004), 154–80. On Detroit metropolitan inequality, see Joe T. Darden et al., *Detroit: Race and Uneven Development* (Philadelphia, PA: Temple University Press, 1990), 3–10.
14 The literature on the role of federal policy facilitating metropolitan housing inequality is vast, see for instance, Kenneth T. Jackson, *Crabgrass Fronter: The Suburbanization of the*

United States (New York: Oxford University Press, 2006), 26. print; Thomas J. Sugrue, *The Origins of the Urban Crisis: Race and Inequality in Postwar Detroit*, Princeton Studies in American Politics, 1st Princeton Classic ed. (Princeton, NJ: Princeton University Press, 1996); Hayden, *Building Suburbia*; Robert O. Self, *American Babylon: Race and the Struggle for Postwar Oakland* (Princeton, NJ: Princeton University Press, 2005); David M. Freund, *Colored Property: State Policy and White Racial Politics in Suburban America* (Chicago: University of Chicago Press, 2010); Richard Rothstein, *The Color of Law: A Forgotten History of How Our Government Segregated America*, 1st ed. (New York and London: Liveright Publishing Corporation, a division of W. W. Norton & Company, 2017); Keeanga-Yamahtta Taylor, *Race for Profit: How Banks and the Real Estate Industry Undermined Black Homeownership, Justice, Power, and Politics* (Chapel Hill, NC: University of North Carolina Press, 2019); Paige Glotzer, *How the Suburbs Were Segregated: Developers and the Business of Exclusionary Housing, 1890–1960* (New York: Columbia University Press, 2020).

15 Self, *American Babylon*, 1.

16 Important works describing diverse forms of suburbanization include Andrew Wiese, *Places of Their Own: African American Suburbanization in the Twentieth Century* (Chicago: University of Chicago Press, 2005); Becky M. Nicolaides, *My Blue Heaven: Life and Politics in the Working-Class Suburbs of Los Angeles, 1920–1965* (Chicago: University of Chicago Press, 2002); Kevin M. Kruse and Thomas J. Sugrue, eds., *The New Suburban History* (Chicago: University of Chicago Press, 2006); and Heather B. Barrow, *Henry Ford's Plan for the American Suburb: Dearborn and Detroit* (Dekalb: Northern Illinois University Press, 2015). For the interactions between suburbanization and mass culture, see Lizabeth Cohen, *A Consumers' Republic: The Politics of Mass Consumption in Postwar America* (New York: Vintage Books, 2004).

17 Westacres brochure, July 1, 1945, Box 9, Folder: Westacres Housing Project, GG Papers.

18 "Westacres," *The Architectural Record*, October 1936, Box 9, Folder: Westacres Housing Project, GG Papers; Westacres brochure, July 1, 1945, Box 9, Folder: Westacres Housing Project, GG Papers.

19 *Greenbelt Towns* (Washington, DC: Resettlement Administration, 1936), Box 9, Folder: Westacres Housing Project, GG Papers.

20 "Westacres," *The Architectural Record*, October 1936, Box 9, Folder: Westacres Housing Project, GG Papers, BHL; Gillette memoirs, undated, Box 9, Folder: Westacres Housing Project, GG Papers.

21 Gillette untitled memoirs, undated, Box 9, Folder: Westacres Housing Project, GG Papers.

22 *Greenbelt Towns* (Washington, DC: Resettlement Administration, 1936), Box 9, Folder: Westacres Housing Project, GG Papers; Aaron Sachs, "Lewis Mumford's Urbanism and the Problem of Environmental Modernity," *Environmental History* 21, no. 4 (October 2016): 638–59.

23 *Greenbelt Towns*.

24 Darden et al., *Detroit: Race and Uneven Development*, 87.

25 CHPC Newsletter, June 1944, Box 20, Folder: "Press Releases, 1944-1946," EC Collection, ALUA.

26 On the environmental causes and consequences of the 1943 riot, see Joseph Cialdella, *Motor City Green: A Century of Landscapes and Environmentalism in Detroit* (Pittsburgh, PA: University of Pittsburgh Press, 2020), 116–19; Patrick D. Cooper-McCann, "The Promise of Parkland: Planning Detroit's Public Spaces, 1805–2018" (Ph.D. Dissertation, Ann Arbor, University of Michigan, 2019), 119–26.

27 "Huron-Clinton Metropolitan Authority: Act 147 of 1939," *Michigan Compiled Laws*, accessed December 19, 2019, www.legislature.mi.gov/(S(zvquxzwnirdgsndwn2z5hieb))/documents/mcl/pdf/mcl-Act-147-of-1939.pdf.

28 Cialdella, *Motor City Green*, 114–15.

29 "Organization History," Huron-Clinton Metropolitan Authority, accessed December 19, 2019, www.metroparks.com/organization-history/.

44 The environmental quest for a livable region

30 "The Huron-Clinton Metropolitan Authority: 1942 Annual Report of the Board of Commissioners, Period Ending June 30, 1942," located in SLM.
31 "The Huron-Clinton Metropolitan Authority: 1942 Annual Report."
32 "The Huron-Clinton Metropolitan Authority: 1942 Annual Report."
33 "The Huron-Clinton Metropolitan Authority: Report of the Board of Commissioners as of December 31, 1945," located in SLM.
34 George Edwards, "The Importance of Planning in Local Government," Box 9, Folder: "Planning, City, 1942–1948," GE Papers, ALUA.
35 Annual Report, Detroit Metropolitan Area Regional Planning Commission, 1949, Box 1, Folder: "Annual Report," SEMCOG-P Collection, BHL.
36 Darden et al., *Detroit: Race and Uneven Development*, 236.
37 Annual Report, Detroit Metropolitan Area Regional Planning Commission, 1949.
38 Sarah Jo Peterson, *Planning the Home Front: Building Bombers and Communities at Willow Run* (Chicago: University of Chicago Press, 2013), 95.
39 (President's Report) R. J. Thomas, *Automobile Unionism (1946): A Report Submitted to the 1946 Convention of the UAW-CIO at Atlantic City, New Jersey, March 23, 1946*, 49. Located in reading room, ALUA.
40 Henry Burdick, "Year's Building Barely Dents Housing Shortage," *Detroit Free Press*, January 13, 1946; Elwin Stouffer, "OPA Chief Aims Blast at Builders," *Detroit Free Press*, February 20, 1946.
41 Thomas, *Automobile Unionism (1946): A Report Submitted to the 1946 Convention of the UAW-CIO*, 50.
42 Housing Act of 1949 (Section 2 and Title 5), Public Law 171, Chapter 338, 81st Cong.; 83 Stat. 434; 42 U.S.C. 1471 et seq.
43 Walter Reuther, "Homes for People . . . Jobs for Prosperity . . . Planes for Peace . . . ," Box 59, Folder 13, UAW-PO-WPR Collection, ALUA.
44 Kevin Boyle, *The UAW and the Heyday of American Liberalism* (Ithaca, NY: Cornell University Press, 1998), 65–67.
45 On the structural barriers to integrating the UAW after World War II, see Kevin Boyle, "'There Are No Union Sorrows That the Union Can't Heal': The Struggle for Racial Equality in the United Automobile Workers, 1940–1960," *Labor History* 36, no. 1 (January 1995): 5–23.
46 *Report of the Board of Commissioners as of December 31, 1945*, Huron-Clinton Metropolitan Authority (1945), located in SLM.
47 David O. Laidlaw, "Creation of the Huron-Clinton Metropolitan Authority," 1947, Box 6, Folder: "Huron-Clinton Metropolitan Authority, 1969–1979," GG Collection.
48 "Huron Clinton Metroparks Information Guide," Huron-Clinton Metropolitan Authority, Box 4, Folder: "HCMA Legislation," MCRC Collection.
49 Henri E. Wittenberg, "$40 Million Tag Put on Belle Isle Expansion Plans," unknown Detroit newspaper, June 28, 1972, article clipping in Box 10, Folder 10, UAW-CRD Collection.
50 "Park Agency's Ideals Challenged," November 30, 1975, *Detroit Free Press*, 12–A, clipping in Box 4, Folder: "HCMA Legislation," MCRC Collection.
51 *The Fourth Biennial Report of the Board of Commissioners as of December 31, 1949*, Huron Clinton Metropolitan Authority (1948/49), located at SLM.
52 *Report of Progress of the Huron-Clinton Metropolitan Authority: Fifth Biennial Report of the Board of Commissioners as of December 31, 1951* (1950/1952), located at SLM.
53 *The Sixth Biennial Report of the Board of Commissioners as of December 31, 1953*, Huron-Clinton Metropolitan Authority, located at SLM.
54 Cialdella, *Motor City Green*, 123.
55 Sarah K. Frohardt-Lane, "Race, Public Transit, and Automobility in World War II Detroit" (Ph.D. Dissertation, University of Illinois at Urbana-Champaign, 2011), 185–87.
56 Meeting Minutes, Executive Committee, SEMCOG, May 31, 1955, Box 2, SEMCOG Collection.
57 Meeting Minutes, May 31, 1955.
58 Meeting Minutes, May 31, 1955.

The environmental quest for a livable region **45**

59 Robert D. Carpenter, "Regional Recreational Perspectives," July 12, 1956, Box 74, Folder 10, SEMCOG Collection.

60 Carpenter, "Regional Recreational Perspectives," July 12, 1956.

61 "Recreation in the Detroit Region, Part I," Detroit Metropolitan Regional Planning Commission, 1958, in Michigan Collections, State Library of Michigan.

62 "A Study of Recreation Facilities and Recreation Needs in the Center and Oakland Subcommunities," Detroit Commission on Children and Youth (July 1, 1955), located at SLM.

63 *The 8th Biennial Report of the Board of Commissioners as of December 31, 1957*, 51, Huron-Clinton Metropolitan Authority, located at SLM.

64 *The 8th Biennial Report of the Board of Commissioners as of December 31, 1957*, 9.

65 *The 8th Biennial Report of the Board of Commissioners as of December 31, 1957*, 51.

66 *Ninth Biennial Report as of December 31, 1959*, 18, Huron-Clinton Metropolitan Authority, located at SLM.

67 *Ninth Biennial Report as of December 31, 1959*, 23.

68 Carpenter, "Regional Recreational Perspectives," July 12, 1956.

69 Memo, Detroit Parks and Recreation Department, July 3, 1946, Box 9, Folder "Parks and Recreation, 1943–1949," GE Collection; Robert D. Carpenter, Remarks at the Supervisors Inter-County Committee meeting, July 12, 1956, Box 74, Folder 10, SEMCOG Collection.

70 Carpenter, "Regional Recreational Perspectives," July 12, 1956.

71 "Recreation in the Detroit Region, Part I".

72 "Proposed Generalized Land Use Plan," City of Detroit, May 1947, Box 8, Folder 10, DUDARP Collection.

73 "Greenbelts," Bulletin Number Two, Detroit City Plan Commission, c. 1954, Box 41, Folder A5–15, DUL Collection.

74 "Greenbelts," Bulletin Number Two.

75 Quoted in William R. Gable, "Michigan Government and the New Urbanism," Box 1, Binder: April 1957–December 21, 1962, SEMCOG Collection.

76 Gable, "Michigan Government and the New Urbanism."

77 Paul Reid, Statement to Senate Select Committee on National Water Resources, October 29, 1959, Box 3, Binder: December 9, 1958 through March 15, 1960, SEMCOG Collection.

78 Meeting Minutes, Sub-Committee on Sewerage and Waste Disposal, Supervisors Inter-County Commissions, September 15, 1955, Box 74, Folder 10, SEMCOG Collection.

79 Meeting Minutes, September 15, 1955, SEMCOG Collection.

80 Unknown newspaper clipping, "Oakland County Gets Pollution Deadline," August 31, 1955, Box 74, Folder 10, SEMCOG Collection.

81 Meeting Minutes, Supervisors Inter-County Committee, Water, Sewerage and Drainage Committee, September 22, 1960, Box 74, Folder 11, SEMCOG Collection.

82 "Staff Papers on Governmental Organization for Metropolitan Southeast Michigan," January 1965, Box 34, Folder 6, SEMCOG Collection.

83 George Galster, *Driving Detroit: The Quest for Respect in the Motor City* (Philadelphia, PA: University of Pennsylvania Press, 2012), especially Chapters 1 and 11. For a discussion of how the automobile dependency was built in to the suburban landscape, see Christopher W Wells, *Car Country: An Environmental History* (Seattle: University of Washington Press, 2014), 253–87.

84 "TALUS and Tomorrow," Detroit Regional Transportation and Land Use Study, Box 2, Folder "Southeast Michigan Council of Governments, 1967–1972," LWV-DDH Papers, BHL.

85 Carl Abbott, *Portland: Planning, Politics, and Growth in a Twentieth-Century City* (Lincoln: University of Nebraska Press, 1983), 268.

86 Lewis Mumford quoted in Statement of John F. Floberg, Hearings Before the Subcommittee on Appropriations, United States Senate, Eighty Sixth Congress, First Session on H.R. 5676 (Washington, DC: Government Printing Office, 1959), 426.

46 The environmental quest for a livable region

87 "Study Design for a Comprehensive Transportation and Land Use Program for the Detroit Region," Box 34, Folder 23, SEMCOG Collection.

88 The concepts of "slow violence" and "slow disaster" have recently animated scholarly discussion of environmental inequality. There are many examples to choose from, but two important examples include Rob Nixon, *Slow Violence and the Environmentalism of the Poor* (Cambridge, MA: Harvard University Press, 2013); Thom Davies, "Toxic Space and Time: Slow Violence, Necropolitics, and Petrochemical Pollution," *Annals of the American Association of Geographers* 108, no. 6 (November 2, 2018): 1537–53.

89 Meeting Minutes, Citizens Advisory Committee on Recreation and Natural Beauty, August 12, 1966, Box 4, Folder: "Citizens Advisory Committee . . . 1966," GG Papers.

90 United States Citizens' Advisory Committee on Recreation and Natural Beauty, *Community Action for Natural Beauty* (Washington, DC: Government Printing Office, 1968).

91 Handbook, "America Could Be Beautiful," Box 4, Folder: "Topical File – Beautification," GG Papers.

92 Bulletin, "Beautification Council of Southeastern Michigan," December 1966, Box 4, Folder: "Topical file – Beautification," GG Papers.

3
FACTORIES, FIELDS, AND STREAMS

To Your Industrial Health!, a labor radio program focusing on worker health and safety, began a 1949 episode with a fictional foundry worker, Sandy, a veteran of World War II and soon-to-be victim of an industrial disease.[1] The narrator intoned, "It was hot in the foundry, wasn't it, Sandy? Hotter than it had been in Guadalcanal. The sweat poured from your body as you worked . . . but you didn't mind it too much. You had some mighty big plans for the future." Hard at work in the intense heat and acute danger of the foundry, Sandy looked forward to his upcoming respite in nature. Sandy planned to tell his wife about getting a cottage in the summer, where he could rest with his family on "a nice beach . . . lots of green grass and blue sky . . . and a heavenly breeze at night," a welcome relief from the hellish foundry. In their apartment, which the summer heat had turned into a "Turkish bath house," the family longed for some time away from the stifling conditions of the city, a place where they could "sleep under blankets" in the cool night air, a place to swim and fish while little Mikey built sand castles on the beach, and Sandy's wife Kay could sit with the baby in the green grass. This, we are led to understand, is a world apart from the factory and city environs, a place where restorative relaxation in nature could relieve the suffering from the industrialized city, and one that provided an opportunity for family togetherness. On the eve of their two-week vacation, Sandy is struck in the middle of the night with "metal fume fever," and moans in agony with symptoms resembling malaria. Sandy perseveres and starts the vacation, but frequent attacks of the fever progressively debilitate him. Forced to turn down time in the rowboat with his son, and bickering with Kay, the quality time with the family and relaxation in nature has been ruined by the poisonous fumes of the foundry.

The innovative labor radio programming, sponsored by the United Auto Workers (UAW) union, illustrates some important features of Detroit's workers and the metropolitan environment after World War II. With increasing leisure time and

DOI: 10.4324/9780429319914-3

48 Factories, fields, and streams

incomes, many workers now had more opportunity to escape the urbanized and industrialized environs of the city. Outdoor recreation provided an opportunity for Baby-Boomer families to find togetherness, or so the programming insisted. Factory work held many dangers, some quite visible, like dangerous machinery prone to malfunction, but silent threats like exposure to toxic chemicals, dangerous air pollution, and cancerous materials in the factory threatened enjoyment of the idyllic escapes for their families. Outdoor recreation like camping, hunting, and fishing provided one route by which industrial workers came to understand environmental conservation. Yet the lived experience of factory work also created an acute awareness of in-plant environmental dangers, many of which spread to the community beyond the factory gates, prompting a growing environmental awareness of industrial pollution and its effects on the community. Despite the rapid growth of middle-class suburbs far from the polluting factories, Southwest Detroit and the downriver industrial suburbs remained thriving neighborhoods for workers.

By the early 1950s, efforts by both working-class sportsmen's groups and their unions to raise environmental awareness began paying dividends. Their efforts transformed the environmental politics of Detroit, fertilizing the grassroots environmental activism that emerged from below in the Motor City and elsewhere. Unionists were increasingly emboldened during the 1950s to demand state action on pollution and improvements in outdoor recreation. Once they reached the limits of local and state action in Michigan, they took their case national, creating an important dialogue on environmental issues even before Rachel Carson published the landmark popular ecology book *Silent Spring* in 1962, and long before the first Earth Day in 1970. Workers pioneered the push for healthy environments *and* industrial prosperity, a middle ground that was unique compared to the broader, emerging environmental movement.[2] As workers paved a middle ground between industrial rapaciousness and strict environmental preservation, they also created an environmental ethos and politics between producer-oriented conservation and consumer-oriented environmentalism. Situated at the point of production (and as beneficiaries of the industrial economy), and as biological members of the ecosystem within the factory and the surrounding community, their unique vantage point gave many industrial workers a distinct environmental activism and politics.[3]

Writing environmental decline, 1945–1952

One environmental writer in Detroit gave voice to the city's working-class environmental concerns. Jack Van Coevering, an outdoors feature writer for the *Detroit Free Press*, did more than any single person in Detroit in the immediate postwar years to call attention to the ruination of lakes, rivers, and wilderness, particularly in terms of the consequences of pollution and poor land use policies for outdoor recreation like camping, hunting, and fishing. Like Genevieve Gillette, Van Coevering insisted on the restorative properties of the great outdoors, and believed that working-class people most needed outdoor recreation and leisure. Working-class environmentalism blended concern over industrial pollution with an interest in preserving outdoors recreation opportunities, and Van Coevering championed this perspective in the *Detroit Free Press*. Workers advocated a balanced approach to environmental regulation, one that urged better regulation of pollution and land use, but which still defended the prerogatives of industry to pollute and exploit nature. They believed that they were uniquely positioned to balance industrialization with conservation of natural and recreational resources accessible to workers. Van Coevering used his *Free Press* columns to promote this viewpoint. In his weekly "Woods and Waters" column and in his investigations of industrial pollution, he exposed industrial abuse of the natural world and highlighted the important conservation and anti-pollution work being done by groups like the Michigan United Conservation Clubs (MUCC). Van Coevering enjoyed a close relationship with Detroit's unions, in particular the United Auto Workers, and was extremely popular with the city's blue-collar workers.

For many Detroit residents, their first foray into environmental activism came from witnessing the industrial abuse of local landscapes, and Van Coevering's Outdoors Page in the *Free Press* provided an inviting platform for them to press their concerns. "Mr. Editor: I know that you are interested in stopping pollution in Michigan waters. I, too, am interested in that. Ecorse Creek is near my home," noted one concerned resident of Ecorse, a working-class suburb in downriver Detroit. "Recently I went to the north bank where the steel mill is located. I found at least six pipes emptying oil scum etc. into the creek. My dog fell into a puddle of oil. He was so sick that I thought he was going to die. . . . The creek empties into the Detroit River three blocks from the mill."[4] The letter indicates one resident noting the connection between industrial pollution, local environmental degradation, a concern with the larger watershed (the Detroit River), and the health of an important household member – the dog. Industrial pollution threatened the ability of residents to safely explore local nature. The health of their families – and pets – depended on a wholesome environment. Van Coevering's "Save Our Streams" series of articles beginning in 1947 called attention to critical water pollution problems throughout Michigan. The "Save Our Streams" column became a starting point for many to discuss pollution, and Save Our Streams committees formed in women's clubs, Grange organizations, and beyond, where they pressed local and state action against pollution and challenged local polluters.[5]

"Save Our Streams" invited readers to write to the newspaper, where Van Coevering's Sunday Outdoors Page provided a forum for their observations, protests, and opinions. The letters offer remarkable grassroots accounts of pollution in the Detroit area and Michigan at large. Edward Speck wrote to complain about the pollution in Monguagon Creek, a small stream in downriver industrial suburb Wyandotte emptying into the Detroit River, where "the pollution becomes so strong that it kills all the fish when they come up to spawn in the spring and takes all the paint off the boats."[6] In addition to pollution observations, readers reported on the anti-pollution activism in which they were personally engaged. Lloyd Eagan wanted Van Coevering to know that the Detroit Sportsmen's Congress had for years been involved in fighting pollution.[7] "We are accused by the

50 Factories, fields, and streams

polluting element of having selfish motives," wrote Eagan, but "the opposition fails to realize . . . that we are first interested in our people, their health and well-being." Letter writers often gave witness to the intersection of public health and recreation concerns in the natural settings of their own communities.

The publicity generated by Van Coevering and the anti-pollution activism of working-class sportsmen and other conservationists produced results. In spring 1949, the Michigan legislature passed anti-pollution laws, which levied $500 per day fines on polluters, abolished the ineffective Stream Control Commission, and established a Water Resources Commission, which would include citizen representatives from industry, municipal leagues, and conservation organizations. The new laws were the result of much bargaining and compromise between industry and conservationists like the Michigan United Conservation Clubs.[8] The sportsmen's imprint on the bills could be found in its definition of pollution as any discharge injurious to fish and game, in addition to human health.[9] Indeed, the new laws went so far as to make it illegal to dump effluent into the water which could give fish an "off taste."[10] Van Coevering gave himself much of the credit for starting the ball rolling on an anti-pollution movement, which he insisted did not exist before the "Save Our Streams" column began in 1947. "At that time, pollution was sweeping Michigan like an all-engulfing wave," Van Coevering explained.[11] "Even ardent conservationists were beginning to think the task of cleaning up a hopeless one." Stories of devastating pollution and dramatic pictures of oil-soaked ducks in "Save Our Streams" generated public outcry and led newspapers across the state to begin regularly reporting on pollution and the environment, argued Van Coevering. The self-congratulations might have been excessive, but the column did much to demonstrate the extent of industrial pollution and its effects on ordinary Detroiters.

Promoting healthy landscapes for the family, 1947–1955

Van Coevering's environmental reporting gave voice to unionists and working-class sportsmen, many of whom belonged to two important institutions in Detroit that led the way in raising environmental consciousness: the Michigan United Conservation Clubs and the United Auto Workers.[12] MUCC was self-consciously organized as an organization supporting the sporting rights of the common man, as opposed to the organizations and clubs catering to wealthy sportsmen. Indeed, many hunting reserves in Michigan operated with exclusionary membership practices or unaffordable dues that limited working-class participation. One of the most acclaimed duck hunting spots in North America, at Pointe Mouilée in downriver Detroit at the confluence of the Detroit River and Lake Eerie, was an exclusive reserve for the rich until the state purchased its 2,600 acres in 1945. MUCC was intimately involved in its purchase, defending the rights of the "little fellows" to sporting lands.[13] Within the UAW, interest in environmental conservation, recreation, and workers' health and safety in the plants combined to form a brand of class-conscious urban environmentalism unique in postwar America.

Operating both inside the factory and as an agent for improved environmental health outside the factory gates, the UAW was a unique institution in the struggle for an improved living and working environment. Building upon its earlier accomplishments in establishing a UAW Health Institute in 1937, which provided access to independent doctors to substantiate work-related health complaints, the union in 1947 turned toward providing better education about on-the-job environmental health risks through a series of radio programs called *To Your Industrial Health!*. Produced in cooperation with the Wayne County Medical Society, the program featured dramatizations of industrial accidents, toxic chemical exposure, and other menacing workplace health issues, often through fictionalized exchanges between a doctor and a worker or a breadwinner (usually a male) and his wife. The first program began ominously, the announcer indicating that the program was directed to those working on dangerous machinery or with chemicals, as the narrator warns, "The industrial hazard is a gun pointed at your health, your pocketbook, your happiness, your family's life!"[14] The program raised important issues regarding exposure to toxic chemicals and in-plant pollution and set the stage for the workers' safety and health activism of the late 1960s and the 1970s.[15]

The program gained more sophistication by the beginning of 1949, turning from fictional conversations – usually between a doctor and patient – to full-fledged plays, complete with sound effects. Not surprisingly, many of the episodes focused on the dangers inherent in foundry work, one of the most dangerous jobs in the UAW shops. A remarkable number of episodes focused on the "silent" health threats, particularly toxic fumes and heavy metals exposure. They dramatized these threats by characterizing them as "mysteries" or "hidden dangers," insisting that workers take the health threat of these materials seriously. The education was designed to challenge the masculine shop floor culture that encouraged male workers to dismiss the danger of health threats that could not be seen. Warning workers that by putting themselves at risk they were putting their families at risk of losing a father or husband, the program leveraged the gender ideal of the male breadwinner. If they could not be convinced to do it for themselves, then perhaps they could be persuaded to take environmental health seriously for their families' sakes.

To Your Industrial Health! illustrated the connection between environmental health at work and family life at home. One key measure of working-class masculinity, according to the programming, was a father's ability to play in nature with his children. Pollution and industrial safety hazards threatened the healthy functioning of a family. In one program, a husband and father enduring excessive noise pollution at work returned home crabby and jumpy, taking out his frustration on the kids and ruining his relationship with them.[16] The second episode of *To Your Industrial Health!* centered on a young family. A beautiful 33-year-old mother provided a stark contrast to the once-vibrant and youthful husband, Sam, now sitting opposite of her, his face "ashen, the blue eyelids cover sunken eyes, the mouth hangs lax and the breath comes into it short and comes out long."[17] Only the prior summer, the woman reminisced, her husband played ball with the kids on Belle Isle, an island park in the Detroit River, teaching them how to swim, and saved a girl by pulling

52 Factories, fields, and streams

her out of the water. He was, she remembered, "a big shouter, a big eater – big Sam." Sam worked at the foundry on the grinder, exposing him to sand. The sand clogged his air passageways, giving him a nagging cough and pleurisy, all a result of silicosis from working in the dusty environment. The silicosis had turned into the early stages of tuberculosis. With no known cure for silicosis, Sam could no longer work and support his family – the realization of the fear of many working men.

In a working-class culture that prized male vitality and toughness, men often ignored – and indeed sometimes embraced – the dangerous and unhealthy working conditions.[18] Factory workers often ignored health malignancies, choosing to tough it out rather than seek professional medical help. The program's fictional Dr. Jay acknowledged that workers' bruised egos often accompanied them to the doctor's office. He lamented that they often failed to "respect" their working conditions, particularly when it included polluted air. Rendering the invisible threat of particulate pollution into realistic stories of suffering and pain for the worker and his family made the menace more tangible and comprehensible. While most men could admit the dangers of an unforgiving piece of machinery, they brushed off the polluted air which caused numerous diseases, including asbestosis, silicosis, tuberculosis, and many others. "The chest houses the very breath of life," the program warned. "Industrial workers ought to respect that house a little better."[19] In order to challenge the male culture of ignoring environmental disease, at times the show adopted a masculine message, arguing that the wife and children depended on the male breadwinner's vitality, and failing to protect one's body as he protected his household, was a dereliction of his manly duties.

At the same time as it endorsed and reframed masculine duty, the program also highlighted the environmental health risks facing women workers, although the characterization of women was more often demeaning than it was empowering. While the women in the program sometimes defied gender stereotypes, at times depicting single mothers, other episodes reinforced belittling caricatures of women. An early episode featured Dotty Hookendrooper, a 32-year-old "blonde and pretty" woman working on a monotonous punch press.[20] Describing the "rapt, beatific smile" adorning Dotty's face, the audience learns that Dotty's mind is not on feeding gaskets into the punch press, but on movie star Clark Gable. Dotty is daydreaming about meeting Gable, who professes his love for her, when the punch press jams without warning, nearly severing her arm. This time Dotty is unharmed, but the message is an indictment of the women who are too busy dreaming of stardom and romance to keep their attention locked on the dangerous machinery. The accidents and health hazards on the job threatened women's femininity and sexuality, the program asserted. "There is no beauty in illness and debility," the narrator began, and then described the plight of a young woman whose dating life suffered from a skin disease caused by contact with factory toxins.[21] Where men were alerted to the threat of injury to their productivity and breadwinning ability, industrial health threats endangered women's beauty and sexuality.

Nevertheless, the program utilized gender inclusive terms when describing many of the threats in the workplace. Poisonous fumes, malfunctioning machinery, and monotonous tasks affected women and men more or less equally in the show. In the first episode, Mrs. Dee, a widow whose husband was killed in Italy during World War II, now supported herself and children, but after three years on the job as an electrotyper, she suffered from pain in her knees, back, and stomach, loss of appetite, and lethargy.[22] She worked a "double-job," coming home from work to take care of her twin children. The doctor suspected lead poisoning, intoning, "there is nothing in the range of industrial injuries more subtle and insidious than metal and acid poisoning." Such workplace pollutants slowly and almost imperceptibly debilitated workers. The use of the female character indicated to listeners the danger faced by men and women alike, and men were not alone in losing the ability to take care of their families as a result of disease and injury. As in this article's opening vignette, work, industrial health, and nature intersected in many episodes. The thoughts of the respite offered by "the cool green waters of the lake . . . and the fish that are waitin' for me" helped Mike to make it through his shift dipping metal in chromium tanks.[23] Yet the daydreams led Mike back to thoughts of his friend on the line, Chubby, also an avid fisherman who Mike remembered as constantly bragging about the size of his fish and looking forward to the next outing on the lake. Mike and Chubby's fishing trip arrived, and the men departed for the cabin. The first night of the trip, before ever making it out on the lake, Chubby woke Mike up with violent coughing. Working in nitrous fumes had finally caught up with Chubby. A healing trip in nature had come too late.

In 1951, the program changed its name to *Danger – Men at Work*. Despite the title change, the program remained a project of the UAW-CIO Health Institute and still called on the same themes as *To Your Industrial Health*. Although it seems that the program ended at the end of 1951, its nearly four years of innovative programming established the UAW Health and Safety Department and the UAW Health Institute as important institutions in the workers' struggle against environmental health threats. A major theme in the programming, "Labor and Management – Allies in Safety," is indicative of the efforts to make safety a cooperative venture between workers and management.[24] Many episodes featured statistics indicating the loss of productivity caused by diseases and industrial accidents, efforts intended to make apparent the economic rationale of promoting a better safety record. Such efforts pointed to the more conciliatory era of labor-management accord in the postwar era.[25]

From the factory to the community

As the UAW highlighted the invisible environmental hazards haunting the workplace, the menace was also frighteningly visible at times, as pollution belched from the smokestacks of the factory. Smoke held nuanced and contradictory meanings for the workers of these factories. What once had been tolerated, even celebrated, as a symbol of industrial prosperity increasingly came under scrutiny by workers and their allies. Detroit, like most major cities, was slow to act on the pall of smog. The early anti-smoke campaigns typically centered on eradicating the nuisance

54 Factories, fields, and streams

which downtown merchants blamed for chasing away customers. Responding to these concerns, the Detroit Common Council passed a set of smoke regulations in 1947, created new funding for enforcement, and established the Bureau of Smoke Inspection and Abatement.[26] Harold Pearson, the new bureau's administrator, argued that Detroit's industrial growth had far outpaced the capacity of officials to respond. These were tentative steps, but the public was simply not yet compelled to push city officials for more stringent air pollution control. The Donora incident, however, would significantly change the national conversation on air pollution.

When Donora, Pennsylvania, residents awoke on October 27, 1948, instead of crisp autumn air, they were greeted with stifling, acrid smog. The smog was bad, but nothing about it seemed alarming to the residents accustomed to the devil they knew. Resident Charles Stacey remembered, "The smog created a burning sensation in your throat and eyes and nose, but we still though that was just normal for Donora."[27] The skies darkened over Donora, resembling "midnight at noon."[28] The zinc and steel plants owned by U.S. Steel held residents hostage. Residents expected the morning smog to dissipate by afternoon, but unusual meteorological patterns trapped the dust, carbon monoxide, fluorides, and sulfur dioxide beneath a layer of cold air. Instead of lifting after a few hours, the smog worsened over the following two days, suffocating Donora for five straight days. By the time the smog lifted, 20 Donora residents lay dead.

Donora exposed the high environmental health risks faced by working-class communities. Politically motivated officials described it as the result of an "atmospheric freak," clashing with the on-the-ground accounts by members of the United Steelworkers.[29] Steelworkers kept the issue alive, forcing investigations by the state. Although workers failed to compel the mills to admit wrongdoing and managed only a meager $256,000 settlement in court against U.S. Steel, they nevertheless prompted a national conversation on industrial pollution and its effects on working-class communities. Donora exposed the problem of plants controlling a monopoly of knowledge about the pollutants their facilities produced. Later, activists would work to ensure a better accounting of toxic chemicals in use at nearby factories.[30]

The incident prompted environmental scientists to investigate "atmospheric contamination and its effects on health conditions" in industrial regions like Detroit.[31] A symposium held at the 1952 Industrial Health Conference reported the results of the Detroit-Windsor Air Pollution Study, a project which incorporated corporate, local, state, federal, and international participants. The International Joint Commission, established in 1909 governed environmental pollution on the U.S.-Canadian border, including Detroit and Windsor, Canada. In 1949, just one year after the Donora disaster, air pollution emanating from Detroit, Windsor, and river vessels prompted the International Joint Commission to create an advisory board to recommend reforms and establish penalties. The group commissioned scientific study to establish the variables that influenced air pollution in the region and measure its effects on environmental health and the economy. The cautious scientists did not assess blame on individual companies or industries, but the gathering of particulate data and types of pollutants provided an important foundation for subsequent research on air pollution in Detroit.

Despite workers' experience with in-plant pollutants, and their suspicions of damaging health effects, public health scientists only slowly revealed scientific evidence tying industrial air emissions to negative community health outcomes. The complexity of disentangling individual sources of pollution and their interactions with consumer waste, automobile emissions, biological waste, and other pollutants bedeviled investigators.[32] The Donora disaster and the research it spawned in industrial areas like Detroit helped public health scientists better grasp the contributions of industry to adverse health outcomes. One of the most important subsequent studies involved establishing the inequalities of air pollution on environmental health in the Detroit region.

William G. Fredrick, head of the Detroit Department of Health, and leading scientist of the health consequences of pollution, produced significant and early examinations of environmental inequality in the city. For one pilot study, Fredrick tested four areas of Detroit; two experiencing high levels of pollution and two with low levels.[33] One of the highs and one of the lows were located in sections of the city that were predominately white while the other high-low pair was in a predominately African-American section of Detroit. Although Fredrick found a relationship between ill health and living in a high-pollution area, he found unsatisfactory the data concerning race-specific effects of pollution.

Further research by Fredrick indicated that African Americans faced higher levels of pollution than their white counterparts. Although they reported fewer ill-health effects from the pollution, Fredrick suggested that the reason was likely due to severe under-reporting of health complaints by the black community.[34] Evidence for this theory was supplied by the fact that the average duration of illnesses reported among African Americans were "consistently greater," suggesting that "only fairly serious illnesses were admitted by non-white respondents." Out-patient clinic records similarly confirmed findings of racial differences in the reporting of illnesses. While far fewer African Americans visited the clinic than whites, the rates of hospitalization for black patients were higher than their percentage in the population would indicate, suggesting a "tendency to ignore minor discomforts," creating misleading survey data. The data indicated that residents living in areas of high pollution experienced more illnesses and more time lost from work. Although the evidence establishing the significance of race was mixed, the investigations provided an important early foundation for studying class, race, and environmental inequality in the Detroit region.

A growing scientific expertise on air pollution and national attention to Detroit's pollution problem led some UAW leaders to confront city officials about their failure to appropriately confront the problem. Roy Reuther, brother to union president Walter Reuther and head of the Political Action Department, took the lead on air pollution. Detroit officials read with embarrassment a May 1955 *New York Times* article that called Detroit's air pollution the worst among the nation's five biggest cities, citing a study by the United States Public Health Service.[35] Reuther

56 Factories, fields, and streams

pushed the city council to take action.[36] He was offended that the city's health officials who were tasked with pollution enforcement seemed to deny that any problem existed when Detroit's frequent smog indicated otherwise.[37] One council member insisted that they were "doing everything possible at the present time in keeping Detroit clean, and . . . seeing to it that the situation is constantly improving."[38] Many officials took issue with the methodologies of air pollution testing and claimed that they were not reliable indicators of how Detroit fared compared to other cities.[39] Reuther urged expansive solutions to pollution, indicating that it would need to be a region-wide effort. The pollution from the downriver suburbs was beyond the reach of Detroit's regulation authority, and so any effective program would need to be metropolitan-wide.[40] Despite officials' denial that "the present level of air pollutants in Detroit is causing acute illness," those living near factories had a different perspective than the officials working at City Hall, removed from the immediate vicinity of factory emissions.[41]

Most working-class families in Detroit needed neither the UAW nor public health officials to explain to them the extent of industrial pollution. They lived, worked, and played in polluted environs, and they were compelled to act as a result of these lived experiences. Water pollution rendered unsafe many of the recreational opportunities available to working-class families. While suburbanites often had access to community swimming pools and recreation centers, lakes and streams served this purpose for city children. The southern section of the Detroit River, significant parts of the Rouge River, and the entire Grosse Isle Shoreline were condemned for swimming in the summer of 1949 by the Water Resources Commission.[42] What seemed like a basic childhood right was undermined by sewage and industrial pollution spilling into water basins. Such visible environmental deterioration significantly contributed to a growing reaction by working-class organizations like the UAW and outdoor sporting clubs.

Fish *and* factories: promoting the environmental middle ground

Many UAW members belonged to one of the Michigan United Conservation Clubs, which became an important mouthpiece for sportsmen – many of whom were working-class men – to voice their concerns about the environment.[43] In Southeast Michigan, MUCC led the anti-pollution charge in the 1950s. Although groups like the National Wildlife Foundation and the League of Women Voters were active in fighting against pollution in Michigan, MUCC remained the only major organization endemic to Michigan, and the only organization with a strong foundation in approaching conservation issues from a distinctly working-class perspective that emphasized restricting pollution of recreational resources.[44]

In Downriver Detroit, water pollution seriously threatened the health of wildlife and the future of fishing and hunting. A concern for birds and waterfowl provided outdoor enthusiasts with deep insight into the state of the environment, representing a very visible indication of the health of an ecosystem. In scenes reminiscent

Factories, fields, and streams **57**

of the oil-soaked birds after high-profile oil spills, the Detroit River was the setting in the late 1940s through early 1960s of several environmental disasters as the river's polluted and oil-slicked waters overwhelmed the waterfowl. One of the first of these disasters occurred in March 1948 near the Pointe Mouilleé Wildlife Refuge in downriver Detroit at the intersection of the Detroit River and Lake Erie, a popular spot for working-class hunters. Incensed at the dead ducks washing up alongshore, victimized by discharges from the nearby steel mills, oil refineries, and chemical producers, sportsmen associated with the Michigan United Conservation Clubs gathered over 1,000 of the corpses, drove them to the Michigan State Capital building in Lansing, and dumped them on the building steps. Media was on-hand to watch the governor gingerly stepping over the massacre. As historian Lisa Fine points out, the dramatic, theatrical protest "would hardly merit our attention" if it had "taken place after 1970," but the working-class composition of the protestors belies the traditional depiction of workers as anti-environmentalist.[45] In the aftermath of the demonstration, Michigan formed the Water Resources Commission, for which MUCC later took credit.[46] Despite the dramatic protest, massive duck and fish kills would occur on the river for the next several years. One of the worst occurred in 1949, when thousands of ducks washed up dead on the banks of the Detroit River. In the summer of 1952, hunters retrieved ducks so soaked in oil they were unfit to eat.[47] Other ducks were too oil-saturated to fly. Conservationists pushed the State Water Resources Commission to investigate the oil sources but found an over-burdened agency too under-staffed and cash-strapped to make much of a difference. Employing only 19 workers, the Commission was overwhelmed by the rapid pace of industrial expansion, yet the state cut its funding.

FIGURE 3.1 A State conservation officer displays oil-sucked ducks, 1948.

Source: Jack Van Coevering Papers, Bentley Historical Library, University of Michigan.

58 Factories, fields, and streams

Overcoming major obstacles, sportsmen made some headway on the pollution problem. These conservationists were key investigators of river pollution who successfully pushed the Michigan Water Resources Commission to act. After months of delays, the Commission investigated the oil pollution and traced its origin to the Great Lakes Steel Company on Zug Island in downriver Detroit.[48] Hunters in the Pointe Mouilleé Wildlife Refuge once again collected many of the 1,255 scaup ducks killed by oil and presented them to pollution officials.[49] State officials determined the actual mortality rate to be much higher than just those ducks collected. Dispatching a new technology invented by the State Water Resources Commission, investigators placed floating skimmers in the river, which collected water samples then analyzed by the commission. Investigators discovered a 40-foot oil slick emerging from a sewer near Great Lakes Steel. When confronted with the evidence, Great Lakes Steel admitted its culpability. "We are only sorry that we cannot come and say that we have the problem licked," admitted Vice President of Engineering D. E. McGuire, adding, "Our old mills were not planned with pollution control in mind. That is where the oil comes from."[50]

Duck hunters and fishermen often remarked on the poor state of the Detroit River, finding that in recent years pollution had become much more visible. Wyandotte resident A. C. Fisher observed, "There is so much oil on their feathers that many of them are unable to fly."[51] Detroit took up a debate that began in a Louisville newspaper that asked, "Fish or Factories?," questioning whether the two might be incompatible in the near future.[52] The factories lining the Rouge River and Detroit River transformed the habitats of fish and fowl. During freezing conditions, ducks sought out the warm water discharges of factories, like the Detroit Edison electric plant, placing the ducks in the direct path of polluted water.[53] Wintertime proved especially dangerous for wildlife, as the water flow of the thoroughly polluted Rouge River slowed to a standstill, turning it into a toxic pool.[54] Given the relative inaction by regulators just a few years earlier, it was a major accomplishment to force the Water Resources Commission to launch investigations into river pollution. The publicity campaigns by working-class sportsmen to improve local habitats would help to form a foundation for the emergence of an environmental movement in Detroit in the 1960s.

Sportsmen and working-class conservationists insisted that it was possible to enjoy natural amenities and resources, in a managed, regulated manner with democratic input from workers to ensure long-term benefit. Increasingly in the postwar period, the wise-use philosophy would clash with the preservationists seeking to protect nature from human activity. As Jack Van Coevering summed up the argument, "In all this, we must admit that city folks often glorify the untouched wilderness. They go all out for unmanaged wild land and grudgingly give in to such 'developments' as fire trails and canoe landings. 'Local' people, on the other hand want to see such country opened up and developed."[55] Working-class conservationists' insistence on the careful, restrained use of nature placed them in the uncomfortable position of rejecting the preservationist ideology as well as the voracious appetite of industry for land and natural resources.

Factories, fields, and streams **59**

Sportsmen developed an understanding of ecology and ecosystems through careful observations. They were among the first to raise the alarm at the synthetic chemical boom in the United States and the damage it had done to local ecosystems. Nearly a decade before Rachel Carson's exposé on pesticides, *Silent Spring*, Van Coevering reported the alarm among outdoor enthusiasts, writing, "America's chemical factories are busy these days turning out carloads of new-fangled poisons for killing weeds, and bugs. Some of these concoctions are comparatively harmless to human beings and wildlife. Others have the incredible potential of poisoning the entire Nation to death through the destruction of its own natural resources, soils and wildlife."[56] The editor of the sportsmen's magazine *Michigan Out of Doors*, Burrell Hendershot, wrote: "A single application of the wrong kind of chemical agent can upset and bring havoc to a wildlife community in short time." Like Rachel Carson, they pointed the finger at synthetic chemicals, including herbicides 2,4-D and 2,4,5-T made by the Dow Chemical Company. For its part, Dow insisted its products were safe to animals and non-toxic. The two chemicals would later gain notoriety for their use as Agent Orange in the deforestation operations by the U.S. military in the Vietnam War. Later studies also determined their carcinogenic nature. While not calling for a stop to the application of all synthetic insecticides and herbicides, they urged a "GO SLOW signal when we are not sure just where new discoveries will take us," and insisted that, more than ever, conservationists could provide leadership in environmental stewardship.[57]

MUCC was not the only group initiating grassroots environmental protests in the 1950s. Naturalists called attention to the environmental consequences of suburban sprawl, particularly the problems caused by poor or nonexistent sewage systems. The Macomb Nature Association organized a hike along Mill Creek in St. Clair County, north of the Detroit metropolitan area, to expose the pollution caused by inadequate sewage systems. Like industrial pollution, suburbanites not only looked to the Water Resources Commission to provide them relief but also encountered an overburdened agency unable to respond to the seemingly limitless sources of pollution. Sewage from residential developments and runoff from farms on the metropolitan fringe created a crisis for the watershed, causing massive fish kills and terrible odors, and destroying the aesthetic and recreational value of places like Mill Creek.[58] But suburbanites were late to awaken to their own environmental crisis, having been "sleeping on their rights too long," wooed into a complacency that their suburban settings would remain pristine. In comparison, Jack Van Coevering indicated, downriver Detroit residents had been much more alert to the consequences of pollution on their local environments.

Van Coevering argued that sportsmen had been among the first Michigan residents to challenge the environmental consequences of suburban sprawl. As Adam Rome argued in his important history of suburban environmentalism, *Bulldozer in the Countryside*, a number of Americans, particularly scientists, urban planners, and government officials, became vigorous opponents of suburban sprawl as a result of a sewage system crisis, destruction of open space as a community resource, and the draining of wetlands.[59] Sportsmen in Detroit followed a different trajectory in

60 Factories, fields, and streams

opposing sprawl. For them, sprawl represented a serious threat to the sports they loved. Where homebuilders saw wetlands as waste and reclamation as an opportunity for profit, hunters, fishers, and birdwatchers often saw them as valuable and delicate ecosystems harboring rare birds, waterfowl, game, and fishing holes. As shoreline, floodplains, and wetlands gave way to residential subdivisions, some questioned whether defying nature's wisdom through reclamation projects was such a good idea. "The drainage bug is biting us badly," wrote Van Coevering, predicting that the fruits of limitless money for reclamation projects would one day be remembered as a testament to human folly.[60] With natural areas in Southeast Michigan quickly swallowed up by suburban sprawl, he asked, "What will people 50 years hence say about us: Did we use the foresight of which we are capable?" His insight revealed a major theme of sportsmen's conservationist ethos – the hubris of human disregard for nature's patterns would wreak terrible ecological consequences and a loss of natural areas close to Detroit.

In 1958, the American Federation of Labor–Congress of Industrial Organizations (AFL-CIO) began promoting conservation of wilderness and natural resources as labor policy.[61] The Michigan State AFL-CIO went on the record opposing the development of a major copper mine in the Porcupine Mountains State Park in the Upper Peninsula. Industry deployed the argument that a mine would provide jobs and relieve the unemployment rate. Yet the AFL-CIO was not moved, arguing that existing mines ought to be providing more jobs, and that short-term economic gain should not be exchanged for "future rights and benefits of the people in the area." The United Steelworkers, the union representing the Upper Peninsula copper miners and the workers at Great Lakes Steel in downriver Detroit (and a CIO affiliate), indicated that they did not oppose development simply for the sake of preservation, but instead argued that the land should be developed as a tourist destination, and could provide a long-term economic benefit in that capacity.[62] Working-class conservationism remained distinct from the preservationist ethos adopted by elite environmentalists. Workers recognized the importance of economic activity and jobs, but attempted to point the way toward a future in which natural resources could be exploited for the long term while preserving sporting opportunities and scenic character. The USW concisely summed up working-class conservation: "Man needs a job which will provide a living wage with conditions which provide [a] wholesome and healthy environment."[63]

Fleeing the often-overwhelming industrial landscapes and pollution, many of Detroit's working-class residents left with their families for the relative peace and restorative relaxation promised by state parks and recreation areas. Business boomed in the parks and campgrounds of northern Michigan. Victims of their own success, many of these sites could not keep up with demand. Visitors complained about run-down, overcrowded, and littered facilities – the same conditions from which they escaped.[64] Michigan's parks and lakes were beneficiaries of the vibrant outdoors culture of Detroit's workers. The outboard motor allowed greater mobility on the lakes and at a price affordable to many workers. Invented in 1910, the motors were for decades plagued with maintenance problems and were notoriously unreliable machines.[65] Yet by the 1950s, improvements made the outboard motor more reliable and affordable so that by the end of the decade, some 30 million Americans enjoyed boating in the summer.[66] "A wife can always tell when her husband is thinking about his other girl friend, his boat," the UAW's periodical *Solidarity* explained in 1958.[67]

Many male workers promoted the wilderness as a place to test their masculinity.[68] Hunting was an act of vigor, argued *Solidarity*, one that could drive men to exhaustion – even death – and was not for the faint of heart, the danger and primal nature of which was indeed part of the appeal for many working men. As one article suggested, "dressing deer is [a] messy job so squeamish shouldn't hunt," and then said if one doesn't have the stomach or ability to properly dress the game, they are "better off shooting at old tin cans."[69] Hunting dangerous game pitted man against nature in a struggle for survival. Cougar hunting was praised because of the danger posed to the hunter. "It is not uncommon for the cougar to stalk the hunter who, in turn, is stalking it," wrote the *Solidarity* outdoors writer Fred Goetz.[70] Hunting animals toward the top of the food chain demonstrated the domination of man over the natural world. The thrill of cougar hunting was unmatched, because the cougar "too, is a hunter of big game – deer, wild sheep, goat, boar, even elk."[71] Likewise, the popularity of fishing in Michigan soared in the 1950s. The magazine *Michigan Conservation* asserted that the pervasive threat of nuclear annihilation had created a longing to "preserve ancient skills."[72] Put another way, masculine survival skills might become necessary in the event the Cold War turned hot. Working-class sportsmen believed that they were preserving essential connections to nature that invigorated men, keeping them from becoming the staid, alienated "organization man" described in the 1956 book of that name by William Whyte.[73]

Conservationists saw it as their responsibility to preserve for "the people" resources which would otherwise be swallowed up by industry.[74] Yet they also saw danger in unlimited access to resources by the people, where recreation would crowd out the industries which supplied income for many workers. Working-class conservation thus saw itself as an important arbiter between the voracious exploitation of natural resources and space by industry, and the overcrowding and uneducated use of wilderness and recreation space by ordinary Michiganders. *Michigan Conservation* suggested that the Space Age would also be the "age of space," as overpopulation; increased competition for land; and overcrowding of hunting, fishing, and camping sites placed great pressure on the state to resolve competing interests.[75] Striking a middle ground became an important mission of conservationists, and one that would at times put them at odds with the preservationist camp of the environmental movement of the latter 1960s and beyond.

Organizing for the environment, 1958–1962

With all the attention being brought to the pollution problems by sportsmen and *Free Press* writer Jack Van Coevering, and despite success in pushing the Water Resources Commission to launch pollution investigations, it certainly seemed

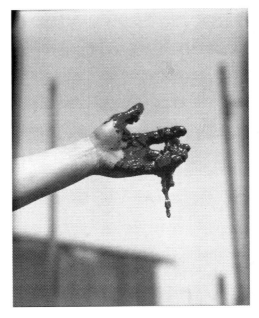

FIGURE 3.2 An unidentified person scoops oil from the Detroit River, 1959.

Source: Jack Van Coevering Papers, Bentley Historical Library, University of Michigan.

to many that they were making serious progress. By the turn of the 1960s, Van Coevering and others looked back favorably on the fifties as the decade in which the nation's consciousness was awakened to the environmental consequences of unmitigated industrialization. But celebrations were cut short by yet another major disaster on the Detroit River in April 1960, this one killing at least 12,000 ducks.[76] Unlike the 1952 oil spill that had an easily identifiable source in Great Lakes Steel, the cause of the mass duck deaths was harder to pin on one entity. A combination of a major raw sewage dump, oil dumping from McLouth Steel, and an "ill-timed return of winter" spelled disaster for the fowl. Investigations and bringing public attention to pollution could only go so far – it was clear a more organized political approach would be necessary. By the early 1960s, MUCC began broadening its activism beyond local and state politics and began demanding more federal regulation of polluters, protection of recreation areas, attention to urban land use, and management of natural resources. Even as Detroit's working-class sportsmen entered a new arena of political activism, they maintained their distinct conservationist perspective.

Working-class conservationists were successful in getting their two institutions to organize against industrial pollution: their sportsmen's associations and their unions, particularly the UAW. Both began forays into participating in political action, including state and national hearings and organizing unionists on environmental issues. Despite the mainstream environmental movement's tremendous success in grassroots organizing on critical environmental issues by the 1970s, the workers examined here helped promote environmentalism sensitive to local pollution issues, the shop-floor environment, and the need to balance industrial activity with a respect for natural resources. Both MUCC and the UAW participated in the growing number of federal conferences in the early 1960s aiming to bring together numerous stakeholders in environmental debates.

The crisis of pollution of Michigan waterways gave working-class conservationists a national platform to air their concerns. At the Joint Federal-State of Michigan Conference on Michigan Water Pollution, among the first of its kind nationally, MUCC deflected criticism that its interest in promoting environmental regulation threatened industrial vitality. "MUCC and other conservation groups have been accused often of standing in the way of progress. Because they have locked horns with industry on other occasions a great hue and cry has gone up that we are keeping industry out and are biting the hand that feeds us."[77] By the 1970s, workers were less likely to push environmental protection due to the threat of factory closures, but here they insisted that "industry and wildlife can live side by side, providing industry will do its part in containing wastes." Still firmly within Detroit's industrial heyday, these representatives insisted that innovation could overcome whatever costs environmental protection might impose. Laurence Braun, a member of the Wayne County Sportsmen's Club and chairman of the Anti-Pollution Committee, echoed the testimony of MUCC.[78] A night-shift worker, Braun gave up his sleep to attend the conference. Braun offered eyewitness testimony on the decline of fish and wildlife near Detroit, asserting the important role of conservationists in working to protect the environment. Like the sportsmen who wrote to the *Free Press* throughout the 1940s and 1950s asserting the authority of their first-hand observations, workers continued to rely on their lived experiences to explain environmental degradation and ecological change. Striking is Braun's deep understanding of fishing and hunting, as he spoke confidently on the types of pollution ("suspended solids, bacteria, and glycerol oils") and the havoc they creaked on ecosystems. "The sport and commercial fishermen are confronted with a reduction of desirable species," Braun warned, "and an increase of the less desirable noxious and rough fish, due to a reduction of the oxygen content in the water." Braun worried that their efforts would be in vain if municipalities, industries, and homeowners did not contribute to managing the pollution problem. A few years henceforth, he feared, the environment would be too wasted to recover.

Environmental degradation continued to threaten working-class families' living and recreational environments, but they were now better organized to confront the environmental threats. Where earlier activism focused on providing natural escapes like campgrounds, safer working environments, and better local and state enforcement of pollution regulation, in the early 1960s, the UAW shifted to pressing for a greater federal responsibility in environmental matters. As the number of outdoor enthusiasts swelled and competed with industry for public lands, the union encouraged federal legislation to ensure a balance between public and private interests. *Solidarity* imagined a fictional working-class family, the Smiths, who, like many

64 Factories, fields, and streams

other working families, looked forward to escaping the "crowded city, the noisy closed-in factory, the harried life," but instead encountered overcrowded recreation sites and places already despoiled by industry.[79] "Every year," *Solidarity* reported, "they seem to be losing a little more of their right to outdoor fun without stepping on other people's toes – or being stepped on." Joe Smith feared that without the government stepping in, "my grandchildren might never remember there ever was an outdoors." The UAW answered Joe by indicating its support for the 1962 Wilderness Bill in the U.S. Senate and the establishment of a National Wilderness Preservation System which would provide a more organized land use system for public land. *Solidarity* further indicated the union's support for preserving natural settings close to workers, like the Indiana Dunes on Lake Michigan and the Sleeping Bear Dunes in Northwestern Michigan, two popular destinations for auto workers.

While the Wilderness Bill failed, and the flurry of environmental legislation would have to wait until the Johnson Administration, the union's shift to pushing for federal environmental legislation established it as an important stakeholder in the debates. The UAW paid earnest attention to the warnings of ecological collapse raised by Rachel Carson's *Silent Spring*. The UAW's official periodical *Solidarity* predicted the significance of the book, arguing that "not since Sinclair's 'The Jungle'; or perhaps even since 'Uncle Tom's Cabin' will an American book have raised so much comment and controversy as 'Silent Spring'."[80] *Solidarity* applauded President John F. Kennedy's decision to form a scientific panel to explore the issues raised in the book. While autoworkers had for years been calling attention to the loss of wildlife and desolation of rivers and lakes on account of industrial pollution, many now applauded the federal government taking an interest in stronger environmental protection. Yet the UAW realized that Congress would not act without feeling political pressure, and so began some of its earliest efforts organizing voters on environmental issues. Pushing for clearer labels on pesticides and increased federal funding for research on hazardous chemicals, the UAW urged voters to insist that their congressmen and state legislators take action.[81] The union's support of expanding the federal government's role in environmental protection was an early indicator of the tremendous support the union would give to Lyndon Johnson's environmental initiatives.[82]

Conclusion

By the time Rachel Carson published *Silent Spring* in 1962, calling attention to the disastrous consequences of DDT and other synthetic chemicals to backyard ecosystems, many of Detroit's workers had already long since sounded the alarm.[83] Environmentalists like David Brower and the Sierra Club gained considerable support by stopping the Federal Bureau of Reclamation from flooding the Dinosaur National Monument on the Utah-Colorado border in the mid-1950s. The victory is often regarded as a major milestone in the emergence of the modern environmental movement. Detroit's workers showed concern both for the wilderness in upstate Michigan and further afield, but more notably they organized on behalf of the local environments where they worked, fished, hunted, camped, let their children swim, built their houses, and walked their dogs – the landscapes closer to home. The efforts of Jack Van Coevering, the UAW, and industrial workers to call attention to the plight of the environment paid dividends by the mid-1960s, as workers grew more organized and aggressive in their fight for healthy and livable communities. As they struggled to fight the environmental degradation of their communities, Detroit's workers likely would have endorsed Jack Van Coevering's parting words in his last column in the *Free Press* in 1965, "The battle will never be won but it is the fight that counts."[84]

Notes

1 "Mysterious Fever and Metal Fume Fever and Health Conditions in Foundries," *To Your Industrial Health!*, Box 9, Folder 30, UAW-HSD Records, ALUA.
2 The literature exploring the urban and industrial origins of environmentalism is now extensive. See, for instance, James Schwab, *Deeper Shades of Green: The Rise of Blue-Collar and Minority Environmentalism in America* (San Francisco, CA: Sierra Club Books, 1994); Andrew Hurley, *Environmental Inequalities: Class, Race, and Industrial Pollution in Gary, Indiana, 1945–1980* (Chapel Hill, NC: University of North Carolina Press, 1995); Robert Gottlieb, *Forcing the Spring: The Transformation of the American Environmental Movement*, rev. ed. (Washington, DC: Island Press, 2005); Robert W. Gordon, "Environmental Blues: Working-Class Environmentalism and the Labor-Environmental Alliance" (Ph.D. Dissertation, Wayne State University, 2004); Scott Hamilton Dewey, *Don't Breathe the Air: Air Pollution and U.S. Environmental Politics, 1945–1970* (College Station, TX: Texas A&M University Press, 2000); Chad Montrie, *To Save the Land and People: A History of Opposition to Surface Coal Mining in Appalachia* (Chapel Hill, NC: University of North Carolina Press, 2003); Chad Montrie, *Making a Living: Work and Environment in the United States* (Chapel Hill, NC: University of North Carolina Press, 2008); Chad Montrie, *A People's History of Environmentalism in the United States* (London and New York: Continuum, 2011); Chad Montrie, *The Myth of Silent Spring: Rethinking the Origins of American Environmentalism* (Oakland, CA: University of California Press, 2018); Josiah Rector, "Accumulating Risk: Environmental Justice and the History of Capitalism in Detroit, 1880–2015" (Ph.D. Dissertation, Wayne State University, 2017).
3 For the working class and its relationship to conservationism, see Louis Warren, *The Hunter's Game: Poachers and Conservationists in Twentieth-Century America* (New Haven, CT: Yale University Press, 1997); Karl Jacoby, *Crimes Against Nature: Squatters, Poachers, Thieves, and the Hidden History of American Conservation* (Berkeley: University of California Press, 2003); Lawrence M. Lipin, *Workers and the Wild: Conservation, Consumerism, and Labor in Oregon, 1910–1930* (Urbana: University of Illinois Press, 2007).
4 "Sportsman Speaks Piece About Ecorse Pollution," *Detroit Free Press*, February 12, 1950, clipping in Box 4, Folder: Sunday Outdoor Page 1950, JVC Collection, BHL.
5 "Why It's Up to You to Help Save Streams," *Detroit Free Press*, July 13, 1947, in *Save Michigan's Streams*, Box 5, Folder: Save Our Streams Columns 1947–1950, JVC Collection. For more on hunting and its relationship to male working-class culture, see Lisa M. Fine, "Rights of Men, Rites of Passage: Hunting and Masculinity at Reo Motors of Lansing, Michigan, 1945–1975," *Journal of Social History* 33, no. 4 (2000): 805–23. For the relationship between conservation and working-class sportsmen in Michigan, see Montrie, *Making a Living*, 97–102.
6 Edward Speck to Van Coevering, in *Save Michigan's Streams*, Box 5, Folder: Save Our Streams Columns 1947–1950, JVC Collection.
7 Lloyd Eagan to Van Coevering, in *Save Michigan's Streams*, Box 5, Folder: Save Our Streams Columns 1947–1950, JVC Collection.

66 Factories, fields, and streams

8 "Woods and Waters," *Detroit Free Press*, April 10, 1949, C–4, clipping in Box 5, Folder: Save Our Streams 1947–1950, JVC Collection.

9 Hub M. George, "Strong Pollution Law Signed by Governor," *Detroit Free Press*, May 19, 1949, clipping in Box 5, Folder: Save Our Streams 1947–1950, JVC Collection.

10 "New Pollution Law Strikes at Greed," *Detroit Free Press*, May 29, 1949, clipping in Box 5, Folder: Save Our Streams 1947–1950, JVC Collection.

11 "New Pollution Law Strikes at Greed."

12 Lisa M. Fine, "Workers and the Land in US History: Pointe Mouillée and the Downriver Detroit Working Class in the Twentieth Century," *Labor History* 53, no. 3 (August 2012): 410.

13 Fine, "Workers and the Land in US History," 409–34, quote on 417.

14 "First Program," *To Your Industrial Health!*, Box 9, Folder 13, UAW-HSD Records.

15 Labor radio is examined in Elizabeth Fones-Wolf, "No Laughing Matter: The UAW and Gender Construction on Labor Relations Radio in Fifties' America," *Labor: Studies in the Working-Class History of the Americas* 8 (Spring 2011): 77–107; Elizabeth Fones-Wolf, *Waves of Opposition: Labor and the Struggle for Democratic Radio* (Urbana: University of Illinois Press 2006). For more on the safety and health activism, and its relation to environmental justice, see Josiah Rector, "Environmental Justice at Work: The UAW, the War on Cancer, and the Right to Equal Protection from Toxic Hazards in Postwar America," *Journal of American History* 101 (September 2014): 480–502.

16 "First Program," *To Your Industrial Health!*, Box 9, Folder 13, UAW-HSD Records.

17 "Only Two Lungs to a Customer . . . 2nd Program," *To Your Industrial Health!*, Box 9, Folder 13, UAW-HSD Records.

18 Jussi Turtiainen and Ari Väänänen, "Men of Steel? The Masculinity of Metal Industry Workers in Finland After World War II," *Journal of Social History* 46 (2012): 449–72; Ava Baron, "Masculinity, the Embodied Male Worker, and the Historian's Gaze," *International Labor and Working-Class History* 69 (2006): 143–60; Ronnie Johnson and Arthur McIvor, "Dangerous Work, Hard Men, and Broken Bodies: Masculinity in the Clydeside Heavy Industries, c. 1930–1970s," *Labour History Review* 69 (2004): 135–51; Stephen Meyer, "Work, Play, and Power: Masculine Culture on the Automotive Shop Floor, 1930–1960," *Men and Masculinities* 2 (1999): 115–34.

19 "Only Two Lungs to a Customer . . . 2nd Program," *To Your Industrial Health*, Box 9, Folder 13, UAW-HSD Records.

20 "When Thoughts Are Killers – 3rd Program," *To Your Industrial Health*, Box 9, Folder 13, UAW-HSD Records.

21 "The Skin Game . . . 4th Program," *To Your Industrial Health*, Box 9, Folder 13, UAW-HSD Records.

22 "First Program," *To Your Industrial Health*, Box 9, Folder 13, UAW-HSD Records.

23 "Death Takes a Fishing Trip – Nitrous Fumes," June 10, 1949, *To Your Industrial Health*, Box 9, Folder 31, UAW-HSD Records.

24 "Labor and Management – Allies in Safety . . . 13th Program," n.d., *To Your Industrial Health*, UAW Health and Safety Department Collection, Box 9, Folder 13, UAW-HSD Records.

25 Nelson Lichtenstein, *State of the Union: A Century of American Labor* (Princeton, NJ: Princeton University Press, 2003), 98–140; Kevin Boyle, *The UAW and the Heyday of American Liberalism, 1945–1968* (Ithaca, NY: Cornell University Press, 1998), 83–106.

26 Newsletter, Citizens Housing and Planning Council, December 1947, Box 1, Folder "Citizens Housing and Planning Council of Detroit," UAW-RD Records, ALUA.

27 Quoted in "Smog Deaths in 1948 Led to Clean Air Laws," *All Things Considered*, National Public Radio, April 22, 2009, accessed February 7, 2020, www.npr.org/templates/story/story.php?storyId=103359330.

28 Benjamin Ross and Steven Amter, *The Polluters: The Making of Our Chemically Altered Environment* (New York: Oxford University Press, 2010), 87–88.

29 Ross and Amter, *The Polluters*, 87–95, quote on 90.

Factories, fields, and streams **67**

30 Lynne Page Snyder, "'The Death-Dealing Smog Over Donora, Pennsylvania': Industrial Air Pollution, Public Health, and Federal Policy, 1915–1963" (Ph.D. Dissertation, University of Pennsylvania, 1994), chapter 6. Scott Dewey also identifies Donora as an important turning point in galvanizing organized labor to engage in anti-pollution politics in "Working for the Environment: Organized Labor and the Origins of Environmentalism in the United States, 1948–1970," *Environmental History* 3, no. 1 (January 1998): 45–63.

31 George D. Clayton, "The Detroit-Windsor Air Pollution Study," *Public Health Reports* 67, no. 7 (July 1952): 658–71.

32 Morris Katz, "Atmospheric Pollution: A Growing Problem in Public Health," *Atmospheric Pollution* 45, no. 3 (March 1955): 298–305.

33 Conference paper, W. G. Fredrick, "The Detroit Pilot Study of Community Air Pollution and Health," at Second Annual Research Planning Seminar of the Air Pollution Medical Program, February 3–5, 1958, Box 6, Folder 9, WGF Collection, ALUA.

34 This possible under-reporting could have any number of causes, including suspicion over the motives of elite white scientists investigating their communities or inability due to lack of access to transportation or income to seek medical treatment. "Analysis of the Last Three Periods. . . . Of the Air Pollution Health Study," February 21, 1957, 1, Box 6, Folder 5, WGF Collection.

35 "Air of New York is Second Purest," *New York Times*, May 5, 1955.

36 Miriani to Reuther, May 16, 1955, Box 64, Folder 31, UAW-PAD-RRF Papers, ALUA.

37 Reuther to Miriani, May 20, 1955, Box 64, Folder 31, UAW-PAD-RRF Papers.

38 Connor to Reuther, June 17, 1955, Box 64, Folder 31, UAW-PAD-RRF Papers.

39 Linsky to Reuther, June 4, 1955, Box 64, Folder 31, UAW-PAD-RRF Papers. Department of Health to Common Council, June 3, 1955, Linsky to Reuther, June 4, 1955, Box 64, Folder 31, UAW-PAD-RRF Papers.

40 Reuther to Beck, June 10, 1955, Box 64, Folder 31, UAW-PAD-RRF Papers.

41 Joseph Molner to Common Council, June 3, 1955, Box 64, Folder 31, UAW-PAD-RRF Papers.

42 "State Lists 50 Rivers and Likes Too Polluted for Swimming This Summer," *Detroit Free Press*, June 22, 1949, clipping in Box 5, Folder: Save Our Streams Column 1947–1950, JVC Collection.

43 Montrie, *Making a Living*, 92; Fine, "Workers and the Land in US History," 410.

44 "Woods and Waters," *Detroit Free Press*, March 14, 1954, clipping in Box 4, Folder: Sunday Outdoor Page 1954, JVC Collection.

45 Fine, "Workers and the Land in US History," 409.

46 MUCC Statement, March 27–28, 1962, in *Transcript of Conference in the matter of Pollution of the Navigable Waters of the Detroit River, Lake Erie, and Their Tributaries Within the State of Michigan*, 945–48. Document 000R62101B. Accessed December 19, 2013, http://nepis.epa.gov.

47 "Oil-Soaked Ducks Point to New Detroit River Pollution Peril," *Detroit Free Press*, November 16, 1952, clipping in Box 4, Folder: Sunday Outdoor Page 1952, JVC Collection.

48 "Set Hearing on Oil Pollution in Detroit River," *Detroit Free Press*, February 22, 1953, clipping in Box 4, Folder: Sunday Outdoor Page 1953, JVC Collection.

49 "State Uses New Weapon in Fight Against Oil Pollution," *Detroit Free Press*, March 1, 1953, clipping in Box 4, Folder: Sunday Outdoor Page 1953, JVC Collection.

50 "State Uses New Weapon in Fight Against Oil Pollution".

51 "Oil Waste Increasing on River," *The Detroit Free Press*, date unknown, clipping in Box 4, Folder: Sunday Outdoor Page 1950, JVC Collection.

52 "Fish or Factories? No Choice Necessary," *The Detroit Free Press*, June 22, 1952, clipping in Box 4, Folder: Sunday Outdoor Page 1952, JVC Collection.

53 Photo caption, *Detroit Free Press*, February 17, 1963, clipping in Box 5, Folder: Sunday Outdoor Page 1963, JVC Collection.

68 Factories, fields, and streams

54 "Oil Pollution Threat to Ducks," *Detroit Free Press*, February 17, 1963, clipping in Box 5, Folder: Sunday Outdoor Page 1963, JVC Collection.
55 "Just Where Would 'Wise Use' of Natural Resources Lead Us?," *Detroit Free Press*, June 29, 1952, clipping in Box 4, Folder: Sunday Outdoor Page 1952, JVC Collection.
56 "Are Chemicals Dealing Death to Whole U.S.?," *Detroit Free Press*, July 13, 1952, clipping in Box 4, Folder: Sunday Outdoor Page 1952, JVC Collection.
57 "Are Chemicals Dealing Death to Whole U.S.?".
58 "Woods and Waters," *Detroit Free Press*, February 12, 1961, clipping in Box 5, Folder: Sunday Outdoor Page 1961, JVC Collection.
59 Adam Rome, *The Bulldozer in the Countryside: Suburban Sprawl and the Rise of American Environmentalism* (New York: Cambridge University Press, 2001), 1–14.
60 Jack Van Coevering, "Woods and Waters," *Detroit Free Press*, July 6, 1952, C4, clipping in Box 4, Folder: Sunday Outdoor Page 1952, JVC Collection.
61 Jack Van Coevering, "Woods and Waters," *Detroit Free Press*, November 2, 1958, clipping in Box 4, Folder: Sunday Outdoor Page 1958, JVC Collection; Dewey, "Working for the Environment," 48.
62 "Miners Seek Answers on Porkies," *Detroit Free Press*, November 23, 1958, clipping in Box 4, Folder: Sunday Outdoor Page 1958, JVC Collection.
63 Quote in "Miners Seek Answers on Porkies".
64 "Age of Space," *Michigan Conservation*, July–August 1959, 1.
65 "Going Boating?," *Solidarity*, April 7, 1958, 6.
66 "Let's Keep It Afloat and Still Have Fun," *Solidarity*, June 30, 1958, 4.
67 "Going Boating?," 6.
68 Fine, "Rights of Men," 810–12; Montrie, *Making a Living*, 98–99.
69 "Dressing Dear is Messy Job," *Solidarity*, November 10, 1958, 7.
70 "Really Big Game: The Cougar," *Solidarity*, February 1965, 10; "Bears Are Exciting to Hunt," *Solidarity*, January 1966, 12.
71 "Are You in Shape to Hunt?," *Solidarity*, September 1965, 12.
72 J. W. Leonard, "Sport Fishing in 1990," *Michigan Conservation*, July–August 1959, 40.
73 William Whyte, *The Organization Man* (Philadelphia, PA: University of Pittsburgh Press, 1956).
74 Editorial, "The New Decade," *Michigan Conservation*, January–February, 1960.
75 Editorial, "Age of Space," *Michigan Conservation*, July–August 1959, 1.
76 "Woods and Waters," *Detroit Free Press*, April 17, 1960, clipping in Box 5, Folder: Sunday Outdoor Page 1960, JVC Collection.
77 MUCC Statement, March 27–28, 1962, in *Transcript of Conference in the Matter of Pollution of the Navigable Waters of the Detroit River, Lake Erie, and Their Tributaries Within the State of Michigan*, Vol. 2, 948, Document number 000R62101B. Accessed March 25, 2021 from Environmental Protection Agency digital archive, http://nepis.epa.gov.
78 Laurence M. Braun Statement, in *Transcript of Conference in the Matter of Pollution of the Navigable Waters of the Detroit River, Lake Erie, and Their Tributaries Within the State of Michigan*, Vol. 2, 862–65, Document number 000R62101B. Accessed March 25, 2021, from Environmental Protection Agency digital archive, http://nepis.epa.gov.
79 "Recreation for All," *Solidarity*, June 1962, 13.
80 Roscoe Fleming, "Our Campaign Against Pests May Be Endangering Us," *Solidarity*, November 1962, 13.
81 "Here's What you Can Do About Pesticide Poisons," *Solidarity*, August 1963, 11.
82 Montrie, *Making a Living*, 106–7.
83 Montrie, *The Myth of Silent Spring*, 104–6.
84 "A Farewell Message from Van Coevering," *Detroit Free Press*, June 27, 1965, clipping in Box 5, Folder: Sunday Outdoor Page 1965, JVC Collection.

4

THE UAW CONFRONTS THE URBAN ENVIRONMENTAL CRISIS

By the late 1960s, the United Auto Workers (UAW) believed the urban crisis was also an environmental crisis – the two could not be separated. The union pursued an environmental activism it called the "War on Pollution," but it went much further than just addressing air and water pollution, to encompass the "total, living environment" of Detroit.[1] The post–World War II era saw the middle-class and elite suburbs over-develop environmental amenities, while pushing environmental hazards to the central city and industrial suburbs. As a result, Detroit's inner city and industrial communities suffered from air and water pollution, a lack of green space, deteriorating physical infrastructure, and impoverished recreational facilities. The UAW, over the late 1960s and into the early 1970s, promoted an environmentalism sensitive to race, class, and urban settings. In doing so, they pioneered a justice-oriented environmentalism that foreshadowed the emergence of the environmental justice movement in the early 1980s. Despite many faults, the UAW's program offered a substantial counterweight to middle-class environmentalism which often marginalized working-class and minority residents.[2]

The route to stalwart UAW liberal environmentalism was years in the making. The UAW supported some modest efforts at pollution control in the mid-1950s, but by the early 1960s, it took a greater role in advocating federal environmental protections. The UAW's initial entrée into full-throated urban environmental activism developed out of union president Walter Reuther's support of President Lyndon Johnson's Great Society.[3] When Johnson launched his Great Society program in May 1964 at the University of Michigan, Walter Reuther shared the stage. Johnson and members of his administration called for a "new conservation" that would embrace the cities as much as the old conservation worked to efficiently manage rural lands, natural resources, beautiful scenery, and wilderness.[4] The *Washington Post* noted the conservationist connection between Theodore Roosevelt and Lyndon Johnson and suggested that Johnson "is probably the first President to

DOI: 10.4324/9780429319914-4

tell Americans they should 'salvage the beauty and charm of our cities.'"[5] Lady Bird Johnson was a driving force for environmentalism within the administration, championing programs like highway beautification, environmental education, and inner-city cleanups.[6] Reuther relished the opportunity for his union to play a leading role in the president's Great Society, including its environmental initiatives.

Olga Madar, environmental crusader

Reuther entrusted the union's environmental initiatives to his Recreation Department director, Olga Madar, whom he had grown to respect for her dogged promotion of racial integration through recreation.[7] Women were often excluded from leadership positions in the UAW, with the union's male leaders insisting that women lacked the fortitude to stand up to management and collectively bargain with nerve. Madar rose through the ranks anyway, navigating the brutal politics of the union, and wisely allied with rising star Walter Reuther. She developed a strong reputation within the labor movement for her advocacy of union recreation programs as an alternative to the company programs – called "corporate welfare" – that once attempted to provide an alternative to the lure of unionism. Her influence inside and outside the union would go far beyond working-class leisure.[8] From her role advocating for working-class recreation, Madar challenged racism and sexism, giving a critical edge to her recreation advocacy. From her

FIGURE 4.1 Olga Madar portrait.

Source: UAW Photo Collection, Walter P. Reuther Library, Archive of Labor and Urban Affairs, Wayne State University.

The UAW confronts the urban environmental crisis **71**

home base in Detroit, Madar led a national campaign that ended official segregation of bowling leagues by race and sex.[9] She developed women's rifle shooting programs in the UAW to challenge sex segregation in the shooting sports.[10] In part as recognition for her work de-segregating bowling, Reuther appointed Madar Director of the Recreation Department in 1947, making her only the second woman appointed to a leadership role in the union. Madar challenged the expectations of what a recreation director could accomplish. Her leadership on environmental initiatives provided a new arena for Madar to promote her vision of social justice.

Late in 1965, Madar and the UAW hosted the United Action for Clear Water conference, cementing the union's status among the forefront of environmental advocacy. Over 1,000 scientists, conservationists, union organizers, and political figures converged on Detroit.[11] Representing the Johnson administration, Secretary of the Interior Stewart Udall addressed the crowd. Udall was instrumental in pushing the Johnson administration to adopt strengthened environmental protections. Reinforcing Johnson's embrace of the UAW on the environment, he applauded the "enlightened leadership and grassroots impetus," claiming that it was evidence of "the genius of two great new waves – the new wave of conservation and the new wave of unionism – and I submit that together these two waves constitute a formidable tide of the future."[12] The UAW "has won its bread," Udall remarked, "and is now intent upon securing its roses."

Conference speakers not only fretted over the looming environmental crisis but also suggested a path forward, with unions and the working class at the forefront of the fight. Chief Enforcement Officer at the Federal Water Pollution Control Administration, Murray Stein, urged the union to adopt a comprehensive conservation program and continue its investment in clean water. "The water pollution issue has the peculiarity of being both a national, nonpartisan, long-range concern," Stein argued, "and a 'bread-and-butter' issue of the greatest immediacy to union members."[13] Walter Reuther seized the moment. He demanded a $50 billion "war chest" to confront air and water pollution.[14] Adopting the war-like rhetoric that would be commonplace for the union's environmental efforts, Reuther compared the sum to the amount "we spend on armaments in one year." Within a very brief period of time, the union turned its attention to the environmental crises members had noticed in the community air and streams, where they witnessed the effects firsthand.

Olga Madar took the show on the road, testifying on behalf of the UAW at the federal "Pollution of Lake Erie and its Tributaries" conference in Cleveland. Detroit's location on the Lake Erie basin and the city's status as one of the lake's worst polluters gave the UAW an opportunity to stand up for regional environmental crises. The UAW's Olga Madar argued that its membership, "particularly those who are fishing and boating and swimming enthusiasts," had been demanding the right to cleaner environments for recreational purposes.[15] After all, she added, nobody needed to tell the UAW's membership that the Detroit River was polluted. "They could tell by the way it looked and the way it smelled, and the fact that

72 The UAW confronts the urban environmental crisis

they can't do any more fishing there."[16] It was her insistence that the working-class citizens often paid the greatest price for industrial pollution that made her a strong, and relatively lonely, advocate for environmental equity in the mid to late 1960s.

The UAW's activism was evident in other industrial unions which confronted the urban environmental crisis in their own locales. The United Steelworkers (USW) fought pollution in Cleveland, Pittsburgh, downriver Detroit, and other USW strongholds. Like the UAW, the steelworkers union reflected on the impact of urban pollution on quality of life. "A relentless river of pollution is surging from our expanding cities and our booming cities," *Steel Labor* remarked. "It is oozing into once clear waters turning them from blue to gray, killing the fish and soiling shores with filth and scum."[17] Adopting the language of Johnson's reform program, the union argued that a "war on pollution is necessary to win this fight."

Echoing the USW, Walter Reuther addressed the union's annual convention in 1966, promising to confront the industries destroying the environment. "Great industries came into being, chewing up resources and spewing forth waste into the atmosphere and into our lakes and streams," Reuther charged. "Industry is our most conspicuous despoiler."[18] To better fight for environmental quality, the union reorganized its departmental structure at that convention, forming the Conservation and Resource Development Department, which would work closely with the Recreation Department. In the same year, Olga Madar led an insurgent effort to get the UAW to admit a woman to its International Executive Board, a goal for which many UAW women had fought following the successful 1962 activist effort to install a black unionist to the board.[19] At the convention in which Reuther significantly expanded the union's environmental agenda, Madar accepted election as the first woman on the executive board. Madar did not celebrate long, but went to work expanding recreational and environmental programs in the union.

Uprising of 1967

In March 1967, the UAW sounded the alarm over the fate of American cities in its periodical *Solidarity*. "Dirty air. Water pollution," and "empty, idle land" were evidence of the urban decay that threatened to destroy American cities. "If our cities continue to decay," warned Walter Reuther, the union's president, "then the economic, political and social fallout will be just as deadly and inescapable as nuclear fallout."[20] If the mood surrounding urban America was pessimistic, the UAW and liberal leaders did not believe Detroit was in danger of the kind of urban uprising that engulfed other cities. In Detroit, the tenor within UAW leadership was one of confidence. Having established the union's leading role as a Great Society ally, UAW and city leaders hailed Detroit as a successful example of a Model City. By many measurements, they had reason for confidence. Detroit's inner city, compared to other major cities, enjoyed relatively high rates of homeownership and neighborhood satisfaction. War on Poverty programs succeeded in putting thousands of Detroiters to work. However, as historian Sidney Fine once argued, though life in other cities might have been *worse* for African Americans, that did not negate the

The UAW confronts the urban environmental crisis **73**

racism, severe poverty, and police brutality that black Detroiters endured. In July, 1967, they struck back.[21]

Six days in July revealed the vast gulf between the promise of the Great Society and its War on Poverty and the realities for Detroit's black population. Detroit police officers broke up an illegal blind pig bar in the early hours of Saturday, July 23, in the 12th street area. An altercation between patrons and police grew to encompass the block, then the surrounding neighborhood, and then large sections of the city south of Grand Boulevard. Miscommunication and political conflict between local, state, and federal actors prevented a concerted response and by the following evening there was no turning back. Fires, which had been an ever-present danger in inner-city housing, turned into a weapon of resistance, as rioters set stores ablaze in commercial districts, which often spread to neighboring houses. Hundreds of buildings were destroyed by fire. Over the course of six days, 43 people died, 2,509 buildings were looted and destroyed, and the destruction cost $36 million in insurable property damage.[22] The destruction left 600 Detroiters homeless.[23]

Detroit's motto, born out of the city's devastating 1806 conflagration and translated from Latin, is: "It will rise from the ashes." Some 159 years later, the city would be asked to rise once again. Journalists, scholars, policymakers, and residents struggled to find meaning in the ashes and searched for the causes of widespread urban unrest. Commentators often discussed the state of the urban environment as a factor producing rebellion in Detroit and other cities, coming close to reflecting the popular Progressive Era notion that urban environments play a role in character formation.[24] Several analysts argued that the poor state of the urban environment led to rebellion. One public health scholar at Wayne State University considered pollution one of the many factors "that adds to the sense of degradation, neglect, and disinterest," which "becomes one of the underlying conditions of the stress syndrome, the riot."[25] Observers were quick to point out that the more immediate problems of unemployment and police abuse were to blame for the rebellion, but a great many suggested that the poor state of the urban environment reflected society's general apathy toward inner-city residents.

Detroit's environmental inequalities garnered attention in the aftermath of the rebellion, and the UAW supported efforts to address these inequalities.[26] The UAW helped establish the Deprived Areas Recreation Team (DART).[27] DART was semi-independent, with funding coming from the UAW and public sources, but was closely associated with the union, with offices in the UAW's headquarters in Detroit, the Solidarity House. Former UAW assistant Mary Williams directed DART with a $340,000 budget from New Detroit, a coalition of activists, civic leaders, and business elites created to address the rebellion. Money was tight, especially compared to the $14 million Detroit Parks and Recreation Department budget, but Williams stretched the budget by incorporating neighborhood participation in recreation projects. Recreational inequalities and the lack of green spaces in the city especially motivated Olga Madar. In August, 1967, she lamented, "The tragic events of the past couple weeks graphically justify the existence of DART." Years later, Madar regretted that groups like DART were not in place before the

74 The UAW confronts the urban environmental crisis

summer of 1967, believing that such programs could have helped solve the "serious derelictions in terms of services based on race in this community."[28] DART fit comfortably into the UAW model of cooperative reform combining the resources of the liberal establishment with the grassroots energies of city residents. For those UAW members concerned that about their dues going to the inner city, the union reminded them that some 40,000 UAW members still lived in Detroit.[29]

DART's signature program was the creation of "vest-pocket parks" – safe, open spaces replacing abandoned lots in the inner city. In this way, they fulfilled the Johnson administration's encouragement of "Green Islands" for urban youth. Reverend William T. Patrick, Jr., of the United Community Services, dramatized the need for positive spaces in the urban environment: "Last July 22nd, the subject of our common interest was called recreation. On July 23rd it became *wreck*-creation." Patrick argued that the tall order in front of them was nothing less than "*re*-creation of a shattered city – *re*-creation of a fragmented society, *re*-creation of faith in the great American promise." The only way to restore faith in the urban environment was to face "problems that have been swept under the rug for generations."

A Vest-Pocket Parks Committee insisted that contractors hire residents of the neighborhoods in which the parks were to be constructed. Environmental improvement, they believed, could offer a significant economic benefit to neighborhoods and provide jobs for the black youths facing severe unemployment rates and deep frustration with the system, thereby making more environmentally and economically sustainable neighborhoods. DART demanded that its contractors "must have a work force which is representative of the ethnic composition of the city, with maximum utilization of area residents on that work force."[30] The goal, DART believed, should go beyond the number of parks built, but rather should define success by "how effectively each local community has been involved in the choice, planning and maintenance of each park site."[31] Although it faced some criticism for a slow pace of planning and construction, DART succeeded in creating at least 14 vest-pocket parks.

Groups like DART showed the growing sense among activists in Detroit that organized and engaged residents could make a difference in fighting environmental inequality.[32] Inequality could take many forms, like the deterioration of the built environment in the inner city, while the suburbs enjoyed comparatively pristine lakes, rivers, playgrounds, and ballfields. In the industrial suburbs, working-class residents often attacked the industrial pollution that burdened their communities while sparing the middle- and upper-class neighborhoods not far from their own. Environmental regulations protected the elites while neglecting the working class.

Shop-floor environmentalism

Although much of the initial environmental advocacy came from UAW headquarters, some union locals pursued their own important environmental initiatives. UAW Local 600, at the massive Ford River Rouge complex in neighboring Dearborn, hosted an aggressive environmental campaign by members. Widely known as among the most independent and radical UAW locals, Local 600, beginning in 1967, took a strong lead in organizing for air and water pollution regulation. Just weeks after the riot, Local 600 organized a pollution conference bringing together state legislators, pollution officials, autoworkers, steelworkers, and concerned citizens to address environmental problems in Dearborn, the home of Ford Motor Company and the River Rouge complex. Local 600 invited State Senator Roger Craig, representative of the Dearborn district, to lead the proceedings. Other invitees included a Ford Company official, a representative of the Greater Detroit Board of Commerce, Dearborn clergy, and several other representatives of the local community, workers, pollution officials, and industry, providing a remarkable portrait of the diverse positions they represented.

Dearborn residents and workers became environmentalists because environmental injustice threatened the health and vitality of themselves and their families. Speaking for workers at the Rouge factory, Vincent Bruno condemned Dearborn's belching factories, such as the Mercer Brick Company for operating a stack that "emanate[d] gasless fumes" with a "very toxicating effect" giving residents "a burning sensation to the eyes, nose and throat."[33] Bruno complained of the lack of concern about pollution from Dearborn officials. Despite the heavily industrialized

FIGURE 4.2 The Ford River Rouge Plant in Dearborn, Mich. When it opened in 1927, it was the largest industrial operation in the world.

Source: Detroit News Collection, Walter P. Reuther Library, Archive of Labor and Urban Affairs, Wayne State University.

76 The UAW confronts the urban environmental crisis

nature of the city, Dearborn lacked a single pollution enforcement official, assigning responsibility for regulating pollution to a boiler inspector. Other Dearborn residents indicated that their concern for the environment was a matter of health and security, rather than merely an aesthetic concern that was common among middle-class environmentalists.[34] More than just a "nuisance," pollution was "particularly frightening" and represented "drastic" health risks, according to Mrs. Hardwick.[35] Others described Dearborn's air pollution as "oppressive" on heavy days.[36] Realizing that pollution abatement would come with real costs, in taxes and in higher priced consumer goods, Hardwick insisted that "[w]e would rather pay this kind of cost than higher doctor bills."[37]

State Senator Roger Craig criticized the inequitable class effects of industrial land uses, noting that when the Ford Company attempted to site a coke storage facility on land adjacent to the Ford Foundation, a "fashionable subdivision in which a number of Ford executives lived," residents of the neighborhood "raised particular Cain."[38] And yet, Craig noted, less-economically secure neighborhoods bore the brunt of the effects of pollution. "The way the Salina community perceived this," Craig observed, "is that what is acceptable pollution in the south end in Salina is not acceptable in the Ford [F]oundation area." Father Lombardi echoed these sentiments and lambasted officials for sacrificing the environmental protection of poor neighborhoods. City officials seemed unwilling to challenge industrial polluters, Lombardi argued, saying that they would rather see heavily polluted neighborhoods razed than protected. "If you can't eliminate the smoke," Lombardi said of the city's strategy, "eliminate the people."

Industry officials wished to see pollution regulation remain primarily a local – and at worst a state – affair, defending the pace of voluntary pollution abatement measures. The representative from Ford, Robert Wiesner, pointed to the $27 million already spent on updating the Rouge Factory and indicated the company's willingness to expend $42 million more to "reduce emissions" at the plant.[39] Wiesner insisted that the relationship between pollution from the plant and health effects for the community was unclear and that further pollution restrictions could not feasibly be met by the company. Voluntary pollution abatement was sufficient, he remarked, based on solid scientific evidence. Industrialists warned against the damaging consequences of "quick [and] haphazard" regulations, threatening an area dependent on industrial jobs with a "time loss of 12 to 36 months or more" to install pollution abatement equipment.[40] Wielding the threat of job loss would become a far more effective strategy for industrialists in the 1970s, but in the late 1960s the power was still firmly on the side of those advocating robust regulations.

UAW Local 600 translated its environmental organizing into a political platform that began 1968 asserting the need for action on air and water pollution, calling it a "menace to society."[41] In the same platform, it opposed the creation of new ghettos resulting from expressway development, and demanded greater action on the slum lords responsible for blight. The urban environment required action just as much as Lake Erie, a "cesspool" for Detroit, Toledo, and Cleveland. The activism of Local 600 complemented union leadership on environmentalism, and the UAW's 1968 convention showed that locals supported the union's environmental agenda.

Adopting a "Natural Resources Policy," the convention made many environmental issues a prominent part of the union platform, reflecting a strong working-class orientation to the environmental issues it supported. Natural resources policy, for the UAW, included expanded low-income housing, mass transit, and "urban renewal programs . . . purged of their obsession with site clearance. . . . The families and neighborhoods in the path of the bulldozers must have a substantial voice in determining their future."[42]

Many union locals by 1968 demonstrated environmental leadership, but they sometimes diverged on which environments needed the most attention. Union leadership led the curve nationally on environmental activism, but workers bitterly noted its absence in the environment most crucial to health and survival: the factory floor itself. Workers critiqued the UAW for failing to aggressively stand up to factories where working conditions were unsafe. At the same time that the union proudly boasted its environmental initiatives, union local newspapers described harrowing environmental conditions at the shops, including exposure to toxic materials, malfunctioning machinery, and hazardous floors. So bad were the environmental conditions that workers at some sites refused to wait for the bureaucratic morass of the UAW and walked out of their jobs in defiance of the management and collectively bargained rules.

A common refrain by disenchanted autoworkers charged that Reuther and union leadership talked a strong game on issues like workplace safety and racial equality, but action did not follow rhetoric.[43] Black autoworkers especially critiqued inaction on workplace environmental issues most likely to affect African American members. Various Revolutionary Union Movements of radical black workers took aim both at the racism of auto companies and the UAW in 1968. According to the Dodge Revolutionary Union Movement newspaper, *DRUM*, body shop workers told the foreman about malfunctioning blowers that were casting lead particles into the air.[44] They pointed out that it was "a definite health hazards [*sic*] . . . [that] could cause lead poisoning." The foreman answered, "What do you want me to do?," he responded. The "dumb sonofabitch," *DRUM* called him. The best way to get management's attention, *DRUM* reasoned, was through a work stoppage, and they connected this to the fight for racial equality in Detroit: "In the streets we have to revolt to get civil rights.," while at the Dodge factory, "we have [t]o walk out to get a fan."[45] Rather than respond to critiques over the inaction on in-plant pollution and health hazards, Reuther and his allies subverted the activism of the Revolutionary Union Movements and called to attention the work being done in the city and on the national political scene. The urban environmental crisis may have started in the factories, but Reuther and UAW leadership were more comfortable addressing environmental issues in the community.

The UAW war on pollution

In 1968, Walter Reuther reflected on the new direction in urban environmental policy the union had undertaken, including the important role of groups like the Pollution Action Line. "Much as Americans enjoy the open spaces, most

78 The UAW confronts the urban environmental crisis

Americans live in cities. In cities often the only open spaces are the streets and the vacant lots. It need not be so. It is possible to have both urbanization and civilization. Beauty, dignity and cleanliness can exist anywhere that like-minded people set themselves to that task."[46] Reuther's comments suggested that pride in one's neighborhood — and cleaning it up — was an obligation of citizenship. In Detroit, the UAW's efforts dovetailed with the mayor's "Keep Detroit Beautiful" campaign, launched in the spring of 1968 aimed at mobilizing "the help of all citizens in keeping our streets and alleys free of litter and dirt."[47] These efforts acknowledged the prevalence of beliefs that the urban crisis was in part the product of inner-city ugliness.[48] Although the Johnson administration was in its final months, the beautification ethos of the Great Society lived on in Detroit. Reuther explained that the union's efforts underscored a new understanding of the "total environment." "The UAW's concern for its members does not stop at the shop door—it extends into the *total environment*," Reuther proclaimed. "At this moment, that environment is deteriorating in several areas at once."[49]

The UAW sought to harness grassroots environmental concern from its members. Prior to the uprising, the UAW started the Pollution Action Line, an effort designed to train citizen observers to spot and report water pollution. Union locals nominated members to serve as observers, who attended training sessions presented by a pollution control expert and took a field trip to Detroit's wastewater treatment plant.[50] Civic participation was significant, according to Morton Sterling, chief of the Detroit and Wayne County Air Pollution Agencies, because "the territory of Puerto Rico has more money allocated for air pollution control than the State of Michigan."[51] The effort was short-lived, but demonstrated a growing interest by union locals in participating in grassroots environmental action. More significant was the UAW's creation of the Downriver Anti-Pollution League (DAPL), which replaced the fledgling Pollution Action Line. Olga Madar's young Conservation and Resource Development Department led the charge. The UAW hoped to mobilize a united front of community members and organizations in affected downriver communities, where pollution had long been accepted as a fact of life, if not a necessary side effect of factory jobs. "We call on students and retired persons, as well as those in the work force, for their ideas on how best to work with church, civic, service, conservation, sportsmen and other groups to achieve a strong and united front to which government and industry will be forced to respond," stated Madar.

Like some of the first environmental activists, the urban progressive reformers of the early twentieth century, Madar's team hit the pavement in downriver communities, canvassing neighborhoods and observing first-hand the pollution menace. As historian Chad Montrie notes, these investigations led them to conclude that race and class affected exposure to air pollution. The team reported, "River Rouge and Ecorse had more black people in the streets," and also happened to have some of the worst pollution-related health problems. In River Rouge, "every morning silvery dust is found on cars, porches, windows" that was very difficult to remove, and "all complain of their inability to open their windows." The downriver town of Ecorse, which also had a significant black population, contained "large numbers

The UAW confronts the urban environmental crisis   **79**

of heavy industrial facilities along [the] river, most seeming to pump dirt into the air." Department staffer Hillel Liebert noticed that in the predominantly white neighborhoods, "Damage from pollution was not very evident, nor were unusually offensive odors." Such investigations were an early step in making clear the connections between pollution and social justice.[52]

Madar's team settled on four downriver communities in which to base operations: River Rouge, Ecorse, Lincoln Park, and Wyandotte. In organizing DAPL, Madar's staff self-consciously attempted to empower residents of Detroit beyond the union's members.[53] Workers here were not always autoworkers, but were often employed in industries including steel, chemical production, petroleum refining, and many more. DAPL organizers argued that the health of workers was disproportionately affected by industrial pollution. Giving working-class citizens the tools to fight back against pollution was the best way to empower them. Madar wrote, "Your Union is confident that UAW members, joining with other citizens and organizations, can develop a plan of action to muster the united strength needed to effectively eliminate harmful pollution." A UAW press release announced the formation of DAPL, alerting residents that they should brace for the "war on pollution," borrowing from the language of the Great Society even after Johnson's departure from office.[54] The Steering Committee, established in December 1969, expressed the goals of the group, which included, "To help all citizens more effectively use their democratic institutions and work with other organizations and groups to make their voices heard; citizens must have more influence over the forces which affect their lives."[55] Often working-class residents felt helpless to resist powerful industrial interests, meaning the most difficult and most important role of DAPL was in convincing Detroiters that they in fact could make a difference in their communities, helping them to overcome fatalism over their working and living conditions. Educating DAPL members meant alerting them to the profound health effects of pollutants and identifying the sources of pollution.

The speed at which Americans turned their attention to environmental problems is dizzying. As David and Richard Stradling observe, Cleveland's Cuyahoga River caught fire many times in the 1960s, and residents and the press barely batted an eye. When it caught fire yet again in 1967, *The Cleveland Plains-Dealer* published a small blurb, and little immediate reaction ensued. Yet over the next weeks and months, it struck a nerve among Clevelanders who started piecing together an understanding of how the urban end environmental crises reinforced each other. The Cuyahoga River's flammability turned into a referendum not only on industrial abuse of the environment but also on the effectiveness of the city's first black mayor, Carl Stokes.[56]

Other events drew significant media attention and sensitized the public to the environmental crisis perpetuated by industry. If the Cuyahoga River disaster only slowly aroused public anger, the Santa Barbara oil spill in January and February 1969 struck a raw nerve with Americans. While drilling six miles off the California coast, Union Oil Company hit a high pressure seam, sparking a blowout and the biggest oil spill in the nation's history to that point. Over the next ten days, at

80 The UAW confronts the urban environmental crisis

least 80,000 barrels spilled into the Pacific, creating an oil slick that hugged 35 miles of coast. Unlike Cuyahoga, the reaction to the catastrophe was swift and aided by a media eager to capture its disturbing pictures of birds, waterfowl, and marine mammals covered in oil. It may have been easy to compartmentalize the Cuyahoga River as an industrial waterway in an industrial zone of an industrial city. This was different. Dramatic pictures of Santa Barbara's tar-blackened beaches beneath the picturesque Santa Ynez mountains invited Americans to imagine their own natural escapes threatened by catastrophe. The industrial pollution that blue-collar workers long encountered now affected the middle class and elites.[57]

From environmental teach-in to Earth Day

Witnessing the Santa Barbara oil spill compelled Wisconsin Senator Gaylord Nelson to act. Nelson and Harvard graduate student Denis Hayes spent months planning an environmental teach-in at the University of Michigan for March, 1970. The university was home not only to Johnson's 1964 commencement announcing the Great Society agenda but also to the original 1965 Vietnam War teach-in. The environmental teach-in would combine the confrontational style of the Vietnam teach-ins with the expansive vision for improving quality of life that Johnson promised. Walter Reuther committed $2,000 in startup money for the teach-in, making it "the largest single financial backer of the Earth Day effort," Denis Hayes later remembered.[58] Meanwhile, Senator Nelson praised the UAW for being "in the vanguard in the nation" on environmentalism.[59]

The Environmental Teach-In that took place over four days in Ann Arbor proved a monumental success, setting the stage for a massive Earth Day turnout one month later. Student leaders planning their own festivities for the upcoming Earth Day poured in Ann Arbor, attending a headline event with speakers running the gamut from Senators Gaylord Nelson and Phil Hart, Democratic presidential candidate Edmund Muskie, environmentalists Barry Commoner and David Brower, and a performance by folk singer Gordon Lightfoot. The 13,000 who witnessed the convention absorbed the ecological messages, but more importantly the political lessons – that the time was ripe for a political movement based on the environmental crisis. The organizers who attended returned to their communities and developed Earth Day into a worldwide phenomenon that engaged millions, and launched environmentalism into a potent political force.[60]

April 22, 1970, marked a new phase in the environmental movement, as it dramatically shifted from the periphery to the center of the national consciousness. What planners initially envisioned as teach-ins occurring in a few cities grew into a national phenomenon. Environmental historian Adam Rome has discovered thousands of events on the first Earth Day. Some 35,000 speakers addressed gatherings, 1,500 colleges and 10,000 schools celebrated, and millions of Americans took part.[61] Strikingly, celebrations crossed partisan lines and other divides, with Republican and Democratic members of Congress holding events throughout the country. From its humble origins at the University of Michigan teach-in, Earth day

The UAW confronts the urban environmental crisis **81**

grew into a demonstration larger than any civil rights march or anti-war protest of the era. Exactly what kind of environmentalism would emerge from Earth Day remained to be seen.

Workers and students clashed over the meaning of Earth Day, exposing the fault lines that would widen over the next several years. *Environmental Action*, a New Left, student-run periodical created by the founders of the original Environmental Teach-In, captured the tension between workers and students. Despite believing that material progress created environmental inequalities felt most keenly by workers, *Environmental Action* was pessimistic that environmental activists and workers would see their causes as linked.[62] Therefore, they argued, "we should not be surprised at minority and poor communities' skepticism of our Earth Day-type admonitions to link arms and fight pollution."[63] DAPL attempted to integrate Detroit autoworkers and union retirees into the activities at the University of Michigan, envisioning bussing workers to Ann Arbor to join the festivities, but after approaching the School of Natural Resources about the proposal, they received a tepid response.[64] Despite the union's early leadership in the environmental movement, Earth Day demonstrated an erosion of union power as environmentalism became a mainstream cause.

Conservative Republicans and business leaders could not resist the growing grassroots movement pushing them to go green. Nixon signed the National Environmental Policy Act in 1969, the Clean Air Acts amendments in 1970, and the Federal Water Pollution Control Act amendments of 1972. Nixon achieved the major legislative victories on the environment that evaded Johnson in the 1960s. Scholars have argued that Nixon's signature on major legislation amounted to a cynical effort to prevent Democrats from capitalizing on the popularity of the movement, but whatever the motives, the environmental legislation transformed environmental politics.[65] Nixon's support of environmental initiatives early in his presidency did not initially threaten blue-collar support, but increasing economic challenges in the early 1970s put environmentalism on its heels. But that still laid ahead.

In the aftermath of Earth Day, revolutionary environmental change seemed within reach. Reuther hoped that Earth Day could be the start of a larger movement and dedicated the UAW's resources to sustaining the momentum. In order to prevent Earth Day from becoming a passing fad, Reuther discussed with Gaylord Nelson the possibility of a student conference on "Man's Living Environment" at the union's Black Lake conference facilities in Michigan. Such a conference, Reuther calculated, would encourage the momentum from Earth Day to become a self-sustaining movement, "so that we could keep the highest level of activity and broadest involvement in the continuing struggle to improve man's environment." The UAW invited 250 participants to its conference grounds for three days in June 1970 believing that the gathering would contribute to the union's efforts to achieve "total community action to end pollution in our environment."[66] Despite persistent conflicts between New Left environmentalists and workers, in the immediate term, the UAW continued to lend its support to the students.

82 The UAW confronts the urban environmental crisis

Shortly after the first Earth Day, UAW leaders at the 1970 convention defended the union's urban environmental outreach. Reuther argued that a broadening of environmental efforts beyond traditional conservation and wilderness preservation was necessary, because "[w]e cannot save our land if we don't manage to save our cities by transforming them into wholesome communities."[67] Reuther delivered a powerful critique of industrial capitalism, arguing that corporate destruction of the natural environment reflected industry's mistreatment of workers. "The indifference to the human element which has for so long polluted the environment of the plants has now created an environmental crisis of catastrophic proportions in the broader community," Reuther remarked, and promised that the union would "discuss the implications of the crisis at the bargaining table."[68] The statement also indicated that UAW would treat environmental and occupational health issues as one in the same, for industrial workers were first exposed to pollutants and hazardous materials before they filtered into the larger community.[69]

Reuther would not get the opportunity to test the union's resolve. On May 9, 1970, while traveling to the union's new Black Lake conference grounds, near Onaway, Michigan, the plane went down, killing the pilot, Reuther, and his wife. For decades, Walter Reuther was nearly synonymous with the UAW. He was irreplaceable, but initial indications from his successor, Leonard Woodcock, suggested that the UAW's environmental initiatives were in good hands. The UAW hosted the United Nations Symposium of the Environment at Onaway in May 1970. Woodcock offered a bold agenda for the UAW's intervention in the urban environmental crisis. "Much of what still passes for environmental concern in the United States is limited to a cosmetic approach: sweeping streets, picking up litter, returning disposable bottlers and beer cans, cleaning debris out of streams," Woodcock argued,

> These are wholesome pursuits, but they do not go to the heart of the matter, and from the standpoint of the poor and the deprived of our urban centers such actions are frivolous middle-class evasions of the need to end deprivation and poverty.

Woodcock issued an alternative approach to environmentalism, a social-justice perspective that held that environmentalists must put "elimination of poverty and deprivation high on the agenda of the environmental campaign" and fight for "distributive justice" in order to achieve "environmental sanity." Woodcock then indicated the UAW's willingness to take the environmental struggle to the bargaining table, promising to combat industry's threat to close factories rather than practice pollution abatement. Very soon after, however, economic pressures put the union on the defensive, and its bold promises on pollution enforcement against factories went unrealized.[70]

A final organizing effort by DAPL provided a dénouement. Using their characteristic approach of organizing volunteers and engaging in the community, DAPL teamed with the UAW and the University of Michigan's School of Natural Resources to conduct an environmental survey of the downriver project area. The results provide a unique snapshot into the values of downriver residents at the end of 1970. They

The UAW confronts the urban environmental crisis **83**

surveyed neighborhoods in Wyandotte, River Rouge, and Ecorse, because their residents lived in "some of the wors[t] air pollution in Michigan." Teams of interviewers from the university, local high school students, and local residents attended a training session before hitting the ground to canvass the neighborhoods. One local newspaper heralded the efforts "to determine the nature and severity of problems pertaining to the environment in the Downriver area."[71]

Surveyors encountered residents significantly dissatisfied with environmental conditions. When asked, "What do you feel are the two or three most serious problems facing this community, that something will have to be done about over the next few years?"[72] In terms of total responses from the three communities, "Crime and Morality" was the top response. However, "All environmental problems except air pollution," and "Air Pollution" were the second and third most prominent answers, beating out racial problems, economic problems, education, housing and population, and transportation and planning. In Ecorse, "All Environmental problems" was an even more popular answer than crime. Despite the wide recognition of their environmental challenges, DAPL struggled to maintain excitement.

DAPL rapidly faded. Not long after DAPL peaked at as many as 1,1000 members, Madar warned that the union could no longer prioritize programs that did not benefit their own membership.[73] Efforts at urban environmental outreach were overshadowed by attempts to stave off environmental blackmail, a threat that had been growing since at least 1971.[74] Rising inflation and a sputtering economy caused many industrialists to claim their factories could not afford to implement pollution-abatement measures to comply with federal law.[75] Doing so, they argued, would force them to lay off employees at a time when the country could not afford a growing unemployment rate. The last instance of a DAPL effort was a call for a meeting on April 13, 1972, of the Wyandotte chapter, hoping to "Revitalize & restructure the DAPL organization," and to plan events for Earth Day III.[76] DAPL ended with a whimper.

Despite the union's early leadership, it quickly lost its status as a pollution fighter. This reflected the success of environmentalism during and after Earth Day, and its adoption by both political parties on the national level. With policy successes like the National Environmental Policy Act, the creation of the Environmental Protection Agency in 1970, and later, the Federal Water Pollution Control Act of 1972, environmentalism was no longer an insurgent movement. National organizations institutionalized many of the gains of the Earth Day era, simultaneously proving the success of the movement, but also sapping the grassroots energy, particularly among workers, that had fueled it. Unsurprisingly, grassroots-focused organizations like the Downriver Anti-Pollution League suffered.

UAW's environmental agenda transformed

Even as the UAW tempered its critiques of industrial pollution, it remained engaged in confronting the urban environmental crisis. In a provocative brochure, "Pollution is not a 'White Thing,'" Olga Madar warned, "The chief victims of

84 The UAW confronts the urban environmental crisis

pollution are the urban poor, Blacks and workers who cannot escape their environment. Unless we join together now to stop those who pollute for profit, our cities will become ugly cesspools of poisonous pollutants."[77] One of the UAW's few black executives, Southeast Michigan regional director Marcellius Ivory added, "The environmental crisis that exists in our urban settlements is everybody's problem. Blacks and whites must work together to correct these evils." The brochure sought to demonstrate the intertwined fates of black and white workers, claiming that

> America's inner cities present the worst concentration of nearly every kind of environmental problem. Polluted air and tapwater, garbage-littered streets and alleys, rats, roaches, the lead paint peeling from tenement walls, overcrowding are all environmental problems that plague the inner city.

The UAW continued its outreach efforts, but did not follow through with any new specific environmental programs in which African Americans or urban workers could participate.

The headwinds against UAW urban environmentalism were too stiff, and the union's activism dwindled. The union faced growing challenges in the 1970s and retreated from its forceful advocacy of urban environmental issues. Walter Reuther's death in May 1970 meant the loss of a leader who had held the union presidency for nearly a quarter century, and who placed a high priority on environmental politics. Olga Madar, who had significantly shaped the Recreation Department and the Department of Conservation and Resource Development, took a step back from UAW responsibilities, helping to organize the feminist Coalition of Labor Union Women, and became its first president in 1974.[78] Reuther's successor Leonard Woodcock managed a historic victory in the GM strike of 1970, in what was the biggest auto strike since the end of World War II.[79] However, this would not be a bellwether for the decade. By 1972, the UAW was shifting away from urban environmental organizing to focus on the needs of its own members. As the UAW imposed "severe financial austerity" during the early 1970s, the organization sacrificed environmental programs.[80] In 1973, the union was forced to accept a humiliating contract following a 1973 strike against Chrysler, in what would establish a significant precedent.[81] The OPEC-led oil price increases and loss of market share to German and Japanese automakers further weakened the American automotive industry.[82] In 1969, Chrysler, Ford, and General Motors had over 1.5 million employees.[83] By 1979, these companies only employed 840,000.

Efforts at urban environmental outreach were thwarted by environmental blackmail, a threat that had been growing since at least 1971.[84] Rising inflation and a sputtering economy caused many industrialists to claim their factories could not afford to implement pollution-abatement measures to comply with federal law.[85] Doing so, they argued, would force them to lay off employees at a time when the country could not afford a growing unemployment rate. Auto companies effectively leveraged the threat of job losses, blaming industry weakness on regulations. Environmental blackmail pushed the UAW and other unions against a wall.

The UAW confronts the urban environmental crisis **85**

Leonard Woodcock attempted a political solution, throwing the union's support behind legislation that would have given financial assistance to workers who lost their jobs due to plant shutdowns resulting from anti-pollution measures.[86] As historian Josiah Rector shows, in the late 1970s, the UAW embarked on a potentially revolutionary campaign seeking full employment legislation that would thwart the effectiveness of environmental blackmail.[87] The efforts did not secure new legislation, but they showed the bold agenda the UAW pushed, leveraging environmentalism to stanch the severe losses in membership and union power.

The UAW and its members offered a unique vision of environmental activism sensitive to race, class, and the urban environment. Working-class environmentalism, however, is only one part of the story of environmental activism in the 1960s and 1970s. Black environmental activism emerged alongside working-class activism, and aimed to improve local landscapes ravaged by blight and industrial pollution. Challenging civic leaders to improve the urban environment to promote a more healthful and sustainable Detroit, African Americans launched vigorous efforts that challenged environmental inequalities and promoted environmental and economic sustainability in a city in crisis. The next chapter reveals how black urban environmental activism at times overlapped with, and at other times, diverged dramatically from, working-class environmentalism, and foreshadowed the emergence of the environmental justice movement.

Notes

1 *Report of Walter P. Reuther to the 21st UAW Constitutional Convention: Part One: UAW in Action*, Atlantic City, NJ, May 4–10, 1968, located at Reading Room, ALUA.
2 On the relationship between unions and environmental activism in the 1960s and 1970s, see Robert Gottlieb, *Forcing the Spring: The Transformation of the American Environmental Movement*, rev. and updated ed. (Washington, DC: Island Press, 2005); Andrew Hurley, *Environmental Inequalities: Class, Race, and Industrial Pollution in Gary, Indiana, 1945–1980* (Chapel Hill, NC: University of North Carolina Press, 1995); Laura Pulido, *Environmentalism and Economic Justice: Two Chicano Struggles in the Southwest, Society, Environment, and Place* (Tucson, AZ: University of Arizona Press, 1996); Robert Gordon, " 'Shell No!': OCAW and the Labor-Environmental Alliance," *Environmental History* 3, no. 4 (October 1998): 460, https://doi.org/10.2307/3985207; Robert Gordon, "Poisons in the Fields: The United Farm Workers, Pesticides, and Environmental Politics," *Pacific Historical Review* 68, no. 1 (February 1, 1999): 51–77, https://doi.org/10.2307/3641869; Robert W. Gordon, "Environmental Blues: Working-Class Environmentalism and the Labor-Environmental Alliance" (Ph.D. Dissertation, Wayne State University, 2004); Scott Dewey, "Working for the Environment: Organized Labor and the Origins of Environmentalism in the United States, 1948–1970," *Environmental History* 3, no. 1 (January 1998): 45, https://doi.org/10.2307/3985426; Scott Hamilton Dewey, *Don't Breathe the Air: Air Pollution and U.S. Environmental Politics, 1945–1970*, 1st ed., Environmental History Series, no. 16 (College Station, TX: Texas A&M University Press, 2000); Chad Montrie, *To Save the Land and People: A History of Opposition to Surface Coal Mining in Appalachia* (Chapel Hill, NC: University of North Carolina Press, 2003); Chad Montrie, *Making a Living: Work and Environment in the United States* (Chapel Hill, NC: University of North Carolina Press, 2008); Chad Montrie, *A People's History of Environmentalism in the United States* (London and New York: Continuum, 2011); Chad Montrie, *The Myth of Silent Spring: Rethinking the Origins of American Environmentalism*

(Oakland, CA: University of California Press, 2018); James Lewis Longhurst, *Citizen Environmentalists* (Medford, MA: Tufts University Press, 2012); J. Rector, "Environmental Justice at Work: The UAW, the War on Cancer, and the Right to Equal Protection from Toxic Hazards in Postwar America," *Journal of American History* 101, no. 2 (September 1, 2014): 480–502, https://doi.org/10.1093/jahist/jau380; Josiah Rector, "Accumulating Risk: Environmental Justice and the History of Capitalism in Detroit, 1880–2015" (Ph.D. Dissertation, Detroit, Wayne State University, 2017); Josiah Rector, "The Spirit of Black Lake: Full Employment, Civil Rights, and the Forgotten Early History of Environmental Justice," *Modern American History* 1, no. 1 (March 2018): 45–66, https://doi.org/10.1017/mah.2017.18.

3 On Reuther, see Nelson Lichtenstein, *The Most Dangerous Man in Detroit: Walter Reuther and the Fate of American Labor* (New York: Basic Books, 1995), 248–70; Kevin Boyle, *The UAW and the Heyday of American Liberalism, 1945–1968* (Ithaca, NY: Cornell University Press, 1995), 185–205, 205; and Stephen Ward, *In Love and Struggle: The Revolutionary Lives of James and Grace Lee Boggs* (Chapel Hill, NC: University of North Carolina Press, 2016), 275–76; Montrie, *Making a Living*, 108.

4 As David Stradling, Robert Gottlieb, Samuel Hays have pointed out, the conservationist ethos certainly was alive and active in Progressive era cities, but the public usually perceived it as a western and rural phenomenon. See David Stradling, *Smokestacks and Progressives: Environmentalists, Engineers and Air Quality in America, 1881–1951* (Baltimore, MD: Johns Hopkins University Press, 1999); Gottlieb, *Forcing the Spring*; Samuel P. Hays, *A History of Environmental Politics Since 1945* (Pittsburgh, PA: University of Pittsburgh Press, 2000).

5 UAW Washington Report, February 15, 1965, Box 586, Folder 3, UAW-PO-WPR Collection, ALUA.

6 Hal K. Rothman, *Saving the Planet: The American Response to the Environment in the Twentieth Century* (Chicago: Ivan R. Dee, 2000), 125–26.

7 Olga Madar Oral History, Interview by Glenn Riggles, August 6, 1985, 24, Box 6, Olga Madar Papers, ALUA. Chad Montrie has written extensively on Olga Madar's pioneering role in labor environmentalism. See Montrie, *Making a Living*, 102–11; Montrie, *A People's History of Environmentalism*, 3, 903–95, 104–8; Montrie, *The Myth of Silent Spring*, 3–5, 104–10.

8 Montrie, *Making a Living*, 103.

9 Olga Madar Oral History, Interview by Glenn Riggles, August 6, 1985, 20–22. Box 6, OM Papers.

10 NRA Brochure, "How to Keep 96 Employees Happy," 1947, Box 1, Folder: Gun Club, UAW-RD Collection, ALUA.

11 *Report of the President Walter P. Reuther to the 20th UAW Constitutional Convention*, Long Beach, California, May 16–21, 1966, 121, located at ALUA; Montrie, *Making a Living*, 108.

12 UAW Press Release, November 6, 1965, Box 17, Folder: UAW Conference Nov. 1965, JVC Collection.

13 Murray Stein, "The Second Battle of Lake Erie," Paper presented at the United Action for Clear Water Conference of the United Automobile Workers, November 5, 1965, Detroit, Michigan. Quote on 10. Document number 000R65105. From Environmental Protection Agency digital archive, accessed March 3, 2010, http://nepis.epa.gov.

14 "$50 Billion 'War Chest' Urged to Fight Water, Air Pollution," *Dodge Main News*, November 20, 1965, located at Reading Room, ALUA.

15 Olga Madar Statement, *Pollution of Lake Erie and Its Tributaries: Proceedings of Conference Held at Cleveland, Ohio on August 3–6, 1965*, 946–63, quote on 953. Document number 905R65105. Accessed February 20, 2010 from Environmental Protection Agency digital archive, http://nepis.epa.gov.

16 Madar Statement, *Pollution of Lake Erie*, 953.

17 "America's Disgrace – Our Polluted Waters," *Steel Labor*, February 1966, 10–11.

18 *Report of the President Walter P. Reuther to the 20th UAW Constitutional Convention*, quotes on 120 and 123, located at Reading Room, ALUA.

19 Nancy F. Gabin, *Feminism in the Labor Movement: Women and the United Auto Workers Union, 1935–1975* (Ithaca, NY: Cornell University Press, 1990), 210–18.

20 "The Race to Save Our Cities," *Solidarity*, March 1967, 4.

21 An indispensable study of the 1967 riot is Sidney Fine, *Violence in the Model City: The Cavanaugh Administration, Race Relations, and the Detroit Riot of 1967* (Ann Arbor: University of Michigan Press, 1989).

22 Figures from Thomas J. Sugrue, *The Origins of the Urban Crisis: Race and Inequality in Postwar Detroit* (Princeton, NJ: Princeton University Press, 1996), 259.

23 Fine, *Violence in the Model City*, 294.

24 See, for instance, Sharon Wood, *Freedom of the Streets: Work, Citizenship, and Sexuality in a Gilded Age City* (Chapel Hill, NC: University of North Carolina Press, 2005), 102–31; and Michael McGerr, *A Fierce Discontent: The Rise and Fall of the Progressive Movement in America* (New York: Simon and Schuster, 2003), 80, 113.

25 Richard A. Prindle, "Health Aspects of the Urban Environment," *Public Health Reports* 83 (July 1968): 617–21, quote on 621.

26 "Cities: The Fire this Time," *Time*, August 4, 1967.

27 Press Release, "Urge UAW Members to Help Build Better Community," August 23, 1967, Box 3, Folder "DART 1967," UAW Conservation and Recreation Departments Collection, ALUA. See also "Seek Recreation for Detroit Areas," *Solidarity*, October 1967, 15. For a discussion of how DART reflected the city's "pivot" to public-private partnership for recreational provisioning, see Patrick D. Cooper-McCann, "The Promise of Parkland: Planning Detroit's Public Spaces, 1805–2018" (Ph.D. Dissertation, University of Michigan, 2019), 142–54.

28 Olga Madar Interview by Glenn Ruggles, August 6, 1985, 45, Box 6, IEB-OH Collection, ALUA.

29 "Recreationally Deprived Areas Program," Box 7, Folder "DART 1967," UAW-CRD Collection.

30 "Vest Pocket Parks General – Daily Log," May 17, 1969. Box 7, Folder 17, UAW-CRD Collection.

31 John Westbrook to Daniel Schwartz, November 5, 1968, Box 7, Folder 17, UAW-CRD Collection.

32 Cooper-McCann, "The Promise of Parkland: Planning Detroit's Public Spaces, 1805–2018," 142–54.

33 Proceedings, Local 600 Air Pollution Conference, August 12, 1967, 1–2, quotes on 1, Box 19, Folder 18, RC Collection, ALUA.

34 Hal K. Rothman showed the significance of aesthetic environmentalism to middle-class Americans in Rothman, *Saving the Planet*, 108–30.

35 Proceedings, Local 600 Air Pollution Conference, 26.

36 Proceedings, Local 600 Air Pollution Conference, 3.

37 Proceedings, Local 600 Air Pollution Conference, 26.

38 Proceedings, Local 600 Air Pollution Conference, 10.

39 Proceedings, Local 600 Air Pollution Conference, 8.

40 Proceedings, Local 600 Air Pollution Conference, 5.

41 "Local 600's 1968 Legislative Program," *Ford Facts*, January 22, 1968.

42 "UAW's 21st Constitutional Convention Adopts Agenda for Action in a Troubled Nation," *Ford Facts*, May 20, 1968.

43 These charges emerged out of frustration over Reuther's red-baiting of UAW opponents in the 1950s, and continued throughout the 1960s. Ward, *In Love and Struggle*, 233–34, 275–77.

44 "Breathing Death," *DRUM* 1, no. 21 (undated), Box 17, Reel 17, Dodge Revolutionary Union Movement Collection, ALUA. See also Heather Ann Thompson, *Whose Detroit? Politics, Labor, and Race in a Modern American City* (Ithaca, NY: Cornell University Press, 2001), 159–91.

45 "The Air We Breathe," *DRUM*, September 1968, Box 17, Reel 17, DRM Records, ALUA.

46 *Report of Walter P. Reuther to the 21st UAW Constitutional Convention*, 224, located in ALUA.

88 The UAW confronts the urban environmental crisis

47 Gerald Remus Statement, *Proceedings Progress Evaluation Meeting Pollution of Lake Erie and It* [*sic*] *5 Tributaries,* June 4, 1968 (Cleveland, Ohio), 55. Document number 905R86100. Accessed March 6, 2010, from Environmental Protection Agency digital archive, http://nepis.epa.gov.
48 *Report of Walter P. Reuther to the 21st UAW Constitutional Convention.*
49 *Report of Walter P. Reuther to the 21st UAW Constitutional Convention.*
50 Andrew Getto to Olga Madar, August 8, 1967, Box 7, Folder 1, UAW-CRD Collection; Olga Madar to PAL Supporters, August 10, 1967, Box 7, Folder 1, UAW-CRD Collection; Olga Madar to PAL Supporters, September 8, 1967, Box 7, Folder 1, UAW-CRD Collection.
51 Proceedings, Local 600 Air Pollution Conference, 20–21.
52 "Summary Log for Sept 10–Nov 8: Hillel Liebert," Box 2, Folder 3, UAW-CRD Collection; Montrie, *Making a Living*, 109–110.
53 Madar to UAW Members and Spouses, December 20, 1969, Box 2, Folder 4, UAW-CRD Collection.
54 Press Release, December 10, 1969, Box 2, Folder 4, UAW-CRD Collection.
55 "News from the UAW," December 10, 1969, Box 2, Folder 3, UAW-CRD Collection.
56 David Stradling and Richard Stradling, *Where the River Burned: Carl Stokes and the Struggle to Save Cleveland* (Ithaca, NY: Cornell University Press, 2015), 144–72.
57 Rothman, *Saving the Planet*, 127–28.
58 Walter Reuther to Gaylord Nelson, December 19, 1969, in Gavin Strassel, "Labor Unions, Earth Day, and Environmentalism," Walter P. Reuther Library, April 20, 2017, accessed August 2, 2018, https://reuther.wayne.edu/node/13723; Denis Hayes Interview, *Michigan in the World*, accessed August 2, 2018, http://michiganintheworld.history.lsa.umich.edu/environmentalism/exhibits/show/interviews.
59 "Calls Threat to Environment Mankind's Most Critical Problem," *Solidarity*, May 1970, 13.
60 James Tobin, "Earth Day Eve," accessed September 30, 2019, https://heritage.umich.edu/stories/earth-day-eve/.
61 Adam Rome, *The Genius of Earth Day: How a 1970 Teach-in Unexpectedly Made the First Green Generation* (New York: Hill and Wang, 2013), 165; Adam Rome, "The Genius of Earth Day," *Environmental History* 15, no. 2 (April 2010): 194–205, 194.
62 "Ecology and Social Justice: Is there a Conflict?" *Environmental Action* 4 (August 5, 1972): 3–6, 5.
63 "Ecology and Social Justice: Is There a Conflict?"
64 Nat Weinberg to Walter Reuther, Inter-Office Communication, March 12, 1970, Box 586, Folder 8, UAW-PO-WPR Collection.
65 J. Brooks Flippen, *Nixon and the Environment* (Albuquerque: University of New Mexico Press, 2000), esp. Introduction.
66 John Yolton to Denis Hayes, April 3, 1970, Box 2, Folder 21, OM Papers.
67 *Report of President Walter P. Reuther to the Twenty-Second UAW Constitutional Convention: Part One: UAW in Action,* 1970, 200, located at Reading Room, ALUA.
68 *Report of President Walter P. Reuther to the Twenty-Second UAW Constitutional Convention,* 196.
69 "Scientists Call In-Plant Pollution 'A Microcosm' of What Is Outside," Box 1, Folder 3, UAW-CRD Collection.
70 UAW Publication, "The Crisis of the Environment: UAW's Views Presented to a United Nations Conference," quotes on 11, Box 3, Folder: Other Organizations: UAW, JL Papers, BHL.
71 "Residents to Be Surveyed," *River Rouge Herald*, October 21, 1970, 1.
72 Environmental Inventory, Fall 1970, 5, UAW-CRD Collection.
73 Membership figure from: Statement of Peter Naccrato, Chairman Downriver Anti Pollution League. Air Quality Standards Hearings, August 19, 1970, Box 2, Folder 6, UAW-CRD Collection.

74 *Report of President Leonard Woodcock to the Twenty-Third UAW Constitutional Convention: Part One: UAW in Action*, April 23rd Through April 28, 1972, Atlantic City, NJ, 140–41, located at ALUA.

75 Scott Dewey argues that the poor state of the economy drove workers to side with management on environmental issues beginning in the early 1970s in "Working for the Environment," 46–47. An important work detailing environmental blackmail in the 1970s is Richard Kazis and Richard Lee Grossman, *Fear at Work: Job Blackmail, Labor, and the Environment* (New York: Pilgrim Press, 1982). Robert W. Gordon, "Environmental Blues: Working-Class Environmentalism and the Labor-Environmental Alliance, 1968–1985" (Ph.D. Dissertation, Wayne State University, 2004), 254–69.

76 DAPL Flyer, Wyandotte Division, for April 13, 1972, Folder 8, Box 2, UAW-CRD Collection.

77 Brochure, "Pollution Is Not a 'White Thing'," September 1972, Folder 13, Box 2, UAW-CRD Collection.

78 Gabin, *Feminism in the Labor Movement*, 225–27.

79 Jefferson Cowie, *Stayin' Alive: The 1970s and the Last Days of the Working Class* (New York: New Press, 2010), 44–45.

80 Leonard Woodcock, "Jobs and the Environment," November 15, 1975, Folder 11, Box 11, UAW-CRD Collection.

81 Thompson, *Whose Detroit?*, 211–12. Thompson argues that the union's quelling of dissenting members, especially black radicals, and its cozy relationship with auto companies, weakened its bargaining power in the 1970s. See also Steve Jefferys, *Management and Managed: Fifty Years of Crisis at Chrysler* (Cambridge and New York: Cambridge University Press, 1986), 188–214.

82 Daniel Yergin, *The Prize: The Epic Quest for Oil, Money & Power*, Free Press trade pbk. ed. (New York: Free Press, 2008), 527–28; Thompson, *Whose Detroit?*, 215–16.

83 Thompson, *Whose Detroit?*, 216.

84 *Report of President Leonard Woodcock to the Twenty-Third UAW Constitutional Convention.*

85 Scott Dewey argues that the poor state of the economy drove workers to side with management on environmental issues beginning in the early 1970s in "Working for the Environment," 46–47. An important work detailing environmental blackmail in the 1970s is Kazis and Grossman, *Fear at Work*. See also Gordon, "Environmental Blues: Working-Class Environmentalism and the Labor-Environmental Alliance, 1968–1985," 254–69.

86 UAW Press Release, October 27, 1972, Folder 14, Box 11, UAW-CRD Collection.

87 Rector, "The Spirit of Black Lake."

5

BLACK ENVIRONMENTALISM IN AN AGE OF URBAN CRISIS

In 1962, Mildred Smith moved into a house on Hobart Street, the third such move as a result of urban renewal projects forcing her out of previous homes. This time, she was determined to stay there, hoping to "finish out [my] years" in the residence.[1] The bulldozer came calling yet a fourth time, as Wayne State University officials sought to remove her and her neighbors to build a new space research center. This time, Mildred Smith refused to budge. The house became a symbol of resistance to the bulldozer. Smith joined with neighbors in the West Central Organization to oppose Wayne State's expansion. Smith put her body on the line, guarding the doorway of nearby 5778 Hobart Street as city officials attempted to push their way in. In what became known as the "Battle of Hobart Street," 21 members of the protest were arrested, generating media attention. In a rare outcome, their resistance to relocation worked. The Detroit Common Council reversed its approval of the university expansion and allowed the homes to remain standing.[2] High school students from wealthy neighborhoods Grosse Pointe and Royal Oak in 1971 helped in the rehabilitation of 5778 Hobart, and in 1974, Grosse Pointe students fundraised $1,000 to build an "environment school" where suburban and inner-city students could collaborate and learn about urban environmental issues. Mildred Smith, who had once guarded the doorway to stop city officials from entering, was now secretary for the neighborhood organization Research Park Council. Smith offered her ringing endorsement of the project, and by now explicitly labeled housing problems as environmental. "Environmental problems are human problems," Smith noted. "We've all got a right to live and we have to live and work together." Their efforts established the Hobart Street Environmental Field Center, an alternative public school which could accommodate 15–40 students.[3] More importantly, it showed the continuities through which housing activism could later be understood as environmental activism.

DOI: 10.4324/9780429319914-5

Housing protests showed that black concern for the environment reflected the inner-city experience. African Americans were influenced by the mainstream environmental movement, but in greater measure developed an organic understanding of the environment resulting from their unique lived experience within Detroit's built environment.[4] In this chapter, I argue that black environmentalism in Detroit developed in reaction to sharpening metropolitan inequalities, worsened by urban renewal, highway development, population loss, and deindustrialization. The urban crisis also presented opportunities for African Americans, who became a majority of Detroit's residents in the 1970s, to assert their vision for the urban environment. Black environmental action started as a rearguard action of defending homes and neighborhoods from the bulldozer. But what started as a defensive effort in many ways became a *proactive* effort launched to make their homes, their neighborhoods, and their workplaces healthier, more livable, and more sustainable. Black environmental activism, in the context of Detroit's well-known struggles in the 1960s and 1970s and beyond, offers the possibility of rethinking postwar environmentalism and writing an alternative history of the urban crisis in Detroit.[5]

Freeway to rebellion

Freeways drained wealth and residents from the central city. Highway development provided an especially convenient tool for urban planners, since they could eliminate slums, improve traffic flow, and support the downtown business district by making it easier to access from the suburbs.[6] Instead of urban renaissance, as historians have demonstrated, freeways often served to further eviscerate central cities, making relocation to the suburbs easier, further encouraged industrial decentralization, and imposed dangerous health hazards next to residential neighborhoods. The freeways displaced mostly African-American residents, thrusting victims into a tight housing market, where residential segregation was enforced by policy, violence, and intimidation.[7] Slum clearance, many insisted, was euphemism for black removal.

The mid-1960s witnessed a greater militancy by black Detroiters on environmental matters, revolving primarily around urban renewal and highway development. While established organizations like the Urban league and NAACP pushed back against the worst harms created by bulldozing neighborhoods, they still operated within a framework that supported slum clearance. Indeed, many middle-class African Americans agreed that the slums reflected badly on all African Americans. Though resistance to highways and slum clearance appeared in the 1950s, the forces supporting their development proved overwhelming, and the acceptance of much of the black leadership in groups like the Urban League facilitated the development of Detroit's highways. Foes of the highways were isolated and lacked a voice.

This time would be different. In late 1964, the Highway Department announced plans to construct an Interstate-96 extension, called the Edward J. Jeffries Freeway, connecting downtown near the Ambassador Bridge to Canada, and extending northwest to the existing I-96 terminus in suburban Farmington Hills.

92 Black environmentalism in an age of urban crisis

The Highway Department believed that much of the region's growth had shifted to the northwestern section, where new retail, industrial, and residential developments had grown rapidly during the 1950s.[8] The highway extension, the agency insisted, would provide a safer, more cost-effective, and speedier connection between the Central Business District and the northwest suburbs. Although significant displacement of people and demolition of homes, businesses, and factories would be required, the advantages would benefit the region as a whole. The freeway took the name of Mayor Jeffries, Detroit's executive from 1940 to 1948. Ironically, Jeffries had once expressed his concern over expressways as Congress debated an early roads bill, the Federal-Aid Highway Act of 1944. Jeffries feared that the urban arteries would benefit the suburbs at the expense of the central city, leaving "nothing . . . but industry."[9] In spite of reservations, Jeffries nevertheless supported highways construction, though his misgivings proved prescient.

Suburban residents usually cheered when the construction of highways facilitated their access to downtown. The whole region benefited, they supposed, when the heart of Detroit was connected by the asphalt arteries to the suburbs. It was easy for them to disregard the consequences on inner-city residents whose neighborhoods lie in the path of destruction. After all, they imagined the neighborhoods as slums – dangerous, disease-ridden, and economically infertile. Certainly, many suburbanites must have thought that it would be a favor to the residents to demolish their blighted blocks. So effective were the images constructed by urban renewal's cheerleaders of a wasteland, that it became easy to imagine many parts of Detroit as a blank slate. Yet again, it was a radical statement for activists to claim that these neighborhoods *mattered*. With a God's eye view of the city, modernist planners condemned neighborhoods with a red marker. Peopling the landscape with narratives and stories of their sacrifices represented an act of resistance – an effort to confront the planners with the human costs of their urban designs.

The highway project prompted a vigorous opposition, shattering the silence that had previously met highway development plans. Just weeks after the announcement, five ministers petitioned the Detroit Common Council, asking for "genuine citizen participation" in the planning process and a public hearing.[10] The council granted their wish for a public hearing, setting aside January 6, 1965. Leading up to the hearing, scores of letters streamed into the offices of Common Council members. Council member Mel Ravitz received letters representing a diverse array of opinions, but on the whole, received more letters from opponents of the project. From the supporters, Ravitz heard from those insisting that "the tax payers want this expressway," insinuating that the heavily black opposition did not pay taxes.[11] Opponents wished that Detroit and the state would seek solutions for transportation problems other than highways, and instead focus on mass transit.[12] One neighborhood of petitioners stressed environmental factors in their opposition to highway construction, arguing that "fumes," "dust," and "noise" would make their area unbearable.[13] No longer would residents be able to hang their clothes outside to dry, and playful children would be greatly imperiled.

The Highway Department had unwittingly sparked a freeway revolt. One group quickly organized to confront the threat: the Jeffries Freeway Action Body (JFAB). Years of promises by the urban renewal proponents had resulted not in a revitalized Detroit, but more segregation, lost neighborhoods and housing, and more highways. Younger activists in the black community saw urban renewal not as an opportunity, but as a Trojan horse, yet one more means for white residents of the region to transfer wealth from the city to the suburbs. They questioned the years of slum clearance and highway constructions as means for promoting urban renewal, particularly in light of the extraordinary sacrifices required of Detroit's underprivileged citizens for whom the benefits of the so-called renewal remained elusive.

Jeffries Freeway Action Body, formed in November 1965, gained support from the younger faction within the Detroit Urban League, particularly its Housing Department.[14] DUL had been an advocate in the 1950s of slum clearance and the relocation of African Americans to new housing during the 1950s, but by the mid-1960s, some of the younger Urban League staffers were no longer willing to concede power to policymakers and planners and became openly resistant to urban renewal and highway construction plans. One Urban Leaguer in particular, director of the organization's housing department Roy Lee Williams, took charge of the emerging opposition to urban renewal. "Merely moving a person out of slum housing," Williams noted, "will not cure the reasons for them being there. It will not even [e]nsure the public that these same people will not be living in slums five years later."[15] The Housing Department promised to "bird-dog" the Jeffries construction, determined to ensure the rights of residents were not violated in the process of relocation.

The Jeffries Freeway Action Body continued its opposition to the new road, holding mass meetings and charging that freeway projects represented "black removal."[16] Lobbying state government for greater legal protections for residents, they pushed authorities to recognize the unique harms created by displacing residents. In November 1966, George Romney signed House Bill 3781, which offered more robust "protections for families displaced from their homes by highway construction projects."[17] Projects affecting 15 or more dwelling units would now have to be found a new home before road construction commenced.[18] The new law, according to the Romney Administration, would enshrine the principle that "majority rule" must be balanced with a concern for "minority rights," keeping at the forefront the "right of the people to be secure in their homes," and a fair opportunity for citizens to appeal decisions that negatively affect them.

In an age in which the bulldozer trampled black neighborhoods, even a weak law like HB 3781 signaled an important achievement. The new legislation demonstrated some sensitivity to the objections raised by protest action groups like JFAB, demonstrating the promise of grassroots action. Romney recognized that those often asked to bear the greatest burden for urban renewal and highway development were "members of low-income families, racial minorities, and senior citizens who may already labor under severe social and economic disadvantages." Future residential dislocation would need to take a more holistic approach to the re-housing

94 Black environmentalism in an age of urban crisis

needs of homeowners and renters. Giving residents just compensation for their properties meant something more than "fair market value," because those displaced residents often entered a tight housing market, where they could find no comparable home. While the legislation still provided the State Highway Department much latitude in displacing residents, it suggested that urban renewal protests did have some effect in altering the discourse and providing limited citizen protections. Uniting people with wholesome green spaces became a major goal of reformers and activists, and one that would gain greater urgency as the long, hot summers of rebellion and violence exposed the enduring racial fault lines of the city.

The West Central Organization

At the same time as residents organized to resist the highway, another radical challenge to urban renewal emerged based on famed radical community organizer Saul Alinsky's efforts in Chicago and elsewhere. Historian Robert Gioielli credits Alinsky and his Industrial Areas Foundation for facilitating grassroots environmentalism in Chicago. Alinksy organized Chicago's ethnic working class and the lower middle class to attack the air pollution that one activist described as "a floating garbage pit."[19] Activists in Detroit, including two members from the Industrial Areas Foundation and advised by Alinsky, developed the West Central Organization (WCO) in the near west side.[20] Alinsky urged a flexible approach that adapted to the needs of local residents, and in Detroit, this frequently meant organizing to improve housing conditions and resist urban renewal projects, or as the *Free Press* termed it, "the do-it-yourself War on Poverty."[21] Officials ran roughshod over residents in the west central area, organizers charged, a section of the city that included Wayne State University and its ambitious expansion plans. WCO operated as an umbrella organization for smaller block groups, clubs, and church congregations, which allowed it to organize and direct the grassroots energy of the city.[22] People of color formed a majority of the WCO's leadership and membership while providing space for interracial and interfaith action.

Detroit officials arrived at 5778 Hobart Street on September 16, 1966, preparing its demolition to make way for construction of a space research center at Wayne State University.[23] When they arrived, they faced a handful of WCO picketers ready to put their bodies in front of the bulldozers to stop the demolition. So began the "Battle of Hobart Street."[24] One WCO member, Mrs. Thomas, a mother with 10 children and a victim of an urban renewal eviction, joined seven clergymen and several others in an attempt to move in to the condemned 7-room home and prevent its bulldozing.[25] Their action called attention to the difficulty with which large families suffered after urban renewal displacement, finding a rental market that rarely met their needs. Once in the home, they barricaded the entrances and ignored the police threats of arrest. Project Manager for the Housing Commission George Weible forced his way into the home past those guarding the entrance, including Mildred Smith, who accused Weible of striking her.[26] Once in the home, Weible smashed the toilets in an apparent attempt to make it uninhabitable.[27]

FIGURE 5.1 West Central Organization members confront Mayor Cavanagh at his home.

Source: Jerome P. Cavanagh Papers. Walter P. Reuther Library, Archives of Labor and Urban Affairs, Wayne State University.

Authorities demolished the steps outside the home, to make entrance more difficult. Weible left, while four WCO members occupied the home overnight. The children and Mrs. Thomas returned the next day, and while she stepped outside to retrieve items from a trailer, the police raided the home, arresting 14, which included Mrs. Thomas and six people guarding the entrance to the house.

Undeterred, more WCO members put their bodies on the line and attempted to re-occupy the home. On September 20, police promised a "get tough" policy against the demonstrators.[28] Picketers attempted to force through a police line and occupy the home. Pushing past the police in a "scuffle," they began repairing porch steps which earlier in the day had been removed by city crews boarding up the home. Police arrested two ministers and five other picketers. WCO members moved from the neighborhood to the city council chambers later that day, demanding that the Housing Department Director Robert Knox more effectively relocate displaced urban renewal casualties. Too often, they charged, slum clearance eliminated homes, and in its place left vacant unused land, attracting neither industry nor housing construction.

The WCO's protests led to the arrest of 21 WCO members under numerous charges, including trespassing and felonious assault, charges which the organization viewed as politically motivated.[29] WCO members, including clergy, descended on Mayor Jerome Cavanagh's home on October 2nd to present a petition to reform the city's treatment of displaced residents.[30] Cavanagh responded to the pressure by

96 Black environmentalism in an age of urban crisis

promising to make available 50 repossessed homes to displaced families at public housing rates, and instructed Detroit's community relations commission to meet with WCO.[31] The organization would not be appeased, and engaged in several more actions, including depositing the destroyed steps from 5778 Hobart on the front yard of Detroit Housing Department Director Robert Knox.[32] Actions like these demonstrated the frustrations of Detroit residents and willingness to engage in more direct action to gain officials' attention. Detroit urban planning scholar June Manning Thomas credits WCO's actions with promoting greater civic participation in urban renewal, and, along with the anti-highway activists, helped promote passage of the legislation Governor Romney signed offering modest protections for residents displaced by urban renewal projects.[33]

Living with rats

Meanwhile, the built environment continued to deteriorate at an alarming rate, and much of the city's housing stock was unfit and unhealthy for habitation. Discrimination in housing markets, poverty, and lack of oversight on apartment owners created a toxic housing mix. Many Detroiters lived with the most unwelcome roommate – the Norway Rat, *Rattus norvegicus*. In the 1960s, urban residents brought the issue to national attention. Historian Malcolm McLaughlin has shown that the war on rats is one forgotten episode of Johnson's Great Society.[34] By the late 1960s, rat infestations had become a "national disgrace" as parents tried in vain to keep their children safe at night from the menacing rodents which were known to leave deep wounds on the faces of infants. As McLaughlin puts it, "Rats were attracted to traces of food or milk left on an infant's mouth and the rat's licking could wake the baby up with tragic consequences. Unable to fight back, infants could be left with deep facial scars after being attacked by rats." There were a handful of cases of rats killing infants. Interested in demonstrating his commitment to alleviating some of the most horrific consequences of blight, conditions which Johnson believed had directly led to the urban uprisings in 1967, that summer he introduced into Congress a Rat Extermination and Control Bill. Johnson expressed dismay at "this national shame" where children and infants "are bitten by rats in their homes and tenements. Some are killed. Many are disfigured for life."[35] Congress rejected the $20 million proposal, stirring much conversation and condemnation over the injustice of environmental conditions in urban America.[36]

Before the rat problem gained national notoriety, Detroit residents struggled to bring the issue to the attention of local authorities and send a message to slumlords that they were fed up with their living conditions. Tenants in a northwest Detroit apartment confronted their landlords, the Goodman brothers, over rat and mice infestations which led to two children being bitten in a 24-hour period.[37] The nine-year-old victim was bitten on the knee, causing him to limp around for days afterward. A three-month-old victim suffered a bite to the heel, and spent the next week vomiting before being taken to Children's Hospital.[38] "The Goodman brothers have been sucking the blood from colored people for too long," said Juanita

Starling, who then went on to criticize city officials for failing to protect residents from slum living conditions, "You call the board of Health with complaints and they find out where you live and do nothing."[39] Frustrated by the lack of response, tenants took matters into their own hands, calling a rent strike against the landlords, asking prospective tenants to look elsewhere. Tenants coped by joking about the rats. Former tenant Willie Crittendon quipped, "Man, I've seen rats here so old they have got but one tooth!," and another joked that they should make the rats pay their share of the rent. "It's a good thing we can joke about this, because we'd go crazy," Crittendon remarked. "But we're dead serious about setting out to break this thing." The rent strike lasted at least a week, and residents reported that the Goodman brothers, embarrassed over the negative press, had made some efforts to clear weeds and debris, and set out rat bait (albeit within easy reach of children), but many residents refused to end the strike until they got "a decent place to live."[40] Despite attempts to evict the strikers, Detroit's Neighborhood Legal Service organization helped the renters defeat the Goodman Brothers in court the following Spring.[41] The rent strike demonstrated a militancy over living conditions emerging in inner-city Detroit.

The West Central Organization led protest actions against slum lords and absentee owners, exposing the deadly consequences of dangerous living conditions. One of WCO's earliest actions rallied 100 protesters to convene on the Detroit Common Council to bring attention to the death of three young boys in a fire at an abandoned house in the Midtown urban renewal area.[42] The demonstrators brought caskets to the Common Council chambers, dramatically demanding more preventive action by the city in renewal areas. An address by the incoming WCO president, Pastor Tom Johnson, in July 1966 highlighted the everyday reality for many of Detroit's inner-city residents. He castigated "dark streets where the services of the city are inadequate," and the "code-violated, rat-infested memorial of slumlords who leave behind . . . the death-trap remembrance that it is not people but money that counts."[43] For Johnson and the WCO, the built environment was more than a quality-of-life issue, for many, it was a matter of survival. Fires were not a new feature of the inner-city built environment, but a new spirit of organized resistance *was* novel. The WCO organized residents of an apartment building after a fire in January, 1967.[44] The fire followed resident complaints of dangerous electric wiring and other maintenance deficiencies to the Siegel Management Company.

Recreation and wreck-creation

Suffering under oppressive environmental conditions, many African Americans by the mid-1960s pressed into parts of the city in which they were once forbidden by tradition, intimidation, and violence. Their actions announced that they, too, had a "right to the city."[45] This resulted in new flare ups of violence between African Americans seizing their right to the city, and the white forces of counterrevolution. Conflicts over public spaces simmered in 1966 and 1967, foreshadowing the outbreak of violence that would occur in July 1967. Violence on Belle Isle, an

98 Black environmentalism in an age of urban crisis

island park in the Detroit River, during the "long, hot summer" of 1966 offered early evidence of the darker days ahead. Both white and black Detroiters sought relief from an unprecedented and prolonged June "heat wave" in one of the few major recreational amenities close to downtown Detroit. Conflicts on Belle Isle forced the city to dispatch extra police officers to control the crowds. Black visitors charged the police with harassment and acting with "overzealousness" in dispersing black crowds. In spite of the police presence, the conflicts continued. In early July, Edward Carter, 21, suffered a gunshot wound after a group of white youths allegedly confronted him, taunting, "What's going on, black boy?" before firing a gun and wounding Carter. This was just one of many racial incidents on Belle Isle signaling what seemed like a deteriorating period of race relations and police-black community relations.[46]

Just weeks before the July 1967 urban rebellion, several high-profile racial incidents put Detroit on edge. An interracial couple moving into white-suburban Warren touched off three days of mob violence directed at the couple. The most serious incident, according to the *Michigan Chronicle*'s managing editor Albert J. Dunmore, however, was the murder of Danny Thomas.[47] At River Rouge Park – a large park system along the river on the western border of Detroit and Dearborn Heights – violence spiked in 1967. When Danny Thomas and his pregnant wife spent the day at park on June 23, relaxing and listening to a phonograph, a group of whites approached the Thomases and one allegedly screamed, "Those boys should kill all n – s." The Thomases fled the park and returned hours later, after midnight, and the situation escalated. They tried to escape in their car, but it failed to start, the apparent result of someone tampering with the wires. Desperate for safety, they sought shelter in a recreation building, but the caretaker of the building refused their entrance. Facing a barrage of rocks and bottles, and enduring the screams of "N – s keep out of Rouge Park," Danny Thomas was attacked and shot three times, and his widow soon after suffered a miscarriage. The black community was angered not merely by the senseless murder but by the lack of attention in the press and inaction by the police department. The only man charged with a crime, Michael W. Palchlopek, was found not guilty by a jury in December 1968. Incidents such as this one exposed to black Detroiters the need to push not only for fair housing and an end to urban renewal programs, but also reinforced the importance of equal access to parks and recreation.

In the wake of a summer of urban uprisings in 1967, Lyndon Johnson appointed the National Advisory Commission on Civil Disorders to investigate. The result of the commission's investigation, the 1968 Kerner Report, famous for its observation that "our nation is moving toward two societies, one black, one white – separate and unequal," argued that environmental conditions in the inner city were one among many contributing factors in creating the urban rebellions.[48] "It must be concluded," the report suggested, "that slum sanitation is a serious problem in the minds of the urban poor." The report connected environmental quality to the psychology of the urban poor, pointing out that "sanitation and neighborhood cleanliness is a crucial issue relating to the stability of their blocks and constituting

Black environmentalism in an age of urban crisis **99**

an important psychological index of 'how far gone' their area is." The poor environmental state of the "slums," it went on, led to "poor health conditions," because, "the level of sanitation is strikingly below that which is prevalent in most higher income areas." Major environmental inequalities were one result of the "separate and unequal" societies.

Access to parks and recreational facilities was a matter of great concern for residents of the 12th street area that erupted. A survey of neighborhood residents just prior to the rebellion found high rates of dissatisfaction with the quality of the neighborhood. The figures are striking: 72% believed their neighborhood unsafe, 92% wanted to move to another neighborhood, and, as an indicator of environmental quality, 80% were unhappy with the recreational facilities close to their neighborhoods.[49] When Detroiters looked outside the city's boundaries, they saw in the suburbs abundant opportunities for play: immaculate ball fields, swimming pools, and well-kept parks. Meanwhile, Detroit's Recreation Department struggled with a declining budget as the city continued to hemorrhage residents and their taxes. Reforming inner-city neighborhoods to provide better recreational services would become an important element of rebuilding efforts.

When given the opportunity, residents turned out in scores to press policymakers to make a stronger commitment to reviving their local landscapes through positive means like parks and recreation, instead of the destructive slum clearance measures favored in the recent past. In 1970, the Michigan Natural Resources Council organized the "Governor's Conference on Urban Leisure." Concerned by both the urban crisis and the environmental crisis, organizers believed that "one of the most urgent aspects of this whole complex of environmental problems is securing proper support for recreation – a major part of bettering our environment."[50] The President of the Michigan Natural Resources Council, Norman Philips, urged that something must be done about recreational inequalities in the state's urban areas, arguing, "One of the most critical needs is to secure the advantages of recreation to the people who need them most, the people who live in the heart of the city." Wayne State University President William Keast echoed these sentiments, pointing out that recreational opportunities were "unevenly distributed" throughout the urban landscape, depriving residents of an important aspect of "human development."[51] Ironically, Keast had recently been the focus of activists' scorn for destroying parks and neighborhoods to expand Wayne State University. Michigan Governor William Milliken also lent his support for the idea that "urban leisure is very much a part of the larger problem of urban crisis. The two are inextricably bound together."[52] Attacking environmental inequalities related to recreation had to be part of the equation for urban revitalization. The inequalities seemed particularly cruel because the impoverished residents of Detroit who most needed relief from "impossible living conditions" found none.

That the urban crisis was also an environmental crisis seemed self-evident to many planners and policymakers. It made little sense to address the urban crisis without addressing the environmental conditions of the city. "What is the use of building new parks and playgrounds when the air in those parks is polluted, or if

100 Black environmentalism in an age of urban crisis

the parks, themselves, become cluttered with debris?," the governor rhetorically asked.[53] Many in the black community insisted that recreation held different meanings for the inner city than it did in the suburbs, arguing that recreation and leisure were essential to their health and well-being. For that reason, some preferred not to use the term leisure, finding that it suggested something non-essential. More than one participant noted that *Webster* dictionary defined leisure as "the condition of having one's time free from the demands of work or duty."[54] But, as Charles Howell, director of the Afro-American Cultural Foundation put it, "I am fifty years old. I have never known a moment of leisure, because, number one, as a black person, number two, as a poor person, there has never been one minute in my life that has been free from the demand of work or duty." Howell illustrated his criticism of bourgeois conceptions of leisure: "We conceive of recreation not simply as play. There isn't a black youngster in the city of Detroit who has the time simply to play." Recreation was essential because it served to "re-create, not just the physical being, but the spiritual being as well – those things that would tend to contribute to the creation of a complete person."

More revealing than the testimony of planners, policymakers, and community leaders, though, was the testimony of ordinary people who donated their time to attend the conference and air their grievances over the state of inner city recreation and the plans being produced. Many displayed their frustration that so much hot air at conferences such as this one had produced minimal results. Others used the opportunity to lambast suburbanites for coming into the city who "take the best job and take the money back to the suburbs."[55] Still others critiqued regional planners for failing to take into consideration the perspective of ordinary citizens.[56] Audrey Hogan took aim at the elite attitudes of planners and policymakers, the self-proclaimed "experts" who claimed know "what Detroit needs" while failing to engage local residents.[57] "You make black people feel ignorant," Hogan insisted, "You make them feel rebellious." The failure to truly address inequalities or to consult local people in planning and policymaking is what created groups like the Black Panthers, Hogan remarked. Money and resources – as well as a devolved system of neighborhood-level policymaking – were necessary to make the inner city a "livable space." Connecting the disastrous system of suburban exploitation of the central city to environmental inequality, Hogan demanded, "While you're putting fish in *your* streams for *you* to fish, drop something in the Detroit River, and clean it out, because this is where we have to fish at." Hogan's remarks were incredibly revealing about the way inner-city residents connected the dots between metropolitan development, recreational inequality, pollution, and environmental inequality, demonstrating a sophisticated understanding of environmental justice.

Earth Day

Urban renewal featured prominently in Earth Day 1970 celebrations at Wayne State University in Midtown Detroit. On April 22, 1970, the Young Prides and People Concerned About Urban Renewal cleaned up trash on a highway, piled it

Black environmentalism in an age of urban crisis **101**

into a truck, and drove it to Wayne State University, in Midtown Detroit, where the university's celebrations were well underway and consumer advocate Ralph Nader prepared to address the crowd. They dumped the garbage on the stage where Nader was ready to speak, and marched around the refuse with signs reading "THIS IS WAYNE'S GARBAGE" and "WAYNE USES POLLUTION TO DRIVE US FROM OUR HOMES."[58]

The demonstrators called attention to Wayne State's expansion into area neighborhoods at the expense of poor and black residents. An activist called Ripple laid out the stakes: "Dig it. By dumping the bags of garbage on the stage where the ecology teach-in was going on, we were asking the audience to consider urban renewal in the same light as ecology." Urban renewal was not merely a social problem – it was also an environmental crisis. "Under capitalism," Ripple argued, "urban renewal is always going to be run in the interest of the same class that pollutes the environment and then tries to convince us that the problem comes from our backyard incinerators and barbeque sets rather than from their smoke stacks." Ripple indicated the class and race dimensions of the environmental struggle, critiquing the Environmental Teach-In for failing to connect with issues important to inner-city residents. Criticizing mainstream environmentalists did not necessarily mean opposing environmentalism, merely the dominant narrative of an environmentalism that was concerned primarily with aesthetics and led by people "who like to commute in from [suburban] Birmingham to a tidy little campus like Wayne without having to notice the neighborhood."[59]

For African Americans, improving the environment was something different than the environmentalism developing throughout the United States, which found vivid expression in the nation's first Earth Day in April 1970. While white, middle-class Americans could envision an environmental politics based exclusively on protecting the natural world, for black Detroiters, activism did not neatly fit into categories. As the Wayne State demonstration suggests, black Detroiters saw the fight for a healthier, safer, and greener environment as inseparable from the fight against slum clearance and other struggles for racial equality. They asked white environmentalists to consider "urban renewal in the same light as ecology," arguing that it was a common struggle against capitalist interests. But would those environmentalists listen?

Early signs did not look promising. The *New York Times* reported on the wedge growing between ecology and African American activists just before Earth Day. They asked the same question that many in black communities expressed, "Isn't the new interest in ecology diverting energy and resources from the difficult and frustrating problems of the inner city?"[60] Cliff Humphrey, founder of Ecology Action, a San Francisco Bay Area organizations, organization, insisted that it did not, that environmental activism "must include Watts as well as the redwoods." Yet in spite of the lip service paid to an environmentalism that included all creatures, Earth Day organizers made little effort to integrate African Americans into the planning, or even to address the black critiques of mainstream environmentalism. As environmentalists groused about over-consumption of the Earth's resources, inner-city

102 Black environmentalism in an age of urban crisis

African Americans reminded environmentalists that this message rang hollow for the underclass of the cities, when they struggled to meet the most basic needs. This did not escape the notice of black intellectuals at the time, like Nathan Hare, founder of the black studies movement on college campuses. "The emergence of the concept of ecology in American life is potentially of momentous relevance to the ultimate liberation of black people," Hare wrote. "Yet blacks and their environmental interests have been so blatantly omitted that blacks and the ecology movement currently stand in contradiction to each other."[61]

Black environmentalism offered an alternative. Although inner-city black residents did not consciously describe themselves as environmentalists, they nevertheless asserted that the places in which they lived, worked, and played mattered. For most black Detroiters, the key question was not how to reduce consumption to protect the environment, but rather, how can improving local environments support a healthy, thriving, and economically sustainable life? This would continue to be a key question as Detroiters entered the 1970s determined to address the urban environmental crisis. That the black perspective on environmentalism disappeared from the larger environmental movement led to a divide that would only be partially resolved by the emergence of the environmental justice movement a decade later. In the meantime, they worked on the ground to combat the growing environmental health threat of abandoned homes pockmarking Detroit's neighborhoods.

Abandoned Detroit

"The city ought to tear down these empty —," the homicide detective grumbled. "They ain't good for nothing but this," he remarked, checking the bodies of two dead women for identification. The two women were found in an abandoned house at 658 Pingree Avenue in Detroit. Directly across the street, at 659 Pingree, only one year earlier, a Detroit Department of Public Works crew tasked with clearing out the abandoned garage stumbled upon the corpse of a man who had been tortured, executed, and stashed under a pile of car parts. These were but two of the city's 10,500 abandoned homes, many of them with collapsed roofs, overgrown weeds, chipping lead paint, rodents and vermin, and unstable foundations, presenting a clear environmental health danger to all residents, and in particular for the neighborhood children who explored the ruins as children tend to do. Along Pingree's alleyways, "across from the body-laden garage was another one that had obviously been used as a 'shooting gallery' – narcotics paraphe[r]nalia was strewn about the floor." Once considered America's first middle-class industrial town, Detroit was now a museum of deindustrialization, abandonment, and white flight. The *Michigan Chronicle* considered the corpses the "'strange fruit' of abandoned dwellings." "Eastside, westside and all over this 'city of homeowners,' dead bodies are being found in dead houses," the tragedy of a deserted city.[62]

Into the urban and environmental crisis stepped the newly elected black mayor of Detroit, Coleman A. Young. In 1923, the Young family climbed aboard a train in

Black environmentalism in an age of urban crisis   **103**

Alabama and joined the Great Migration to one of the major destinations for black southerners, Detroit.[63] They joined a swelling black community attracted to the city to take advantage of the economic opportunities and relative sense of freedom. Once the Youngs reached Detroit, they encountered something different from the "land of opportunity" they expected, as segregated residential policies and practices confined their living choices and they settled in the Black Bottom area in Detroit's East Side Colored District. The overcrowded and dilapidated housing conditions the Youngs encountered shaped the political consciousness of Coleman Young and helped him to understand the economic, social, and environmental challenges of inner-city living, experiences that would shape his political activism and, eventually, his mayoral aspirations. Young learned from his father how to hustle to survive, and during Prohibition, there was no shortage of opportunity to make money bootlegging from Windsor, Ontario across the Detroit River, or running theft rings or illicit gambling operations. The money was so good, Young remembered, it was a wonder that he gave it up for the difficult labor at Ford's River Rouge Complex. In 1937, Young worked as an organizer for the brand-new United Automobile Workers, and pushed the union to confront racial inequality on the shop floor and in the ranks of leadership. His brashness made him enemies in the union leadership, and in 1948, his alleged connections to communism got him swept up in Walter Reuther's red-baiting crusade.[64] Young's defense of working-class African Americans helped him build a reputation in Detroit's black east side that would later help his political ambitions. His service as a state legislator in the 1960s further established Young as an up-and-coming activist-policymaker with an aggressive leadership style that inspired many African Americans.[65]

Coleman Young squared off in the 1973 Detroit mayoral election against a white police commissioner, John Nichols, at a critical juncture. After the rebellion of 1967, and continuing abandonment of the city by white residents, the future of the city was up for grabs, and Young seized the moment. White conservatives made one last stand to claim the city by consolidating around the law-and-order politics of Nichols, who promised chaos and crime should the black candidate prevail.[66] Meanwhile, Young promised to reform the police department and made urban revitalization a central part of the campaign.[67] White liberals, unions, and black Detroiters helped Young win by 4% over Nichols, signaling an urban realignment toward black leadership in the city.

Many of the first generation of black mayors of major cities shared a concern for urban environmental issues, often arising out of their lived experiences as African Americans in the inner city. In Cleveland, the city "where the river burned," Carl Stokes confronted the "crisis in the urban environment," by addressing what he saw as interconnected social and environmental issues.[68] This ecological approach to solving the urban crisis, as David Stradling and Richard Stradling argue, reflected a new kind of urban policymaking. The approach was repeated in places like Gary, Indiana, where Richard Hatcher, speaking in front of a 1970 rally, noted that it was the everyday struggles of a blighted environment that kept mothers up at night fearing "rats which may bite their children" and "roaches which crawl over

104 Black environmentalism in an age of urban crisis

and spoil . . . food."[69] Improving the housing and other environmental conditions of Gary's black neighborhoods became a central part of Hatcher's environmental agenda.[70]

The mayor faced several immediate and pressing challenges, seemingly none as large as stemming the inter-related and deteriorating financial and physical condition of the city. White residents continued to flee the city for the suburbs. A steady stream that began in the 1950s turned into a wave after the 1967 rebellion and showed no sign of letting up as Young took the oath of office. If Detroiters expected Young to coddle those who remained, he quickly disabused them of the notion. He thundered: "To all the dope pushers, to all rip-off artists, to all muggers. . . . It's time to leave Detroit. . . . Hit Eight Mile Road. I don't give a damn if they're black or white, or if they wear Superfly suits or blue uniforms with silver badges. Hit the road."[71] White residents in the city and suburbs took it as a declaration of war, that he was sending "a virtual armed invasion" to the suburbs, Young later remembered. It signaled the beginning of a tumultuous relationship between Detroit and the suburbs, which disavowed responsibility for the city's crises. Once Detroit became a black majority city led by a black administration, they abandoned it, with some white suburbanites insisting that the city would return to wilderness.[72]

The job of stopping abandonment was made considerably harder by dwindling city coffers. As factories moved to the global South and homeowners fled for the suburbs, the tax base significantly shrank. The cycle kept reproducing. Some of the challenges may have been eased with a more activist federal government in the city, but federal funds dried up and the Nixon administration reorganized the relationship between localities, states, and the federal government under a program called "New Federalism." Under this program, the federal government would devolve many of its responsibilities in urban renewal and environmental services and instead providing block grants to the cities. Under the arrangement, localities would have more autonomy, but urban activists at the time saw the program as something more sinister – the first step in defunding cities, according to the National League of Cities.[73] Just as the first black mayor won the right to govern the city, federal policies made big city leadership even more difficult.

Even the modest attempts to create sustainable neighborhoods were under threat from the austerity politics that witnessed declining federal aid to cities and shrinking city budgets. Residents went to great efforts to clean neighborhoods, but as the number of abandoned houses continued to rise, keeping a neighborhood livable grew more challenging. After a long struggle by the East Side Concerned Citizens to clean up and revitalize the neighborhood, they finally got the ear of Young. It took a walk-out at a City Council session to get noticed, but Young set up a dialogue with the group and promised a more concerted effort among city departments to identify and solve the community's concerns. The East Side Concerned Citizens succeeded in getting the city to commit to a massive clean-up campaign and the demolition of a dangerous building.[74] In case after case, neighborhood residents banded together in order to force a more robust response to the neglect of

Black environmentalism in an age of urban crisis **105**

their neighborhoods. But they were doing so as the city possessed fewer resources to tackle abandoned houses and essential services.

Abandoned houses, which often became property of the federal Department of Housing and Urban Development (HUD), increasingly threatened the environmental quality of neighborhoods in the 1970s. At the end of 1975, Detroit had the largest percentage of HUD-owned houses. In fact, 16% of all HUD-owned houses in the nation could be found languishing in Detroit.[75] Frustrated by the lack of HUD speed as it sat on an inventory of 2,000 abandoned houses, Coleman Young promised to take demolition into his own hands. He warned HUD that the city would begin demolition within 48 hours, "with or without federal approval."[76] Local HUD administrator Elmer Bickford fired back that the city must not destroy federal property, and would owe HUD $14,000 per house destroyed. Ever the fighter, Young returned the volley, saying, "Not only will we not pay, but we will insist that HUD reimburse the cost of demolition."

In late 1975, the city apparently bulldozed five HUD-owned houses on accident. When tensions rose between Young and regional HUD chief Donald Morrow, Young knocked down two more – on purpose – in October 1975.[77] The two sides avoided further escalation when Morrow backed down on the threats, each side agreeing that court battles would not solve the difficult housing issues facing the city. The gauntlet was laid down temporarily, but did not solve the larger pressures inflaming each side. Slowly, Young and Detroit activists yielded HUD progress. By early 1976, HUD was beginning to see its inventory of homes drop.[78] Speaking at the beginning of 1977, Young claimed, "HUD has finally begun to move." He claimed that city threats to bulldoze HUD properties caught the agency's attention. "HUD is beginning to meet its first obligation – to remove the waste and wreckage of its failures. The second obligation still remains: to heal the terrible wounds and to help rebuild a city."[79] "But last year HUD was working against us. This year we have HUD's attention. . . . Next year, HUD will be working for us," Young declared in his own inimitable way.

Mayor Young has been characterized as a politician who fought against environmental protection, fearing that it created unnecessary burdens for attracting reinvestment.[80] This is only part of the story. Young focused on neighborhood-level environmental issues if they did not seem to threaten urban reinvestment.[81] He championed a "neighborhood conservation" approach, once popular in the 1950s, to reforming the built environment and tackling land use challenges. Far less destructive than slum clearance, neighborhood conservation kept people in their homes, raised property values, and promised stability in rapidly deteriorating neighborhoods – at least in theory. In response to dwindling financial resources, Coleman Young encouraged civic participation in neighborhood governance and citizen-led beautification efforts to heal the scarred landscape.[82] Pledging $2 million in city fund for beautification efforts, he nevertheless emphasized that it was not the city but the citizens themselves that would revitalize the environment, block by block. In his first year in office, as many as 100,000 residents and 700 block clubs participated in the clean-up efforts, an outpouring of support that the

106 Black environmentalism in an age of urban crisis

Michigan Chronicle proudly claimed was a rare demonstration of "widely enthusiastic support."[83]

Throughout the 1970s, citizen-led neighborhood clean-up operations attempted to restore a sense of community, boost property values, and eliminate the piles of rubbish that provided havens for vermin and reduced aesthetic value of the neighborhoods. The black Environmental Protection and Maintenance Department's (EPMD's) director, Nathan Bridges, championed the role that African Americans could perform in cleaning up the nation's cities, and noted the changing national urban political landscape, with African Americans now holding important positions of power in city government, a sea change from just a few years earlier. Bridges remarked that at a Milwaukee conference on litter problems just a few years earlier, the only three black delegates at the meeting were all from Detroit, but now, African Americans played a prominent role in cleaning up cities. Like Coleman Young, Bridges moved with his family from the south and settled in the Black Bottom neighborhood, working his way up from a laborer in the Department of Public Works to become executive administrator of the EPMD. Bridges became a nationally recognized advocate for the Keep America Beautiful campaign, and worked on the Board of Directors of Keep Michigan Beautiful, and locally on the Keep Detroit Beautiful Committee.[84]

While the city provided some top-down leadership on improving the landscape, much of the effort came from the grassroots. It was an approach to making a livable city that geographer Kimberley Kinder has called "DIY Detroit."[85] In a city that fails to provide essential services, residents have consistently responded by "making do" and creating a shadow landscape of services like upkeeping abandoned lots by planting gardens and organizing garbage clean-up drives. With the city's budget stretched perilously thin, ordinary residents put their own stamp on their blocks. By the end of the decade, according to one estimate, some 150,000 volunteers and 1,200 block clubs participated in the annual clean-up drives. Yet residents could not evade the stereotype from a noisy clique of suburbanites that black residents were apathetic to the environment.[86] Images of abandonment and decay obscured the Herculean efforts of Detroiters to make their neighborhoods healthy, sustainable, and livable.

Detroit has been the subject of much fascination with urban agriculture efforts to transform abandoned blocks into productive community gardens and small-scale farms, creating jobs and addressing hunger in the so-called food deserts.[87] Some of the first efforts to re-think abandoned land as a community resource occurred during Young's administration. HUD and city officials attempted to turn vacant properties over to users who could maintain the properties. HUD advertised its inventory of vacant lots as "a place to build a parking space, grow vegetables, have a playground for your children, and increase the value of your property," for as little as $250 for a 30-foot wide lot.[88] Turning abandoned lots into vegetable gardens was an idea that had much popular support behind it. In an effort to encourage neighborhood residents to take care of vacant lots, Young championed a "farm-a-lot" program, in which the city provided permits to build gardens on vacant lots.[89] The city even provided free seeds, including carrots, beans, assorted greens, and turnips.

The community gardening efforts showed the possibilities for turning abandonment into an asset. By 1977, some 1,000 city-owned lots in Detroit had been converted to vegetable and flower gardens, along with many youth gardens funded by the United Community Services.[90] Michigan State University and the U.S. Department of Agriculture contributed seeds and fertilizer to low-income residents, with some 1,500 Detroiters taking advantage of the program in 1977 alone. Senior citizens, who especially confronted a lack of recreational resources, could get help preparing seed beds. The city was interested in greatly expanding this program, but ran up against brick walls when trying to find additional sources of funding. Yet even with limited resources, many of the programs were successful in generating interest among senior citizens.[91] The gardening programs were an especially bright spot in many otherwise-bleak landscapes, reflecting creative approaches to addressing the urban crisis.

By the end of the 1970s, Detroit was still a long way off from creating the healthful and sustainable landscape for which so many activists and policymakers had worked. Many residents withdrew in resignation over the lack of progress and feelings of powerlessness to intervene in the environment. "Ain't nobody gonna do nothing anyhow," one Detroit student reported to a group investigating ways to improve urban recreation.[92] Many residents would no doubt agree with investigators who reported that "recreation is woven into the fabric of urban existence" to make a complex "urban cloth," and saw recreation not as an isolated part of their lives, like many middle-class suburbanites, but one part in the holistic system of daily life.[93]

In neighborhoods lacking conventional recreational facilities, residents, especially children, made their own, creating a shadow landscape of environmental amenities, often in hazardous places.[94] Vacant houses, buildings, and factory sites provided "unofficial and uncontrolled recreational facilities," but they also provided "havens for undesirables." Investigators for a national urban recreation study interviewed children, who provided important evidence for how they worked around a lack of conventional facilities and how to fix the system. "Near our house there is a packing company and nobody runs it," said one fifth grader, "But there's dogs in the yard. Kids go in there and start fires. There's been two fires in one morning. It is dangerous too. Maybe you could make it a recreation center." Children recognized that the deserted city offered myriad opportunities for play, if only some effort could be put into "clean[ing] up the park," turning lots into camping spots, "polluted [sic] city and water cleaned, vacant buildings into recreation centers." Such opportunities, another fifth grader suggested, would help "so people can stop killing people like those gangs [and] can stop acting a fool." The significance of recreation for childhood development was not lost on the interviewees, and one junior high student baldly pointed out, "We . . . know that conditions now determine conditions later."[95]

The 1970s witnessed environmental organizations becoming an important part of the political landscape in Washington, DC, as they grew their lobbying apparatuses and focused on national policy.[96] While these mainstream environmental

108 Black environmentalism in an age of urban crisis

organizations did show some interest in organizing inner-city and working-class residents, the coalition remained weak. The neglect of the black and urban experience left environmentalism to defend a narrower range of priorities, often those most prized by middle-class and elite white suburbanites. Nevertheless, black residents in Detroit continued to work to improve their local environments. Through community gardens, vest-pocket parks, urban agriculture, block clean-ups, and other creative efforts, Detroiters made gallant and creative efforts to turn back the tide of urban crisis. Despite the significant challenges confronting Detroit, residents often expressed a surprising degree of optimism in the city and in their neighborhoods, even at the end of the 1970s. Some two-thirds of Detroit residents reported that they were "almost" satisfied with their neighborhoods, which matched the rate of suburban residents finding satisfaction in their neighborhoods.[97] A plurality of respondents claimed that the most important asset to their neighborhoods were the people living there. In the 1970s, even when the city's future looked bleak, there was a dedicated citizenry that worked to make the city a more sustainable and healthier place to call home.

Notes

1 "Mildred Smith Fought City Hall – and Won," *Detroit Free Press*, February 3, 1982.
2 "Grosse Pointers Donate to Environment School," *Michigan Chronicle*, September 7, 1974.
3 United States Congress, *Models and Strategies for Change: 1975*, Senate Committee on the Judiciary, Subcommittee to Investigate Juvenile Delinquency (Washington, DC: Government Printing Office, 1976), 1045.
4 The classic treatment connecting suburban sprawl and environmentalism is Adam Rome, *The Bulldozer in the Countryside: Suburban Sprawl and the Rise of American Environmentalism* (New York and Cambridge: Cambridge University Press, 2005). Other works that treat suburban sprawl and the rise of ecological consciousness include Kenneth T. Jackson, *Crabgrass Frontier: The Suburbanization of the United States* (New York: Oxford University Press, 1987); Christopher C. Sellers, *Crabgrass Crucible: Suburban Nature and the Rise of Environmentalism in Twentieth-Century America* (Chapel Hill, NC: University of North Carolina Press, 2013); Dolores Hayden, *Building Suburbia: Green Fields and Urban Growth: 1820–2000* (New York: Random House, 2009).
5 For African American environmental history, particularly in cities, see Andrew Hurley, *Environmental Inequalities: Class, Race, and Industrial Pollution in Gary, Indiana, 1945–1980* (Chapel Hill, NC: University of North Carolina Press, 1995); Dianne D. Glave and Mark Stoll, eds., *"To Love the Wind and the Rian": African Americans and Environmental History* (Pittsburgh, PA: University of Pittsburgh Press, 2006); Dorceta E. Taylor, *The Environment and People in American Cities, 1600–1900s: Disorder, Inequality, and Social Change* (Durham, NC: Duke University Press, 2009); Carolyn Finney, *Black Faces, White Spaces: Reimagining the Relationship of African Americans to the Great Outdoors* (Chapel Hill, NC: University of North Carolina Press, 2014); Robert Gioielli, *Environmental Activism and the Urban Crisis: Baltimore, St. Louis, Chicago* (Philadelphia, PA: Temple University Press, 2015); David Stradling and Richard Stradling, *Where the River Burned: Carl Stokes and the Struggle to Save Cleveland* (Ithaca, NY: Cornell University Press, 2015); Colin Fisher, *Urban Green: Nature, Recreation, and the Working Class in Industrial Chicago* (Chapel Hill, NC: University of North Carolina Press, 2015); Dianne D. Glave, *Rooted in the Earth: Reclaiming the African American Environmental Heritage* (Chicago: Chicago Review

Press, 2010); Brian McCammack, *Landscapes of Hope: Nature and the Great Migration in Chicago* (Cambridge, MA: Harvard University Press, 2017).

6 *I-96 Freeway: Detroit Metropolitan Area Corridor Planning Study* (1964), Vol. I, Michigan State Highway Department, Box 8, Folder 15, MR Collection, ALUA.

7 Raymond Mohl, "Stop the Road: Freeway Revolts in American Cities," *Journal of Urban History* 30 (July 2004): 674–706, 677; Thomas J. Sugrue, *The Origins of the Urban Crisis: Race and Inequality in Postwar Detroit* (Princeton, NJ: Princeton University Press, 1996), 47–48.

8 *I-96 Freeway: Detroit Metropolitan Area Corridor Planning Study: 1964: Volume I*, Box 8, Folder 15, MR Collection, ALUA.

9 Roger Biles, "Expressways Before the Interstates: The Case of Detroit, 1945–1956," *Journal of Urban History* 40, no. 5 (2014): 843–54, quote on 844.

10 Petition to the Common Council, November 23, 1964, Box 8, Folder 16, MR Collection.

11 June to Ravitz, December 8, 1964, Box 8, Folder 16, MR Collection.

12 Arthur Rosen to Mel Ravitz, Box 8, Folder 16, MR Collection.

13 Archdale and Longacre Petition to Mel Ravitz, November 10, 1964, Box 8, Folder 16, MR Collection.

14 Progress Report, Jeffries Action Body, February 11, 1966, Box 53, Folder A17–14, DUL Records, BHL.

15 Roy L. Williams, *Quarterly Report*, Department of Housing, October–December 1965, Box 51, Folder A17–1, DUL Records.

16 Alan Kamens to Roger Craig, August 31, 1966, Box 53, Folder A17–16, DUL Records.

17 Press Release, Governor Romney Office, November 2, 1966, Box 53, Folder A17–17, DUL Records.

18 Press Release, William Milliken, November 10, 1966, Box 17, Folder 10, MR Collection.

19 Robert Gioielli, *Environmental Activism and the Urban Crisis: Baltimore, St. Louis, Chicago* (Philadelphia, PA: Temple University Press, 2014), 104–36, quote on 112.

20 Sidney Fine, *Violence in the Model City: The Cavanagh Administration, Race Relations, and the Detroit Riot of 1967* (East Lansing: Michigan State University Press, 2007), 30.

21 "The Man Behind It," *Detroit Free Press*, August 22, 1965.

22 "City's Poor Get Dynamic Organizer," *The Detroit News*, August 15, 1965, clipping in Box 2, Folder 2, DC Papers, ALUA.

23 "7 Seized in New Bid to Break Into House," *Detroit News*, September 20, 1966, clipping in Box 2, Folder 2, DC Papers.

24 "Detroit Poor Leave Barricade, Present Grievances to City Hall," *The Michigan Daily*, October 16, 1966, accessed September 18, 2018, https://digital.bentley.umich.edu/midaily/mdp.39015071754191/435.

25 "14 Arrested as WCO Invades Home in Protest on Renewal," *Detroit Free Press*, September 18, 1966, clipping in Box 2, Folder 2, DC Papers.

26 "Protesters Occupy House to Block Renewal Project," *Michigan Chronicle*, September 24, 1966, clipping in Box 2, Folder 2, DC Papers.

27 "Protesters Occupy House to Block Renewal Project."

28 "7 Seized in New Bid to Break into House."

29 "WCO Explains Protests, Urban Renewal Arrests," *Michigan Chronicle*, October 1, 1966.

30 Photograph, "(26874) West Central Organization (WCO), Petitions, 1966," ALUA, accessed September 20, 2018, http://reuther.wayne.edu/node/13965.

31 "Plan Proposed to House the Poor," *Detroit Free Press*, September 21, 1966, clipping in Box 2, Folder 2, David Cohen Papers, ALUA. June Manning Thomas.

32 "Protesters Leave a Gift for Knox," *Detroit Free Press*, November 7, 1966.

33 June Manning Thomas, *Redevelopment and Rave: Planning a Finer City in Postwar Detroit* (Detroit: Wayne State University Press, 2013), 108–11.

34 Malcolm McLaughlin, "The Pied Piper of the Ghetto: Lyndon Johnson, Environmental Justice, and the Politics of Rat Control," *Journal of Urban History* 37 (July 2011): 549. Keeanga-Yamahtta Taylor, *Race for Profit: How Banks and the Real Estate Industry*

110 Black environmentalism in an age of urban crisis

Undermined Black Homeownership (Chapel Hill, NC: University of North Carolina Press, 2019), 25–28.

35 Lyndon Johnson Statement, July 20, 1967, accessed September 16, 2018, www.presidency.ucsb.edu/ws/index.php?pid=28359.

36 McLaughlin argues that the rat crisis should be seen within a framework of environmental justice, demonstrating how "urban decay that encouraged rat infestation represented a diffuse, pervasive, and nonetheless pernicious form of environmental blight," in "The Pied Piper of the Ghetto," 544. The rat control efforts mark the near intersection of environmental and civil rights goals that would later be credited to the environmental justice movement.

37 "Rats Bite Children, Tenants Call Strike," *Michigan Chronicle*, September 24, 1966.

38 "Bitten Baby in Hospital, Rent Strike to Continue," *Michigan Chronicle*, October 1, 1966.

39 "Rats Bite Children, Tenants Call Strike."

40 "Bitten Baby in Hospital."

41 Fine, *Violence in the Model City*, 69.

42 "100 Picket Council on Fire-Trap Houses," *Detroit News*, July 1, 1965, clipping in Box 2, Folder 2, DC Papers.

43 Tom Johnson, Installation Address, July 15, 1966, Box 2, Folder 5, DC Papers.

44 "Fire Tragedy Spurs Tenants to Protest Slum Conditions," *West Central Action News*, January 1967, in Box 2, Folder 2, DC Papers.

45 Phrase borrowed from Henri LeFebvre, *Le Droit à la Ville* (Paris: Anthoropos, 1968).

46 "Belle Isle – Trouble Spot," *Michigan Chronicle*, July 9, 1966.

47 Fine, *Violence in the Model City*, 148–50, quotes on 149.

48 *Report of the National Advisory Commission on Civil Disorders* (Washington, DC: U.S. Government Printing Office, 1968), quotes on 1, 138.

49 Fine, *Violence in the Model City*, 153.

50 *Governor's Conference on Urban Leisure: Papers and Discussions Presented at 14th Annual Conference* (Michigan Natural Resources Council, 1970), 1, Michigan Collections, SLM.

51 William Keast Statement, *Governor's Conference on Urban Leisure*, 2.

52 William Milliken Statement, *Governor's Conference on Urban Leisure*, 3–5.

53 Milliken Statement, *Governor's Conference on Urban Leisure*, 5.

54 Charles Howell Statement in *Governor's Conference on Urban Leisure*, 44–45.

55 Nora Griffith comments, *Governor's Conference on Urban Leisure*, 47.

56 Unidentified comments, *Governor's Conference on Urban Leisure*, 19.

57 Audrey Hogan comments, *Governor's Conference on Urban Leisure*, 50.

58 Ripple (Red), "Trashin' Wayne," *Fifth Estate*, April 16 to April 29, 1970.

59 Ripple (Red), "Trashin' Wayne".

60 Steven V. Roberts, "The Better Earth: A Report on Ecology Action," *New York Times*, March 29, 1970.

61 Nathan Hare, "Black Ecology," *The Black Scholar* 1, no. 6 (April 1970): 2–8, quote on 2. See also Gioielli, *Environmental Activism of the Urban Crisis*, 141–42; Stradling and Stradling, *Where the River Burned*, 177.

62 Bill Black, "On the 'Strange Fruit' of Abandoned Dwellings," *Michigan Chronicle*, March 24, 1973. Redaction in the original.

63 Coleman A. Young and Lonnie Wheeler, *Hard Stuff: The Autobiography of Coleman Young* (New York: Viking, 1994), 15–16, 22–23.

64 Wilbur C. Rich, *Coleman Young and Detroit Politics: From Social Activist to Power Broker*, *African American Life* (Detroit: Wayne State University Press, 1989), 66–68.

65 Heather Ann Thompson, *Whose Detroit? Politics, Labor, and Race in a Modern American City* (Ithaca, NY: Cornell University Press, 2004), 193–97.

66 Thompson, *Whose Detroit?* 197–98.

67 Young and Wheeler, *Hard Stuff*, 197–201.

68 Stradling and Stradling, *Where the River Burned*, 1–18.

69 Hurley, *Environmental Inequalities*, quote on 111.

70 Hurley, *Environmental Inequalities*, 130.

71 Young and Wheeler, *Hard Stuff*, 200.

72 On the white historical memory of getting pushed out of Detroit, see Rebecca J. Kinney, *Beautiful Wasteland: The Rise of Detroit as America's Postindustrial Frontier* (Minneapolis, MN: University of Minnesota Press, 2016), 1–37.

73 William E. Farrell, "Nixon's 'New Federalism' Scored by Ohio Representative at Urban Parley," *New York Times*, December 4, 1973.

74 "Massive Revitalization Program Launched on the City's Eastside," *Michigan Chronicle*, December 6, 1975.

75 Larry Plump, "HUD's Binford Lashes Council Critics, News," *Michigan Chronicle*, November 15, 1975.

76 "HUD, Absentee Cops Stall Stires Mayoral Crackdown," *Michigan Chronicle*, October 25, 1975.

77 "HUD Backs Down on Threat to City," *Detroit Free Press*, November 5, 1975.

78 "HUD Finally Cutting Backlog of Vacant Homes," *Detroit Free Press*, April 26, 1976, 4–A.

79 "Major Boom Expected with Transit System, Housing," *Michigan Chronicle*, February 12, 1977.

80 Laurie E. Adkin, *The Politics of Sustainable Development: Citizens, Unions and the Corporations* (Montreal: Black Rose Books, 1998), 260.

81 Abstract to the Application for Federal Assistance, Department of Housing and Urban Development, February 19, 1975, Box 20, Folder 21, NDI Collection.

82 "Neighborhood Halls Are Red Tape Slicers," *Michigan Chronicle*, October 22, 1977.

83 "Let's Pitch In and Clean Up Our City," *Michigan Chronicle*, May 11, 1974.

84 Nathan Bridges, "He's Literally 'Anti' About Litter," *Michigan Chronicle*, February 21, 1976.

85 Kimberley Kinder, *DIY Detroit: Making Do in a City Without Services* (Minneapolis, MN: University of Minnesota Press, 2016).

86 Letter to the Editor, Helene R. Lesky, *Detroit Free Press*, July 16, 1973, 6A; Letter to the Editor, A. Lucia, *Detroit Free Press*, January 28, 1973, 8–A.

87 David Runk, "Detroit Leads the Way in Urban Farming," *Christian Science Monitor*, April 28, 2010, accessed December 2, 2010, www.csmonitor.com/The-Culture/Gardening/2010/0428/Detroit-leads-the-way-in-urban-farming; Danielle Nierenberg and Amanda Stone Letter to the Editor, "Eat Locally Processed Food to Support Health, Communities," *Detroit News*, December 9, 2010. See also Joseph Cialdella, *Motor City Green: A Century of Landscapes and Environmentalism in Detroit* (Pittsburgh, PA: University of Pittsburgh Press, 2020), 136–61.

88 HUD Advertisement, *Michigan Chronicle*, October 7, 1973.

89 "Free Seeds Available to City Lot Gardeners," *Michigan Chronicle*, May 10, 1975; and Darcelle Kanoyton, "Novice Gardener is All Thumbs . . . Green!," *Michigan Chronicle*, August 9, 1975.

90 *National Urban Recreation Study: Detroit/Ann Arbor* (Washington, DC: Bureau of Outdoor Recreation, 1977), 77–78.

91 "Planting Time," *Michigan Chronicle*, June 16, 1979, A2.

92 *National Urban Recreation Study: Detroit/Ann Arbor*, 1.

93 *National Urban Recreation Study: Detroit/Ann Arbor*, 6.

94 The idea of shadow landscapes is derived, in part, from Michel De Certeau's conception of vernacular cityscapes. I see this act as a type of "poaching" of an illicit recreational resource through trespassing, an act of hidden resistance to urban decay. *The Practice of Everyday Life*, trans. Steven Rendall (Berkeley: University of California Press, 1984), 91–110.

95 *National Urban Recreation Study: Detroit/Ann Arbor*, 13, 89–90.

96 Samuel P. Hays with Barbara D. Hays, *Beauty, Health, and Permanence: Environmental Politics in the United States, 1955–1985* (Cambridge, UK: Cambridge University Press, 1987), 6–7.

97 *National Urban Recreation Study: Detroit/Ann Arbor*, 81.

6

ENVIRONMENTALISM IN THE FRAGMENTED METROPOLIS

In 1972, two years after the nation's first Earth Day, Michael Brough, a graduate student in the School of Natural Resources at the University of Michigan, surveyed the battle lines of a fight over a proposed Southeast Michigan "Super Sewer." The controversy pitted concerned local residents, some environmental scientists, and suburban governments against powerful institutions like the Army Corps of Engineers and regional planning agencies. Each side blamed the other for the supposed environmental catastrophes that would occur if the sewer was built or abandoned. Suburban opponents combined not-in-my-backyard (NIMBY) language with the rhetoric of environmental protection and utilized opportunities for civic participation under the National Environmental Policy Act (NEPA) of 1969 to fight unwanted development. Brough found both genuine environmental concern and "pecuniary self-interest" motivating suburbanites. Evaluating the comparative environmental claims of each side, he admitted befuddlement, asking, "Will the real villain please stand up?" His confusion suggests the difficulty of disentangling the motives and agendas of suburban environmentalists, whose activism often entailed both authentic environmental concern and cynical self-interest.[1]

"Metropolitan environmentalism" held the promise of unifying the region through the common pursuit of environmental sustainability. As the popular ecologist Barry Commoner invoked in 1971, "everything is connected to everything else."[1] Yet metropolitan environmentalism was a fragmented affair.[2] Suburbanites expressed a growing commitment to environmental politics as a means to control local built and natural environments in ways that supported a high quality of life in the suburbs, based in part on access to green spaces, freedom from toxic waste and other environmental hazards, and local control over their community landscapes. State and regional authorities dominated the efforts to improve suburban quality of life. By the early 1960s, grassroots efforts to improve the environment joined those of planners and policymakers to create a durable force advocating for the suburbs.

DOI: 10.4324/9780429319914-6

As suburban homeowners grew more empowered to defend their homes and their local environments, residents of the central city saw their power to improve the built and natural environment eroded by population loss, disinvestment, deindustrialization, and physical decay. Suburban and city residents each possessed an impulse to improve the environmental quality of their surroundings, but the fates of city and suburban environments diverged dramatically in the 1970s. Unlike the black residents of Detroit and the working-class residents of the industrial suburbs, each of whom engaged in environmental activism focused on the livability of their homes and neighborhoods, suburban environmental activists more often practiced a Not-In-My-Backyard environmentalism protecting property values and quality-of-life in their communities. Asserting "local sovereignty," suburban homeowners attempted to gain more control over their properties. In Detroit's suburbs, environmental activism was often inseparable from fears that the environmental problems – and the people they associated with the urban crisis – might be headed toward their backyards. Suburban environmentalism meant exclusion – of unwanted people, land uses, and environmental hazards.

Citizens opposed to super sewer

A proposed regional sewer interceptor system known as "Super Sewer" demonstrated the changing terrain of homeowner environmentalism, environmental regulations, and regional politics. Detroit suburbanites selectively embraced aspects of environmentalism that allowed them to assert local control of landscapes and property while rejecting sacrifices that purportedly benefited the region. In the late 1950s, Detroit area planning agencies began serious discussions regarding the need for a centralized sewer system to manage urban development. By 1964, a system serving the downriver area of Detroit was operational, yet the need for a system serving the burgeoning western and northern suburbs through the southern suburbs was apparent.[3] The Detroit Regional Planning Commission in September 1967 proposed a 90-mile-long interceptor sewer system that would serve Wayne, Oakland, and Washtenaw counties.[4] The eight-foot-wide sewer line would begin near Bloomfield Hills in the far northwest corner of the metropolitan region, then proceed southward to Romulus, where it would connect with a second section of the sewer line in Ypsilanti, and then turn southeast toward a massive treatment plant at Pointe Mouillée on the Lake Erie shoreline. The treatment plant would process 121 million gallons of raw sewage per day. Due to projections of continued suburban development, some planners expressed concerns that this was the last possible chance to develop an effective, metropolitan-wide system.

A region-wide sewer system, experts hoped, would help to reduce the nonpoint pollutants emptying into the Huron watershed and eventually depositing in Lake Erie, a Great Lake that had endured much of the brunt of industrial effluent for a century, while chemical fertilizers from farms emptied into the watershed. Yet it was the chemical revolution embraced by consumers that contributed to much of the pollution burden after World War II. Banning phosphate detergents became a

114 Environmentalism in the fragmented metropolis

major goal of environmental activists in the late 1960s and early 1970s. Scientists discovered that the phosphorus content of popular detergents contributed significantly to the eutrophication of the Great Lakes, a condition in which excessive nutrients lead to algal blooms. Lake Erie, a once-blue lake, now cast a green pall. Jeremiads proclaiming the "death of the Great Lakes" were common, while an NBC documentary asked, *Who Killed Lake Erie?*[5] The Environmental Protection Agency (EPA) concluded that banning phosphate in consumer detergents would benefit environments and reduce loads on sewer treatment systems.[6]

The Super Sewer was one answer to the Great Lakes water crisis, purporting to relieve the pollution burden on the Huron River and Lake Erie, with a 90% phosphorus removal rate.[7] A major undertaking, the Super Sewer was projected to cost $200 million, though the regional planning agency, the Southeast Michigan Council of Governments (SEMCOG) planned it with the expectation that the federal government would kick in a significant chunk of the money. If the system met a few qualifications, such as approval of the Michigan Water Resources Commission, met water quality standards, and was approved by SEMCOG, the project could recover 55% of the cost from the federal government.[8] Yet some in the region still did not believe that the deal made financial sense, even with so much money coming from Washington.

The provisioning of water, sewer, and other environmental services had long been a contested issue in the metropolitan region. The Detroit Metro Water Department in particular drew the ire of suburbanites who saw an incompetent, wrathful agency constantly raising its rates, which many presumed to be the result of misuse of funds, if not a punitive action aimed at the suburbs. After the Michigan Water Resources Commission indicated that it would force the Ann Arbor area to join the Super Sewer system, residents pushed back, arguing that Ann Arbor was well equipped to handle sewage treatment on its own – and at a cost considerably less than joining Super Sewer. Ann Arbor, their estimates showed, could enlarge its handling capacity at a cost of roughly $23 million, much less than the $90 million they believed it would cost to join the new sewer system.[9] Planners expected Super Sewer to provide a more orderly system of metropolitan development by making sewage services more efficient and consistent across a wider area, creating an economy of scale for the region and ending the patchwork of smaller sewage treatment facilities.[10] Some planning officials sounded the alarm at the uneven pattern in the politics and economics of annexation of quickly urbanizing unincorporated areas on the suburban fringe. Too often, they pointed out, townships were quick to gobble up "lucrative" developments into their tax bases while leaving out undesirable developed areas.[11]

Many suburban residents deeply opposed the regional project, organizing the group Citizens Opposed to Super Sewer (COSS) to prevent its construction and instead support local treatment plants. The executive committee of the organization demonstrates the unique coalitions created by suburban land-use activism, which included a University of Michigan professor of natural resources, a construction executive, graduate students in environmental communications and water

Environmentalism in the fragmented metropolis **115**

resources, and an advertising executive.[12] The COSS reflected the growing interest of suburban homeowners in quality-of-life environmentalism, a growing call for local sovereignty, and the changing regulatory terrain. Containing expertise in science and business professionals, the executive committee demonstrated the changing strategies for effecting local advocacy in the 1970s.

New environmental laws created opportunities for civic participation. Environmentalism gained potency in policy and law with the passage of NEPA and more locally the Michigan Environmental Policy Act. The COSS deftly navigated the new regulatory terrain. Navigating the new regulatory apparatus required expertise, time, and resources. As a federally funded project, to meet NEPA obligations, the EPA produced an Environmental Impact Statement (EIS) in 1973. When authorities produced the EIS, the citizens group denounced what they saw as misleading and incomplete information. NEPA furthermore provided for public hearings, which the EPA granted at Michigan representative Marvin Esch's urging.[13] Opponents packed the April 1973 hearing, decrying everything from increased taxation to pollution concerns.[14] Another opponent, a local real-estate agent, wrote directly to the head of the EPA to demand that he investigate the "folly of the gigantic project."[15]

The COSS made ecological arguments as well as emotional appeals to stop the Super Sewer. Its scientists insisted that Super Sewer would do irreversible harm to Lake Erie, a body of water that by the early 1970s was in a severe state of eutrophication and on the verge of "death." Despite the 90% phosphate removal claims of Super Sewer, an alternative local patchwork of sewage treatment promised 95% removal, a considerable benefit to Lake Erie, the COSS claimed. Furthermore, they argued, the reduced water flow under the Super Sewer would fail to flush pollutants and biological materials which could make the Huron River unfit for recreation. "What canoeist will want to boat in a cesspool?" one opponent asked.[16]

Representing local business and political interests, opponents argued that Super Sewer would sacrifice power to Wayne County. Said one of Washtenaw County's commissioners, "It's high time this county got its dander up. I'm sick and tired of hearing that if we're going to get any federal money we have to do things Wayne County's way."[17] The COSS argued that regional infrastructure programs like the Super Sewer created a "concentration of power, responsibility. . . [which] is politically and socially unsound."[18] The Super Sewer controversy became a symbol of larger anxieties over the distribution of political power in the region. Suburbanites and their political representatives often embraced regionalism when it required little sacrifice, but growing cultural detachment from the central city led them to abandon a sense of shared responsibility for the region.

The fear of urban crisis spilling into the suburbs animated opposition to the urban sprawl and uncontrolled land use supposedly encouraged by the Super Sewer. Urban sprawl imperiled the bucolic nature of much of the service area, opponents warned, threatening "neon commercial strips jammed onto the treeless, steril [sic] monotony of quick-buck housing," and called the project a "Super Hoax."[19] The COSS warned that the project jeopardized solving the urban crisis by encouraging

116 Environmentalism in the fragmented metropolis

further decentralization, threatening the suburban containment strategy for the urban crisis. Michigan House of Representatives Democrat Phil Mastin put it most clearly, arguing that unregulated land use threatened urban stability, meaning that "massive overdevelopment resulting in critical population losses in already established communities will occur. What once was only a Detroit problem is now becoming a suburban problem."[20] Concerns emerged from suburbanites that they would be subsidizing environmental services in the city of Detroit, particularly as the city's population base continued to shrink.[21] Many suburbanites feared that the urban crisis was soon headed for their communities.

Conflicts surrounding the Super Sewer dragged on for more than a decade, as different interests pressed for their own solutions to break the stalemate. The stall tactics of the COSS and other opponents forced an increasingly embattled SEMCOG to defend itself against accusations that some suburbs were being overburdened while polities, including the city of Detroit, got the better end of the deal. Grassroots opposition stalled Super Sewer long enough for Detroit to become embroiled in its own financial troubles. As the graduate student Michael Brough observed, "the ability to cause delay is a politically potent weapon."[22] By 1978, the proposed Super Sewer had been cut down from 90 miles to a more modest 50-mile-long project, dropping the contentious Ann Arbor region from the service area.[23] Coupled with dwindling federal resources for such projects, the sewer was no longer viable on its own. A major grant from the EPA and bond issue eventually funded the scaled-down project, but many suburban residents could still celebrate their successful withdrawal from the regional Super Sewer.[24] Indicating the prevailing local outlook, once the Ann Arbor region was cut from the proposal, the COSS's activism largely fizzled out. Although they pressed arguments in defense of the Huron River watershed, Lake Erie, and the entire metropolitan region, it was the local threat that energized the organization. The Super Sewer controversy both resulted from – and contributed to – a growing disillusionment over regional governance, as suburbanites argued against expensive regional infrastructure and advocated local control.

Parks and metropolitan conflict

Like regional provisioning of environmental services, parks and green spaces became a fraught metropolitan issue by the early 1970s.[25] The Huron-Clinton Metropolitan Authority (HCMA) operated a system of eight regional metropolitan parks called Metroparks, several hundred to several thousand acres, on the suburban fringe, preserving major stretches of land from suburban development.[26] During its nearly three decades in existence, the HCMA had enjoyed broad support from the suburban residents who could easily drive to the system of parks encircling the region, enjoying a day of leisure, family togetherness, and a natural setting. By the early 1970s, however, the consensus on building large regional parks collapsed, fueled by Detroit city residents protesting parks inequalities and suburban residents who feared the sprawl and black residents the parks would bring to their backyards.

Environmentalism in the fragmented metropolis **117**

The proposed 4,000-acre Mill Creek Metropark, located some 55 miles east of downtown Detroit, became the epicenter of conflicts over parks provisioning and inequality. Had the Metropark been proposed a decade earlier, it likely would have been greeted enthusiastically, with little sustained opposition. Preserving large open spaces from development was a high priority for the HCMA while land remained abundant enough on the metropolitan periphery.[27] Parks built by the HCMA in 1957, 1958, and 1964 faced little opposition, despite in some cases being developed in similar suburban environments as Mill Creek.[28]

The popularity of the parks grew rapidly in the 1950s and 1960s, and earlier park development proceeded with little recorded opposition.[29] Yet this popular agency could not escape the growing antisprawl and antiregionalism movement gaining steam by the end of the 1960s. While a 4,000-acre park might have seemed to some to be an effective antidote to sprawl by encouraging the preservation of open space, those living around Mill Creek saw it differently. A Metropark, they charged, would bring more traffic, more strip development, and would rob farmers of land and many homeowners of their property. Opponents often betrayed a fear that a park would bring unwanted people from Detroit, a city on the cusp of becoming majority African American. The homeowners in Mill Creek resisted a built environment resembling the city, which they had abandoned for the rural-like environs far from central Detroit, and they resented that the city was coming their way.

Local residents organized the Mill Creek Research Council (MCRC) to stop the park. A fear not only of the city but also of the urban crisis which they saw enveloping Detroit suffused the MCRC's rhetoric. The context of the urban crisis was never far from the minds of Metropark opponents. As one opponent remarked, "We are now in a troublesome period of greatly increased crime, epidemic drug use, crowded highways, lawless young people, sharp racism: HCMA's assignment should now be reviewed in the context of the seventies and eighties."[30] While arguing that low-income people would be ill served by a park 55 miles from the inner city, the author betrayed also a fear that a park development would spark conflicts during a period of "sharp racism." Better to create smaller parks closer to low-income people, the author wrote, "reducing the danger of conflict, and dispersing congestion and traffic problems." A farmer similarly made the case that a park would draw in "people from Detroit" and insisted that "[t]hey would not do it for us."[31] As Detroit became a majority black city during the 1970s, it was hard to miss the racial implications of the farmer's resentments.[32] Still another farmer lamented the threat of "cancerous urbanism" creeping into his backyard.[33] It is difficult to assess the sincerity of concerns expressed by opponents like MCRC President David Bacon, who insisted that the HCMA should shift its strategy to provide "'backyard' parks and playgrounds [which would] be more heavily used by the residents of Detroit, specifically those living in low-cost housing areas."[34] Sincere or not, the MCRC attempted to capitalize on arguments regarding regional environmental inequalities to resist development of the Metropark.

Opponents critiqued the state's power to take property through eminent domain. One opponent's rhetoric was typical: "It is unfair to take one man's land,

118 Environmentalism in the fragmented metropolis

home *and* business for another man's pleasure without fair compensation," wrote the anonymous author, claiming that in addition to the land, residents of the area would be forced to subsidize the use of the park by nonresidents.[35] Said one furious resident, "It appears that areas are picked off one at a time, causing each area to fight its own local battle to preserve 'Liberty and Justice for all' while at the same time being required (through taxes) to pay for the costs of having their property condemned."[36] Other residents highlighted their long tenure in the area, some whose families had lived on the land for over 100 years.[37] They believed that their property rights should not be so blithely dismissed.

Many of the opponents argued against eminent domain for parks on the grounds that it was un-American.[38] Donald Laier, a farmer near Mill Creek, saw the HCMA's targeting of farmland as unpatriotic, arguing, "when you lose respect for the soil you lose respect for our American flag."[39] "Taking away our land is taking our liberty," Laier wrote. "Private ownership of land is a fundamental of human freedom and that has a very high value." The populist rhetoric ended with a threat, comparing the anger of farmers to the uprising of Native Americans at Wounded Knee, "If you have read about the Indian trouble in South Dakota, wait until we string our bows for HCMA." "I object to the park because I would like to see this more rural way of life continue," remarked a Lima Township resident.[40] The director of the Michigan Department of Natural Resources Gene Gazlay characterized the reaction of area landowners as "hostile."[41] Despite intense opposition, the HCMA and its supporters remained steadfast in their conviction that urban development was headed for the Mill Creek area, whether a park was established there or not, and maintained that preserving open space should be a high priority while it was still affordable to the state.[42]

The MCRC deftly reached across spatial lines to demonstrate their shared interests with inner-city residents to stop the park's development. While the COSS remained a largely local suburban effort, the MCRC effectively mobilized groups across the metropolitan area, reaching for support outside and inside Detroit's borders. The MCRC argued that the HCMA robbed the central city of tax money while returning few benefits.[43] In early 1972, the MCRC enlisted the help of UAW Vice President Olga Madar, the fierce advocate for working-class recreation in Detroit who became an anti-pollution and environmental equity campaigner. The UAW's Recreation Department jumped into action after HCMA secured a contentious ballot measure in the August 1972 elections, Proposition D, doubling the mill levy from 0.25% to 0.5% on property taxes in part to build new parks like Mill Creek. The ballot measure ultimately failed, but it energized many residents to demand that the HCMA provide more parks and services within Detroit.

Despite the failure of the tax measure, it sensitized many Detroiters to the inequality of environmental amenities in the urban core, alerting them to policies that perpetuated inequality. While many historians have focused on the suburban, conservative tax revolts of the 1970s, urban taxpayers in cities like Detroit likewise demanded metropolitan equity in the services paid for by their tax dollars.[44] The UAW and other urban allies became a major thorn in the side of the HCMA,

Environmentalism in the fragmented metropolis   119

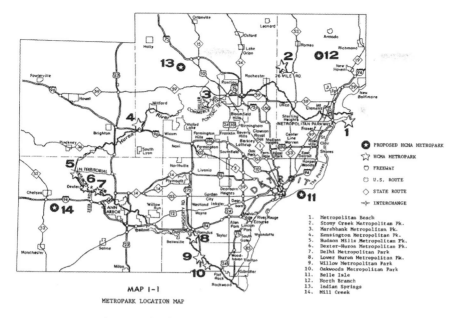

FIGURE 6.1   Map showing the distribution of HCMA Metroparks.

Source: Number 14 is the proposed Mill Creek Metropark. *Mill Creek Metropark: Final Environmental Impact Statement* (Washington, DC: Department of the Interior, 1978), 5.

threatening to stand in the way of all proposed park developments until the agency started demonstrating some interest in addressing the recreation needs of Detroit residents. The proposed Mill Creek Metropark, located an inaccessible distance for many Detroiters, prompted a backlash from urban residents and their allies, as the HCMA's insensitivity to the city's needs was made even more obvious.

Charleen Knight, a UAW representative from the Recreation Department, challenged the HCMA supporters who demanded more suburban parks. At the Department of Natural Resources hearings over the proposed Mill Creek Metropark, she denounced the inequalities of park space for Detroit's residents who paid into the Metropark system but did not derive a fair share of its benefits. "The City of Detroit spends millions of dollars every year for recreation for the Parks and Recreation Department," Knight said, "but they do not have enough money to do the job that needs to be done in the City of Detroit."[45] Of the $5.1 million in millage collected by the HCMA, nearly $2.9 million came from Wayne County. Despite financing the operation of the parks, many Detroit residents simply had no way to enjoy the parks, as only one of the ten parks was accessible by public transportation from Detroit. Compounding the public transportation problem, Knight pointed out, 1970 census figures showed that some 28% of Detroit's residents had no access to an automobile. Not only did Detroit's residents finance the development and operation of parks, but also thousands of residents could not even travel

120 Environmentalism in the fragmented metropolis

to enjoy them. Detroiters lamented that they were helping to subsidize the suburban exodus, financing environmental amenities on the suburban fringe which they could likely never enjoy.

The UAW's fight on behalf of disadvantaged Detroit residents for improving environmental equity was not new, but came on the heels of significant efforts in the late 1960s and early 1970s challenging major industrial polluters, as examined in Chapter Four. Olga Madar, a UAW vice president and head of the Recreation Department, supervised the efforts to improve the environment by making public agencies and politicians more responsive to the working-class and African-American residents often left out of urban policymaking. The UAW's ongoing involvement in urban policy in 1973 and beyond shows the surprising continuities of UAW urban engagement in the context of auto industry weakness and declining membership. Challenging environmental inequality in the inner city, in particular promoting access to environmental amenities for poor and working-class Detroit residents, became an integral part of the UAW's environmental and urban policy agenda.[46]

City planners started taking notice of the efforts by the UAW and its urban allies to promote environmental equality, and by late 1973 proposed efforts to reduce the gap in environmental amenities between the central city and the suburbs. The challenge, however, was in getting regional planners and suburban governments to recognize their role in facilitating environmental inequality. The creation of new parks within the central city, Detroit planners reasoned, would help redress the imbalance in environmental amenities and make the city more attractive for reinvestment, helping to reverse the trend of population loss and disinvestment. City officials noted that Detroit was far below the national average in recreational acreage per person. While the 65 largest U.S. cities averaged seven acres per thousand residents, Detroit could claim only 3.8 per thousand. For inner-city residents, however, acreage per capita was only one measurement of environmental amenities. The National Recreation Center recommended one recreation center per 20,000 residents, but at one per 47,000, Detroit's recreational services were well below the recommended rate. "While provisions for recreation are below standard for the City as a whole," the study pointed out, "lack of acreage is most severe in inner-city neighborhoods where recreation space dips as low as 0.1 acres/1,000 population." Inflation, rising wages, and reduced city budgets meant that the parks and recreation budget was spread thin, requiring the layoff of one-third of its employees in 1973. In that same year, the AFL-CIO organized a "Day of Mourning for Detroit's Dying City Services," lamenting the decline in "areas of rat-control, garbage pickup, recreation, public transportation," and other indicators of environmental health.[47] By almost any measurement, environmental amenities and services were spread too thinly among too many people in Detroit, and without some outside funding, it was unlikely that the situation would change, threatening one strategy for the revitalization of the city.[48]

Several members of the Detroit Common Council expressed their frustrations at the clear inequities in park provisioning, but lamented that they had no leverage over the HCMA to force it to change its development policies, because the mill levy that funded the agency was paid by residents directly to the state.[49] The council invited agency director David Laidlaw to a May 1973 meeting, demanding to know why his agency had failed to provide parks or park funding for Detroit. As city budget deficits increased, and upkeep of Belle Isle slipped, city officials asked HCMA to supplement the park's funding.[50] Councilmember Carl Levin asked, "Do you have monies now that you could use for maintenance at Belle Isle?" To which Laidlaw responded, "Yes, but the policy of our board has been that if we start with some monies you would expect us to take over everything." The council expressed frustration with Laidlaw's canned and offensive answers, going as far as to threaten that a lawsuit might be the only way to change the HCMA's practices. One councilmember lashed out at Laidlaw, blaming the HCMA for "destroying the concept of regionalism not only as far as parks were concerned" but also "other areas such as transportation," and setting a model for supposed regional cooperation that only benefitted the suburbs. The UAW as well as city leaders charged that the future of regional cooperation was at stake.

As Detroit's residents fled the city to the suburbs in the 1950s and 1960s, the power within the HCMA likewise shifted, and the needs of suburbia took precedence over the politically marginalized residents of the city. An examination of the members of the HCMA's board suggested to the UAW that the lack of representation of Detroit residents on the board – and the abundance of suburban representatives – meant that its priorities were skewed toward serving suburban residents. Not long after the contentious city council meeting, the UAW began brainstorming ways for Detroit to withdraw from paying into the HCMA system. The union offered two solutions: Detroit could ask the state legislature to modify the Enabling Act of 1939, which seemed like a long shot, or, they could ask the legislature to alter the composition of the HCMA's governing board so that its membership would better reflect the demographics of the metropolitan region.[51] The very concept of regionalism, in which super-agencies supposedly represented all parts of a metropolitan area, was being challenged. The lack of central-city representation in the HCMA, the UAW argued, violated residents' taxpayer rights and the democratic rights of citizens. "All we are asking for here is fair play," argued UAW Recreation Department staff member Tom Howie. "One man, one vote. What could be more fair than . . . citizens in a democratic society demanding their sacred rights?"

State representative William Brodhead, who enjoyed significant support from Detroit's African American community, echoed many of the UAW's and MCRC's charges. "No person," he remarked, "questions the need to preserve our natural recreation areas before they are bulldozed over and turned into new subdivisions." The problem, Brodhead argued, is that the HCMA needed to provide for the citizens neediest of access to parks. "The teenage son of a Warren factory worker, the Pontiac senior citizen and the Detroit central citizen, among countless others, are denied the ability to enjoy HCMA parks." For Brodhead, the HCMA as a regional agency must equitably serve all of its constituents, with a sensitivity to those with limited access to green spaces. The HCMA served an important purpose, Brodhead

122 Environmentalism in the fragmented metropolis

reasoned. "What many people seek is not to destroy the HCMA, but rather to make it more responsive to the people it is supposed to serve." The HCMA, however, remained unresponsive to the charges, simply echoing the familiar refrain that it was in the business of meeting regional needs and focused on development for the expanding suburban population.[52]

Meanwhile, the MCRC continued its lobbying efforts, forcing public hearings in the state capital.[53] The turnout forced the hearing into a larger venue at the House of Representatives chambers. Opponents repeated many of the arguments they had been making for years – the loss of agricultural land, tax concerns, the overbearing nature of the HCMA, the park's inequalities for disadvantaged residents, and the ecological effects of further damming the Huron River. Director of the Michigan Department of Natural Resources Gazlay characterized the hearing as divided but promised the department's approval of the Mill Creek Metropark pending an environmental impact statement.[54] MCRC still had time to make its case.

The Environmental Impact Statement process, which could take years from the draft to the final document, gave well-organized opposition a tremendous boost, allowing groups like MCRC to organize and gain more allies. They took the fight to county commissioners and other regional policy makers, highlighting what they saw as the urgency for the future of a rural setting lose to Detroit. Highlighting the loss of 4,000 acres of farmland, one MCRC board member implored county commissioners, "For the good of our community; for the good of our country; for the salvation of all humanity, help us stop this proposed Mill Creek Park now."[55] SEMCOG, the regional planning commission for Southeast Michigan, withdrew its support of the park in February 1973, apparently in response to the concerns highlighted by MCRC and its urban allies.[56] Noting the lack of low-income people with access to automobiles, SEMCOG noted that its mission in the 1970s should reflect the need to deliver recreation to traditionally underserved populations.[57] The opportunity for dissenting opinion to be entered into the EIS record allowed MCRC a more formalized process to direct the anger and energies of local residents.

The MCRC defeated the Mill Creek Metropark. In June, 1979, the Michigan Department of Natural Resources withdrew approval of Mill Creek Metropark. Director Howard Tanner called it an "unnecessary and inappropriate conversion of a vital resource."[58] The surprising coalition of suburban homeowners, farmers, and Detroit unionists and residents proved formidable. Although they held different reasons for opposing a new Metropark, they successfully deployed arguments regarding the ill effects of metropolitan inequality, ecological change, and suburban sprawl for the region. In the process, they demonstrated the changing political terrain in the wake of the environmental movement, as environmental politics asserted differing metropolitan agendas.

Toxic nation

Fears of the city's environmental hazards spilling into the suburbs grew more prominent in the late 1970s as the anti-toxics movement came to animate suburban environmentalism. Increasingly in 1970s Detroit, two trends collided in spectacular ways: the deindustrialization of the region increased its pace, and the emerging recognition of the "chemical wasteland," left in its wake.[59] Over the course of the 1970s, Americans' fears of exposure to toxic materials increasingly gained prominence. Most Americans, however, were far less concerned about how workers in hazardous industries fared than they were with the specific effects on their families through the products they consumed and the remnants of hazardous production affecting their neighborhoods. The toxics movement became a thoroughly "backyard" affair for most Americans.

Policymakers in the 1960s and 1970s slowly responded to swelling public anxieties over industrial chemicals and atomic radiation. Rachel Carson's *Silent Spring*, published in 1962, called to Americans' attention the disastrous ecological and human health effects of everyday chemicals like dichloro-diphenyl-trichloroethane, the pesticide known infamously as DDT. A burgeoning antinuclear movement, led in part by mothers fearing their children's safety from nuclear testing radioactive fallout, further exposed the silent killers in our midst. Policymakers were slow to respond to the outcry, despite popular groups like the Audubon Society pushing for a ban on DDT. During the Lyndon Johnson presidency, the federal government took tentative action to limit toxic contaminants, such as passage of the Federal Water Quality Act of 1965 and the Atomic Energy Commission establishing limits on radionuclides emissions for new power plants.[60] Toxic control remained primary a state-based affair. Congress passed the Occupational Health and Safety Act in 1970, creating the National Institute of Occupational Safety and Health. This became an important clearinghouse for scientific knowledge related to workplace toxic chemicals and their effects on health. Despite new legislation and institutions relevant to workplace health, industry fought back hard against detailing the materials used in industrial processes, leaving workers to piece together the health effects of their exposure, including high cancer rates.[61]

Despite the growing concerns over workplace toxic hazards and the ecological effects of synthetic chemicals, it took a series of major disasters and near misses to energize suburbanites to the hazards in their own backyards. During the 1970s, high-profile crises like mercury in fish, DDT in Lake Michigan, toxic polychlorinated biphenyl (PCB) in waterways, and Hooker Chemical Company's contamination of groundwater forced Michigan to act.[62] It was the Hooker Chemical Company's discharges that played the greatest role in pushing the development of an anti-toxics movement in Michigan in the years to come. In Western Michigan, near the Lake Michigan shoreline, Hooker Chemical manufactured chemicals like C-56 and C-59 commonly used to make pesticides.[63] Growing evidence showed that manufacturing byproducts leached into the groundwater and lodged in tissues of fish and wildlife, which eventually wended up the food chain to affect human health. By the mid-1970s, foul odors around the plant garnered the suspicion of nearby residents, and one activist gathered evidence from community members to present to state authorities. One whistleblower employee alerted investigators to thousands of drums of C-56 behind the plant, which his bosses had instructed be

124 Environmentalism in the fragmented metropolis

dumped there. Attorneys for the state sued Hooker in 1979, and collected $1 million, with another $14.5 million reserved for clean-up. According to Michigan environmental historian Dave Dempsey, it was then the "biggest pollution settlement in the history of the state."[64]

The same Hooker Chemical company fouling Western Michigan fired up the famed mother-turned-environmental justice activist Lois Gibbs in 1978, in Niagara Falls, New York in a neighborhood that would soon become a household name: Love Canal. It was there that Hooker Chemical dumped 21,000 tons of waste onsite between 1942 and 1953, after which it deeded the land to the local Board of Education.[65] The deed absolved the Hooker company of responsibility for the site. Building a school and housing on top of the contamination did not end the threat. Residents reported health problems, black sludge seeped into basements, and in May 1978, Lois Gibbs began organizing her neighbors.[66] She heard stories of miscarriages, unexplained illnesses, babies born with deformities, and mentally handicapped children.[67] In a matter of three months, Gibbs and the residents forced the state to begin relocating families. Meanwhile, testing showed alarming levels of dioxin that reached as high as 5.3 parts per billion, when, as historian Elizabeth Blum puts it, the chemical is "so toxic it is usually measured in parts per *trillion*."[68] The episode launched Gibbs into national recognition as she launched the Citizens' Clearinghouse for Hazardous Waste and traveled the country organizing residents against toxic hazards.

Nearly simultaneously as the Love Canal story gained national attention, an equally transformative event was taking place in Warren County, North Carolina, as residents and officials discovered approximately 240 miles of roadways contaminated by dumped PCBs. In August 1978, national news outlets reported the Warren County dumping and compared it to Love Canal.[69] For two weeks, in violation of the Toxic Substances Control Act (TSCA) of 1976, a waste hauling company dumped PCB.[70] North Carolina and Federal authorities responded by cleaning up the roadways and constructing a landfill in Warren County to permanently house the contaminants. Residents denounced the decision, angry that the predominantly black county should become the dumping grounds for toxic waste, an act, they claimed, representing environmental racism. Stymied by the court system, the Warren County activists began a campaign of non-violent resistance. As construction trucks approached the new landfill, they laid their bodies on the line, sprawling on the roads and preventing the trucks from proceeding. After six weeks of delays and stand-offs, the landfill was completed. But importantly, as environmental sociologist Eileen McGurty shows, it became the birthplace of a national environmental justice movement to defy environmental racism.

Less than two weeks before a major milestone called the City Care conference launched in Detroit, a nuclear reactor at Three Mile Island in Pennsylvania partially melted down. Along with the Love Canal poisonings, the events fed media frenzies, not unlike the Cuyahoga River fire and the Santa Barbara oil spill a decade earlier. Toxic waste fears gained further momentum when the Chemical Control Corporation of Elizabethtown, New Jersey, exploded in the Spring of 1980,

Environmentalism in the fragmented metropolis **125**

despite repeated warnings and condemnation of the site by New Jersey officials in 1979. On April 21, some 40,000 drums of chemicals caught fire and exploded, burning for ten hours, and spreading dangerous smoke around the area.[71] The disasters galvanized the public to demand action from elected officials. Congress responded by passing the Comprehensive Environmental Response, Compensation, and Liability Act (CERCLA) in December 1980, which provided $1.6 billion for the so-called Superfund.[72]

Unsurprisingly, many residents of the heavily industrialized Southeast Michigan region eagerly awaited action on what they saw as toxic health threats close to home. The *Detroit Free Press* ran numerous editorials and stories, some critical of the paltry Superfund, calling it a "super-flop"[73] and a "minifund."[74] The new Reagan presidential administration inspired little confidence for toxic cleanup, as his EPA Administrator Anne Gorsuch cut Superfund spending and reduced priority sites.[75] In spite of the cuts, a thirst for action remained, leading local television station WXYZ to broadcast two hour-long specials, "Time Bomb . . . The Menace of Toxic Waste" and "Time Bomb II . . . The Toxic Menace Continues." The first special prompted viewers to write 1,500 letters to the station, which the correspondent Jerry Stanecki would later read to a state Senate committee.[76] The initial 100 Superfund sites listed by the EPA contained only one in Michigan, a toxic landfill in Gratiot County over 100 miles from Detroit. It spoke to the enormity of the toxic waste problem nationally that no Southeast Michigan sites were initially listed, but the coming years would see Detroit become well-represented on the list.

City Care

In numerous areas throughout the United States, an awakening to the proliferation of toxics quickly emerged. Although Southeast Michigan did not initially break news on the same level as Love Canal or Warren County, it nevertheless influenced the growing anti-toxics and environmental justice movements. An important national event called the City Care Conference, held in Detroit in April 1979, brought together approximately 700 environmental, urban, civil rights and other activists and experts to shape the urban-environmental agenda for the future.[77] The Sierra Club took a leading role in organizing the conference, securing $200,000 in federal grants, and partnering with the Urban Environment Conference (UEC) and the Urban League.[78] As historian Robert Gioielli argues, the Sierra Club's leadership on urban environmental issues reflected the group's emphasis in the 1970s on expanding its activities to move away "from an upper-middle-class wilderness club," to one that could have a broader message and political efficacy.[79] The Sierra Club insisted that such urban advocacy was a logical outgrowth of its mission. "In sponsoring this conference," staff noted, "the Sierra Club is not setting out in a new or unfamiliar direction. Environmentalists have long been active in such issues – green areas, clear air, clean water, safe energy, proper land use." Now is the time, the Sierra Club insisted, to putting its might into "making our cities livable," with the "active cooperation of city residents, labor unions, businesses and

126 Environmentalism in the fragmented metropolis

minorities." Coming on the heels of TSCA, environmental disasters, and swelling public concern over toxic contaminants, the conference held the promise of uniting disparate metropolitan agendas to significantly improve the health and viability of cities and their residents in the 1980s.

Months of planning led up to the April 1979 conference. Organizers focused extensively on developing neighborhood-level programs to support environmental sustainability in cities. The steering committee emphasized the need to develop programs supporting "neighborhood environmental enterprises and jobs," centering economic justice as a key to neighborhood stability.[80] The conference divided attendees into numerous "core groups" focused on a single issue.[81] Groups included "Jobs-Survival," local organizing, "Inner City Outings," urban sustainability, energy conservation, civic participation, inner-city housing, political processes, and beyond. Over 20 core groups assembled, discussed their theme, and passed resolutions providing recommendations to present to the general conference. Breaking the conference into smaller discussion groups allowed a proliferation of ideas to emerge from the working groups, preventing conference organizers from dictating the conversations. The hyper-local focus of most of the core groups diverged from the trend of major environmental organizations creating large political lobbying apparatuses at the national level to influence federal policy.[82] In an age of rapid physical deterioration of Detroit's inner-city neighborhoods, such a focus spoke directly to the city's residents who for years clamored for economic opportunities to maintain their neighborhoods despite disruptive urban renewal programs. For instance, one group proposed "economically and environmentally sound programs to revitalize inner city neighborhoods with minimal human displacement."[83] Focusing on environmentally sustainable economic development and jobs indicated the importance of addressing economic and environmental sustainability as two sides of the same coin, particularly when recruiting urban and civil rights allies.

Metropolitan inequality amidst the urban crisis emerged as a major focus of the attendees. Vernon Jordan, the president of the National Urban League, emphasized how metropolitan inequality manifested in an urban environmental crisis. "With the advancement of technology and the subsequent urban sprawl," Jordan said, "the urban areas have borne the brunt of air and water pollution, auto-dominated transportation, restricted housing opportunity and deteriorated neighborhoods."[84] Some attendees read a report from Detroit Human Rights Department official James Bush on "Redlining, Disinvestment, and Overbuilding the Suburbs," which emphasized the need to combat redlining by "reforming the public subsidies and the housing industry practices that *greenline* the suburbs by steering people, jobs and investment beyond the city limits."[85] Naming the phenomenon *greenlining* emphasized the way that policy and industry combined to make the suburbs more green and livable to drive investment to the suburbs. It re-cast the redlining practices by banks, insurers, builders, and government which underdeveloped the inner city as an explicitly environmental concern. Discussion groups followed Bush's lead by highlighting recommendations for the general conference to adopt, such as developing urban parks and recreation,[86] banking investment transparency, equitable

Environmentalism in the fragmented metropolis **127**

regional planning, federal funding for inner-city jobs and housing,[87] mass transit,[88] and highway disinvestment.[89] Their recommendations emphasized that environmental conditions of the city could not be separated from the processes that created the urban crisis.

Toxics only represented a small part of the conference agenda, but participants signaled the growing role that they might play in the 1980s. Discussion participants emphasized the need for industry to disclose its hazardous materials and their "health and safety effects . . . on workers, local population, and the environment."[90] EPA Deputy Administrator Barbara Blum warned of the "entire communities which may be sitting on top of chemical time bombs."[91] Michigan Governor William Milliken warned of the "throwaway society" that found it easier to "abandon neighborhoods and move to the suburbs" and "bury toxic chemicals" than to face up to the environmental consequences of their actions.[92] Workshops at the conference highlighted the most serious environmental challenges confronting cities, like the toxic exposures urban Americans were surrounded by, like lead-based paints, asbestos, and the improper disposal of industrial chemicals.[93] As Love Canal showed, public health advocates faced the enormous challenge of educating residents to the health hazards of toxic wastes. Many residents in polluted neighborhoods simply never connected their health challenges to those of their neighbors or were too disempowered to organize around illness prevention. Conference participants emphasized that health surveys and community organizations and churches could provide the evidence and the political power to effect change.

Detroit possessed a contingent of residents, policymakers, and activists at the conference, but it was not yet clear whether the vibrant discussions and promises of urban, environmental, and working-class advocate cooperation could lead to lasting changes. Very quickly after the conference, the federal headwinds changed. Ronald Reagan's election and subsequent hostility to federal environmental regulations and de-funding urban programs placed environmental organizations and urban allies on the defensive.[94] In 1984, the parent organization for City Care, UEC, had lost federal funding sources and was forced to shutter.[95] Detroit was a city desperately in need of the bold action that City Care attendees had imagined. Despite the optimistic energy, Detroit's urban environmental crisis took decades to create, and could not easily be undone. The toxic legacies of industrialization had come home to roost.

Toxic metropolis

Groups like the Sierra Club, East Michigan Environmental Action Council, Ann Arbor Ecology Center, the UAW, and later the new Michigan Citizens Against Toxic Substances and Evergreen Alliance organized increasingly in the 1980s around the health threats of toxic materials. In Detroit, the fates of two waste incinerator struggles, one in central Detroit and the other in southwest Washtenaw County, show the diverging fates of environmental struggles in the central city and metropolitan fringe.

128 Environmentalism in the fragmented metropolis

Attracting investment back into the city was the number one priority for Detroit Mayor Coleman Young, environmental concerns be damned. As Young later wrote in his autobiography, in 1980, the unemployment rate in Detroit reached 18% as a whole and 30% for African Americans in the city.[96] The Young administration went to great lengths to cajole General Motors into building a new plant in the Poletown neighborhood, called the GM Hamtramck-Detroit Assembly Plant. As urban planning scholar June Manning Thomas argues, it took Young's tremendous political skill and popularity among black Detroiters who had suffered tremendously from plant closures, to thread the needle on the contentious project.[97] Using eminent domain, the city forced out 4,000 people and required it to "buy and bulldoze 1,300 houses, 16 churches, 2 schools, a hospital, and 114 small businesses."[98] Young understood the optics. The city's first black mayor, himself and his family once the victims of eviction for slum clearance in the Black Bottom neighborhood, now inflicting its disruptive wrath on Detroiters. The Poletown Neighborhood Council protested, taking the case to the state supreme court, which ultimately upheld Detroit's use of eminent domain. Last ditch efforts by famed activist Ralph Nader and a small group of Poletown residents to force an Environmental Impact Statement for the project failed in federal court. After displacing 4,000 residents, the GM plant opened in 1985, employing 3,400 workers.[99]

The displacement of residents in order to construct the Poletown plant attracted little attention from area environmental activists despite the clear environmental and social consequences of its construction. Apathy in this project contrasted starkly against the uprising of environmentalists, civil rights activists, and others who organized to stop the construction of the world's largest waste-to-energy incinerator. The combination of activist energies, not seen since the City Care Conference, showed the promise of a broad-based fight for environmental justice. Yet the battle also demonstrated the limitations of environmental justice activism in an unequal and fractured metropolis. Planning began in 1975, seeking solutions for the city's waste, with excess capacity that could be sold to bring revenue to a cash-strapped Detroit.[100] The city applied for a permit in 1983 through the Michigan Department of Natural Resources for a new waste-to-energy incinerator, called the Greater Detroit Resource Recovery Facility (GDRRF), and in 1986 issued bonds of $438 million to pay for the project.[101] Detroit was ripe for exploitation by the hazardous waste industry. As historian Josiah Rector notes, "losses in tax revenues from capital flight and population loss, combined with the Reagan administration's cuts in aid to cities, made the Young administration increasingly reliant on public-private mega-projects, financed through the municipal bond market."[102] Without Coleman Young's determined advocacy for the incinerator, it could never have been built.[103]

The Evergreen Alliance organized in 1986 to mobilize inner-city residents to oppose the incinerator. It connected "environmental economics and racism" and labeled Detroit's neighborhoods as "sacrifice zones," borrowing from – and contributing to – the energies and language of the emerging environmental justice movement.[104] Wayne County's air, the group noted, was burdened by the nation's

Environmentalism in the fragmented metropolis **129**

highest level of hazardous chemicals and suspected carcinogens. By 1988, the Evergreen Alliance was a lively organization. It held concerts, pickets, a Great Lakes Conference, held a mock funeral for the excess deaths the incinerator would cause, published a booklet that sold 20,000 copies, and engaged in international cooperation with Canadian residents across the river in Windsor.[105] At a sit-down protest at the gates of the incinerator in May 1988, 19 protesters were arrested. The organization brought attention to the "Evergreen 19" and showed support by rallying at the court. The protestors were subsequently acquitted.[106] It was a vibrant and thriving community effort.

Despite the vocal local support that Evergreen Alliance and similar groups possessed, Coleman Young consistently blamed outside agitators. The charge had some foundation. Local affiliates of national organizations like the Sierra Club, Environmental Defense Fund, and Audubon Society joined the fight to stop the incinerator.[107] It was the type of inner-city environmentalism that the Sierra Club had promised at the City Care conference and was now putting into action. Sierra Club possessed the political lobbying skill and the resources of a national organization, while local activists supplied the energy. Along with the local North Cass Community Union, the groups filed a lawsuit under the Michigan Environmental Protection Act, alleging that the incinerator violated its "duty to prevent or minimize environmental degradation by planning and constructing the incinerator without adequate air pollution control equipment," and other violations.[108] Construction of the incinerator had occurred through a permit based on faulty MDNR evidence. When the agency asked the city to install more expensive scrubber technology to control emissions, the city refused.[109] The plaintiffs sought relief on the basis that the incinerator was not using the Best Available Control Technology as required under the Clean Air Act. The court was not moved. The ruling in *Detroit Audubon Society v. City of Detroit* (1988) allowed the construction of the incinerator to proceed. The court rejected the plaintiffs' case in part because the city had operated under a valid permit under the Clean Air Act, despite the later evidence to the contrary, and had invested many millions of dollars under a valid permit. In its decision the court stated that it would not "set aside the Clean Air Act's permitting scheme."[110] In 1989, the incinerator began transforming 3,300 tons of garbage into energy every day.[111] It was a devastating blow to the environmental groups, but activists and organizations persisted in their opposition.

Groups like the Sierra Club pressed for greater emissions control as the plant began operations. As activists warned, the incinerator exceeded levels of safe mercury emissions. The Michigan Air Pollution Control Commission (MAPCC) temporarily shuttered the Detroit incinerator in April 1990 for violating mercury limits, and soon after issued a consent order requiring installation of acid gas scrubbers.[112] Mayor Young blasted the decision. "This is Earth Week," he said. "They wanted a sacrificial lamb to lay at the altar of the environment and they got the big one – Detroit." Young was not wrong that the commission often harbored resentment of Detroit and its residents. The long-serving MAPCC Commissioner Nicholas Kachman argued that Detroiters did not care about the environment. Detroiters, he said, did not like trees

130 Environmentalism in the fragmented metropolis

because criminals hide behind them.[113] They cared nothing about animals except for the rat problem. "They are afraid to go outside." Ten percent of kids were crack babies, and "they remember things for about two minutes. So you teach two plus two over and over again." Therefore, Kachman insisted, "They don't know what the hell mercury is about." More important to Kachman was making sure the incinerator provided jobs for residents. "There's other problems besides the mercury level." Such statements only further justified Young's efforts to cast outside agencies and activists as racists. As historian Josiah Rector points out, there is little evidence that Detroit's black residents supported the incinerator, but Young nevertheless deftly leveraged the urban/suburban racial divide.[114]

Forced to pay for expensive emissions control technology, the City of Detroit swallowed the bitter pill, placing the city's finances in further precarity. Ultimately, the city was forced to sell the incinerator to private investors, but the burning continued. Maturity of the plant did not lead it to better manage toxic emissions. From 2013 to 2018, the *Detroit Free Press* found, the Michigan Department of Environmental Quality cited the company 750 times.[115] Meanwhile, activist organizations like Zero Waste Detroit continued to press the city to stop the incinerator. Finally, in March 2019, facing political pressure and untenable financial conditions, operators permanently closed the incinerator. Although a particularly dramatic example of the fate of a hazardous facility siting in Detroit, many others, albeit at smaller scales, began operations during the 1980s and 1990s in Detroit. Other smaller incinerators fared differently. Residents, activists, and policymakers in the central city community of Highland Park successfully united to resist the siting of a medical incinerator.[116]

Toxic backyards

The toxic battle took a different course in an overwhelmingly white rural community near Detroit. The waste management company Envotech eyed an 1800-acre site in Augusta Township 12 miles south of Ann Arbor, for a toxic waste landfill, deep well injection, and incinerator. The area surrounding the site was overwhelmingly white, with less than 7% African-American residents, whereas Detroit was 75% African American by 1990.[117] As proposed in 1989, the $45 million facility would be home to the second largest toxic waste landfill in the country.[118] This site, known as the Arkona Road Landfill, had been subject to illegal dumping in the 1970s. The Department of Natural Resources for Michigan named it as the fourth most polluted site in the state.[119] Building the new facility required two phases. The first phase involved the cleanup of the Arkona Road Landfill, an illegal toxic waste dumping ground, before construction of its own facilities. Transferring responsibility for cleanup to Envotech offered an attractive arrangement to state regulators, facilitating cleanup of a dangerous environment through private capital.

Many in the region rejected the plan. Residents, environmentalists, UAW locals, and the UAW Toxic Waste Squad quickly coalesced into a formidable opposition in 1989.[120] They created the Michigan Citizens Against Toxic Substances

Environmentalism in the fragmented metropolis **131**

(MCATS) organization to coordinate their opposition. By 1991, the organization was capable of summoning 700 people to a high school to present public comment to the Michigan Department of Natural Resources in opposition to the company's Arkona Road Landfill cleanup plan.[121] The organization fought against what it saw as misleading claims by Envotech, such as its assertion to a nearby newspaper that "there is no health impact" of the incinerator or landfill and it "won't hurt area property values either."[122] Negative health and property value effects were central arguments of MCATS, which distributed fact sheets to promote its own interpretation of the facts. MCATS shared information intended to frighten area residents, including exhaustive lists of the dangerous chemicals it would emit, and warning that a spill might force the nearby prison to release prisoners into the community "without security." MCATS publicized data that emissions from the incinerator could affect residents as far as 30 miles away.[123] Explaining the long reach of the health hazards helped to recruit suburban Washtenaw County residents and environmental organizations to fight the siting.

Surrounding communities showed formidable solidarity in opposition to the plant. In August 1992, residents of Augusta Township voted to approve a tax millage to fund the fight against the Envotech hazardous waste site.[124] By a two-to-one margin, voters approved the tax. Milan and York similarly passed taxes to oppose the site, and all three communities joined together in the AMY (Augusta, Milan, York) coalition. Both area newspapers, *The Saline Reporter* and *The Milan News,* each rallied its readers to fight against the facility, organizing petition drives, publicizing town halls, and printing extensive anti-Envotech stories and editorials.[125] MCATS held a 10K "Clean Air Classic" run, picnics, and other community events, helping the organization to publicize its cause and engage the community in the struggle.[126] The solidarity translated into civic participation at public hearings. Michigan DNR hosted a public hearing on September 15, 1992. In the weeks leading up to the event, MCATS members passed out 110,000 flyers to households in Washtenaw County, urging awareness of Envotech's plans. As a result, as many as 4,000 people showed up for a town hall at Lincoln High School to voice their opposition to the company's clean-up plan for the Arkona Road Site, which included the deep-well injection.[127] By March 1993, MCATS counted over 70 organizations with resolutions against the toxic site, including the Washtenaw County Board of Commissioners, the Washtenaw County Republican Party, numerous cities and townships, 14 UAW locals, and two NAACP local affiliates. Opposition traversed usual partisan lines.

Residents demonstrated their anxiety over the changing landscape and economic make-up of the region as factories shuttered, including the nearby General Motors Willow Run Assembly, which ceased operations in 1993. They feared that the post-industrial economy meant that unwanted land uses would increasingly locate in their communities, like the federal prison and hazardous waste facilities. Economic uncertainty gave Envotech a wedge, claiming that it would bring much needed jobs to the area. The jobs blackmail was a consistent tactic used by corporations siting hazardous facilities through Michigan and the United States.[128] More

132 Environmentalism in the fragmented metropolis

important than jobs, however, was the threat that a hazardous waste facility would imperil their property values. MCATS published estimates from university studies that found within six miles of the site, homes would lose $12,000 for each mile closer to the incinerator, so that homes neighboring the landfill would be worth $72,000 less than those located six miles away.[129] "Residents of the area have already been denied home equity loans," MCATS warned, "specifically because of the proximity to Envotech's Existing Arkona Road Landfill." They thundered: "The results would be devastating!!!"

Children from Milan Middle School joined a letter-writing campaign to the governor, describing their homes and "small, nice, and friendly little town," and how the Envotech site would threaten their lives.[130] Said one 13-year-old student, whose home sat two and a half miles from the proposed site, "I like to wake up in the morning and know that I have a very remote chance of getting cancer walking from my house to the school. That could all change if there is toxic substances blowing in the air."[131] Many of the children noted that the waste could threaten water resources, but one seventh grader vividly noted, "When the company that first owned the land tried to build, everywhere they dug it filled with water. If Michigan is the Water Wonderland why would we want to fill our water with toxins [?]"[132] One jokester wrote, "We don't want to have kids with two heads either."[133] The students echoed the themes that MCATS had promoted to residents: the inevitability of seepage into groundwater, the possibility of cancer, and the 30-mile radius of contamination.

In 1996, the EPA considered an appeal by petitioners including the UAW, MCATS, and the AMY coalition of governments opposing the licenses granted to Envirotech for deep-well injection of hazardous leachate from the Arkona Road Landfill.[134] MCATS argued that residents' rights as taxpayers were being violated by Envotech, by dismissing the will of the community. MCATS demanded, "The people's right not to have these wells in their community should be respected. The people of August, Milan, and York all pay higher taxes, voluntarily, in order to oppose Envotech."[135] The midwestern EPA region insisted that, despite the impassioned pleas from residents, it could only narrowly rule based on regulations of the Safe Drinking Water Act, "and local opposition alone is simply not a factor that the Region may consider in its permit decision."[136] The AMY coalition made environmental justice central to its appeal, leveraging the 1994 President Clinton Executive Order 12898 that established environmental review of developments that disproportionately burdened low-income and minority residents. Evidence that the siting represented an environmental injustice against a protected group, however, was flimsy, but it showed the extent to which Envotech opponents could appropriate environmental justice to serve their own interests. The EPA ruled that "minority or low-income populations were only minimally, if at all, affected by the permits."[137] The agency rejected nearly all of the petitioners' objections, and it appeared the last-ditch effort to stop the siting had failed.

In an abrupt reversal in 1998, the waste company, now going by the name EQ, abandoned the development. After nearly a decade of conflict, opponents

Environmentalism in the fragmented metropolis **133**

could celebrate. The residents who successfully stopped the dump and incinerator held advantages that opponents of the Detroit incinerator did not possess. Significant unity from Augusta Township, Milan, and York Township helped, including the taxes that paid for the legal battles. Over in Detroit, Mayor Coleman Young threw the weight of city government and his own personal power behind the project, overcoming what was a formidable opposition. When historically white advocates like the Sierra Club and Audubon Society joined the anti-incinerator cause, he could claim that the opposition did not represent black Detroiters and their interests. As Detroit suffered from high unemployment and tenuous city finances, the promise of jobs and revenue offered a salve. The rural and suburban residents could resist the job appeals made by Envotech, and the threat to property values was far more frightening than the economic stimulus the company offered. In Washtenaw County, residents possessed land and lives that inherently *mattered*. Despite the Milan incinerator proposing a much smaller environmental health impact than Detroit's incinerator, the health of the former was highly valued. Meanwhile, much of Detroit had become a sacrifice zone, where devalued black residents, unwanted land uses, and environmental hazards were "packed in."[138]

Conclusion

The post-World War II exodus of white Detroiters to the suburbs and the remarkable sprawl of Southeastern Michigan generated conflicts regarding the distribution of environmental amenities and hazards. Particularly after the passage of the National Environmental Policy Act, relatively wealthy suburbanites could effectively flex their political will and ensure that their communities retained control of their local environments. Far less successful at dictating the quality of their environment were the residents of Detroit, the majority of whom were black. As other chapters have shown, the decay of their local environments did not occur because residents lacked the will to improve their living conditions. Though metropolitan environmentalism offered the promise of uniting suburban, urban, civil rights, and labor activists as the City Care conference tantalizingly suggested, economic and political disadvantages in the urban-industrial core hindered the quest for metropolitan environmental equity and sustainability.

Notes

1 Michael B. Brough, "The Southeastern Michigan Wastewater Treatment System Controversy," 4, Box 1, Folder: "Office Material: 1972 (1)," Coll Collection, BHL. Barry Commoner, *The Closing Circle: Nature, Man, and Technology*, 1st ed. (New York: Knopf, 1971), 33. For a discussion of how Commoner and ecological ideas influenced critiques of the suburban built environment, see Adam Rome, *The Genius of Earth Day: How a 1970 Teach-In Unexpectedly Made the First Green Generation* (New York: Hill and Wang, 2013), 9, 136. See also Commoner's significance for the urban environmental crisis in Robert Gioielli, *Environmental Activism and the Urban Crisis: Baltimore, St. Louis, Chicago* (Philadelphia, PA: Temple University Press, 2014), 46–48; David Stradling and

Richard Stradling, *Where the River Burned: Carl Stokes and the Struggle to Save Cleveland* (Ithaca, NY: Cornell University Press, 2015), 10–14.

2 Andrew Busch invokes the term "metropolitan environmentalism" to describe the land use activism and opposition to sprawl within Austin, Texas. Andrew M. Busch, *City in a Garden: Environmental Transformations and Racial Justice in Twentieth-Century Austin, Texas* (Chapel Hill, NC: University of North Carolina Press, 2017), 163.

3 *Volume II: Draft Environmental Impact Statement: Huron Valley Wastewater Control System Facilities Plan*, 1, U.S. Environmental Protection Agency Region V, Document EIS791225F, accessed from EPA digital archive February 26, 2013, http://nepis.epa.gov/.

4 "Comments on the Water Resources Commission Ruling," Box 1, Folder: "Office Material: 1968," COSS Collection; Memo, Washtenaw County Metropolitan Planning Commission, April 15, 1968, Box 1, Folder: "Office Material 1972 (1)," COSS Collection; Position Paper, "Southeastern Michigan 'Super Sewer' Controversy," Box 1, Folder: "Office Material 1973 Miscellaneous (1)," COSS Collection.

5 Rome, *The Genius of Earth Day*, 123; William Ashworth, *The Late, Great Lakes: An Environmental History* (Detroit: Wayne State University Press, 1987).

6 G. R. Alexander, Jr., "The Rationale for a Ban on Detergent Phosphate in the Great Lakes Basin," *CIBA Foundation Symposium* 57 (September 13–15, 1977): 269–84. PubMed PMID: 249680; "Phosphates in Detergents and the Eutrophication of America's Waters," *Hearings*, Ninety-first Congress, first Session, December 15–16, 1969 (Washington, DC: U.S. Government Printing Office, 1970); Cited in Chris Knud-Hansen, "Historical Perspecitve [*sic*] of the Phosphate Detergent Conflict," *Conflict Research Consortium*, February 1994, accessed April 19, 2017, www.colorado.edu/conflict/full_text_search/AllCRCDocs/94-54.htm.

7 "Local Group Tells Why It Opposes Super Sewer," *Ann Arbor News*, April 3, 1973, accessed March 9, 2017, http://oldnews.aadl.org/node/89197.

8 Brough, "The Southeastern Michigan Wastewater Treatment System Controversy," 2-3.

9 Position Paper, "Comments on the Water Resources Commission Ruling," Box 1, Folder: "Office Material: 1968," COSS Collection.

10 "The Southeast Michigan Wastewater Treatment Controversy," 6–7.

11 Memo, Washtenaw County Metropolitan Planning Commission, April 15, 1968, Box 1, Folder: "Office Material 1972 (1)," Citizens Opposed to Super Sewer Collection, BHL. Mansel Blackford explores similar patterns in *Columbus, Ohio: Two Centuries of Business and Environmental Change* (Columbus, OH: Trillium, 2016), 104–14.

12 "Local Group Tells Why It Opposes Super Sewer," *Ann Arbor News*, April 3, 1973, accessed March 9, 2017, http://oldnews.aadl.org/node/89197.

13 Marvin Esch to William Ruckelshaus, April 16, 1973, Box 1, Folder "Office Material 1973 Correspondence," COSS Collection.

14 'Super Sewer Draws Flood of Criticism," *Ann Arbor News*, April 5, 1973, clipping in Box 1, Folder: "Office Material 1973 Correspondence," COSS Collection.

15 Newton to Ruckelshaus, April 19, 1973, Box 1, Folder "Office Material 1973 Correspondence," COSS Collection.

16 "Super Sewer/Super Hoax," March 2, 1973, Box 1, Folder "Office Material Misc. 1973 (1)," COSS Collection.

17 Brough, "The Southeastern Michigan Wastewater Treatment System Controversy," 9.

18 Position Paper, "Super Sewer," Box 1, Folder: Office material 1972 (1)," COSS Collection.

19 "Super Sewer/Super Hoax," March 2, 1973, Box 1, Folder "Office Material 1973 Correspondence," COSS Collection.

20 Philip Mastin, "Land Use and Coordinated Planning," Box 1, Folder: "Office Material Miscellaneous 1973 (1)," COSS Collection.

21 "Wayne County Gets Approval for 'Super Sewer,'" *Ludington Daily News*, October 6, 1979.

22 Brough, "The Southeastern Michigan Wastewater Treatment System Controversy," 25.

Environmentalism in the fragmented metropolis **135**

23 *Volume II: Draft Environmental Impact Statement: Huron Valley Wastewater Control System Facilities Plan*, XI, U.S. Environmental Protection Agency Region V, Document EIS791225F, accessed from EPA digital archive February 26, 2013.

24 "Rouge Seeks State Money," October 6, 1988, *Westland Observer*, accessed May 24, 2017, http://westland.lib.mi.us/pdf/observers/1988-10-06.pdf.

25 On Metroparks and their relationship to the urban environmental crisis, see Joseph Cialdella, *Motor City Green: A Century of Landscapes and Environmentalism in Detroit*, History of the Urban Environment (Pittsburgh, PA: University of Pittsburgh Press, 2020), 125–35.

26 "Guidelines for Levels of Function and Responsibility for Public Outdoor Recreation in Southeastern Michigan," Detroit Metropolitan Area Regional Planning Commission, March 1966, Box 1, Folder: "Mill Creek . . . Clippings 1966," MCRC Collection, BHL.

27 *The Fourth Biennial Report of the Board of Commissioners as of December 31, 1949*, Huron-Clinton Metropolitan Authority (1948/49), Michigan Collection, State Library of Michigan, Lansing, Michigan; *The Sixth Biennial Report of the Board of Commissioners as of December 31, 1953*, Huron-Clinton Metropolitan Authority, Michigan Collection, State Library of Michigan.

28 "Authority Information and Current Facilities for 1965," Huron-Clinton Metropolitan Authority, Box 11, Folder 23, DUDARP Collection, ALUA.

29 Annual Report, "Progress in Regional Planning," Detroit Regional Planning Commission, 1959, Box 1, Folder: "Annual Report," SEMCOG-P Collection, BHL.

30 Untitled Paper in Box 3, Folder: "Correspondence 1969–1970," MCRC Collection.

31 Weber and Weber to Washtenaw County Board of Commissioners, November 25, 1970, Box 3, Folder: "Correspondence 1969–1970," MCRC Collection.

32 The U.S. Census showed Detroit with a 43% black population in 1970, a proportion which rose to 63% by the 1980 census. "Table 23. Michigan – Race and Hispanic Origin for Selected Large Cities and Other Places: Earliest Census to 1990," United States Census Department, accessed May 18, 2017, www.census.gov/population/www/documentation/twps0076/MItab.pdf.

33 Sutton to Ellison, May 27, 1974, Box 4, Folder: "HCMA – Record of Opposition," MCRC Collection.

34 Bacon to Oakland County Clerk, December 15, 1970, Box 3, Folder: "Correspondence 1969–1970," MCRC Collection.

35 Untitled Paper in Box 3, Folder: "Correspondence 1969–1970," MCRC Collection.

36 Letter to the Editor, June 1971, clipping in Box 4, Folder: "HCMA – Record of Opposition," MCRC Collection.

37 Letter to the Editor, *Ann Arbor News*, March 16, 1973, clipping in Box 4, Folder: "HCMA – Record of Opposition," MCRC Collection.

38 S. M. H. Letter to the Editor, August 9, unknown year, unknown newspaper, clipping in Box 8, Folder: "Mill Creek Metropark – Clippings," GG Papers, BHL.

39 Letter to the Editor, *Ann Arbor News*, March 1973, clipping in Box 4, Folder: "HCMA – Record of Opposition," MCRC Collection.

40 "Right of Owning Private Property Must Be Considered," *The Ann Arbor News*, March 19, 1973, clipping in Box 4, Folder: "Mill Creek . . . Record of Opposition," MCRC Collection.

41 Position Statement, Michigan DNR, May 10, 1973, Box 3, Folder: "Mill Creek . . . Correspondence 1973," MCRC Collection.

42 Statement by Genevieve Gillette, DNR Hearing, March 15, unknown year, Box 8, Folder: "Mill Creek Metropark – Reports, etc.," GG Papers.

43 McCalla to Madar, January 21, 1972, Box 3, Folder: "HCMA Correspondence 1972," MCRC Collection.

44 See, for instance, Robert O. Self, *American Babylon: Race and the Struggle for Postwar Oakland* (Princeton, NJ: Princeton University Press, 2003), 256–90.

45 Charleen Knight, Statement to DNR, n.d. [c. March 1973], Box 10, Folder 5, UAW CRD Collection, ALUA.
46 E. D. O'Brien to Olga Madar, September 24, 1971, Box 2, Folder 1, UAW-CRD Collection, ALUA.
47 "Minutes of the Regular Meeting: Metropolitan Detroit AFL-CIO," *Detroit Labor News*, April 5, 1972.
48 "Structure for an Overall Program Design for the City of Detroit," 215, Dec. 31, 1973, Box 216, Folder 14, NDI Collection, ALUA.
49 Madar to Jeffrey, May 25, 1973, Box 56, Folder 20, MJ Collection, ALUA.
50 Joseph Cialdella points out that in 1970, Detroit's budget deficit reached $22.5 million, while spending $1.5 million on Belle Isle maintenance and upkeep. Cialdella, *Motor City Green*, 127–28.
51 Tom to Olga and Milly, August 21, 1973, Box 56, Folder 20, UAW-CRD-MJ Collection, ALUA.
52 Charleen Knight Letter to the Editor, "Park Planners Ignore Detroit's Needs," *Detroit Free Press*, July 9, 1973; William Brodhead Letter to the Editor, *Detroit Free Press*, July 4, 1973.
53 "Mill Creek Park Opponents Optimistic," *The Advisor*, February 28, 1973, clipping in Box 3, Folder: "Mill Creek . . . Correspondence 1973," MCRC Collection.
54 Position Statement, Michigan DNR, May 10, 1973, Box 3, Folder: "Mill Creek . . . Correspondence 1973," MCRC Collection.
55 Sylvester Weber to Washtenaw County Board of Commissioners, December 9, 1974, Box 2, Folder: "Mill Creek . . . 1975 Report," MCRC Collection.
56 James Trainor to David Laidlaw, February 27, 1973, Box 3, Folder "Mill Creek . . . 1975 Report," MCRC Collection.
57 "Tomorrow Today: Fifth Annual Report," January 1973, Southeast Michigan Council of Governments, Box 4, Folder: "Mill Creek . . . SEMCOG," MCRC Collection.
58 "State Refuses Creation of Park in Washtenaw," *Battle Creek Enquirer*, June 7, 1979.
59 Phrase borrowed from Dave Dempsey, *Ruin and Recovery: Michigan's Rise as a Conservation Leader* (Ann Arbor: University of Michigan Press, 2001), 220–44.
60 Samuel P. Hays and Barbara D. Hays, *Beauty, Health, and Permanence: Environmental Politics in the United States, 1955–1985* (New York: Cambridge University Press, 1987), 177–85.
61 Josiah Rector uses the concept of "popular epidemiology" to show how autoworkers discovered high rates of cancer resulting from their employment and demanded the "right to know" about workplace carcinogens. Josiah Rector, "Environmental Justice at Work: The UAW, the War on Cancer, and the Right to Equal Protection from Toxic Hazards in Postwar America," *Journal of American History* 101, no. 2 (September 1, 2014): 480–502, 495–96, https://doi.org/10.1093/jahist/jau380.
62 Dempsey, *Ruin and Recovery*, 220–21.
63 Dempsey, *Ruin and Recovery*, 226.
64 Dempsey, *Ruin and Recovery*, 229.
65 "Hooker Chemicals Named in Suit," *Lansing State Journal* (April 29, 1980): 3.
66 Eileen McGurty, *Transforming Environmentalism: Warren County, PCBS, and the Origins of Environmental Justice* (New Brunswick, NJ: Rutgers University Press, 2009), 40–41.
67 Elizabeth D. Blum, *Love Canal Revisited: Race, Class, and Gender in Environmental Activism* (Lawrence: University Press of Kansas, 2011), 24–30.
68 Blum, *Love Canal Revisited*, 28.
69 McGurty, *Transforming Environmentalism*, 41–42.
70 McGurty, *Transforming Environmentalism*, 1–5.
71 *Superfund Record of Decision: Chemical Control, NJ* (Washington, DC: Environmental Protection Agency, 1987), 1–3. Accessed from nepis.epa.gov, June 4, 2020; McGurty, *Transforming Environmentalism*, 42.
72 "Superfund: CERCLA Overview," Environmental Protection Agency, accessed June 4, 2020, www.epa.gov/superfund/superfund-cercla-overview.

Environmentalism in the fragmented metropolis **137**

73 Frank Greve, "Super-Flop?," *Detroit Free Press*, August 19, 1981.
74 "Minifund?," *Detroit Free Press*, November 30, 1980.
75 Greve, "Super-Flop?."
76 Mike Duffy, " 'Time Bomb II' Is a Dynamite Idea," *Detroit Free Press*, August 19, 1981.
77 "City Care Starts with More Aide – Conyers," *Detroit Free Press*, April 9, 1979.
78 Gioielli, *Environmental Activism and the Urban Crisis*, 163–65.
79 Gioielli, *Environmental Activism and the Urban Crisis*, 163.
80 Memorandum, February 7, 1979, Box 4, Folder 44, UEC Collection, ALUA.
81 Box 4, Folder 46, UEC Collection.
82 Samuel P. Hays, *A History of Environmental Politics Since 1945* (Pittsburgh, PA: University of Pittsburgh Press, 2000), 104–6.
83 Core Group P Recommendations, Box 4, Folder 46, Urban Environment Conference Collection, ALUA.
84 "Major Urban Conference," *EPA Journal Reprint*, October 1978, in Box 4, Folder 49, UEC Collection.
85 James A. Bush, "Redlining, Disinvestment, and Overbuilding the Suburbs," in Box 4, Folder 45, UEC Collection.
86 Core Group H Recommendations, Box 4, Folder 46, UEC Collection.
87 Core Group I Recommendations, Box 4, Folder 46, UEC Collection.
88 Core Group K Recommendations, Box 4, Folder 46, UEC Collection.
89 Core Group M Recommendations, Box 4, Folder 46, UEC Collection.
90 Core Group L Recommendations, Box 4, Folder 46, UEC Collection.
91 Barbara D. Blum Statement, Box 4, Folder 50, UEC Collection.
92 William Milliken Statement, Box 4, Folder 50, UEC Collection.
93 Workshop 4: Preventing Environmental Disease in the home and the Neighborhood, Box 4, Folder 50, UEC Collection.
94 Gioielli, *Environmental Activism and the Urban Crisis*, 168–71.
95 Josiah Rector, "The Spirit of Black Lake: Full Employment, Civil Rights, and the Forgotten Early History of Environmental Justice," *Modern American History* 1, no. 1 (March 2018): 60.
96 Coleman A. Young and Lonnie Wheeler, *Hard Stuff: The Autobiography of Coleman Young* (New York: Viking, 1994), 239.
97 June Manning Thomas, *Redevelopment and Race: Planning a Finer City in Postwar Detroit* (Detroit: Wayne State University Press, 2013), 161–66.
98 Young and Wheeler, *Hard Stuff*, 245.
99 Young and Wheeler, *Hard Stuff*, 249; Thomas, *Redevelopment and Race*, 165.
100 Nicholas Leonard, "The Detroit Incinerator Primer: Construction, Design, Operation," *Breathe Free Detroit*, undated, accessed July 2, 2021, www.ecocenter.org/breathe-free-detroit.
101 Case No. 87-CV-71577-DT, Box 8, Folder "Det. Inc. Chron Detroit 1984–1986, SCMC Collection, BHL.
102 Josiah Rector, "Accumulating Risk: Environmental Justice and the History of Capitalism in Detroit, 1880–2015" (Ph.D. Dissertation, Wayne State University, 2017), 259–95, quote on 261.
103 Bunyan I. Bryant and Elaine Hockman, *Michigan: A State of Environmental Justice?* (New York: Morgan James Pub., 2011), 137.
104 Collective Statement, Box 3, Folder 9, TWS Collection, ALUA.
105 Newsletter, January 17, 1989, Box 3, Folder 9, TWS Collection; Newsletter, June 1988, Box 3, Folder 9, TWS Collection; Bryant and Hockman, *Michigan*, 135.
106 Bob Campbell, "Incinerator Protestors Acquitted in Jury Trial," *Detroit Press*, undated clipping in Box 3, Folder 9, TWS Collection.
107 Press Release, September 21, 1989, Box 8, Folder "Det. Inc. Chron Detroit 1984–1986, SCMC Collection.
108 Case No. 87-CV-71577-DT, Box 8, Folder "Det. Inc. Chron Detroit 1984–1986, SCMC Collection.

138 Environmentalism in the fragmented metropolis

109 Dempsey, *Ruin and Recovery*, 271.
110 *Detroit Audubon Society v. City of Detroit*, February 24, 1988, accessed July 1, 2020, https://elr.info/sites/default/files/litigation/19.20170.htm.
111 William E. Schmidt, "Ideas and Trends: Trying to Solve the Side Effects of Converting Trash to Energy," *New York Times*, May 27, 1990.
112 Bill Mcgraw et al., "Incinerator Vote was a Betrayal, Mayor Says," *Detroit Free Press*, April 19, 1990, in Box 3, Folder 5, TWS Collection; "Blowing Smoke," *Detroit News*, April 19, 1990, Box 8, Folder: "Detroit Incinerator. . . (1990–1994)," SCMC Collection; Richardson to Mackris, July 3, 1990, Box 8, Folder: "Det. Inc., Corr. 1989–1991 (1/2)," SCMC Collection.
113 MAPCC Meeting Transcript, March 19, 1991, 172–174, Box 3, Folder, 6, TWS Collection.
114 Rector, "Accumulating Risk," 276–78.
115 Keith Matheny and Kat Stafford, "Detroit Renewable Power Waste Incinerator Pollutes," *Detroit Free Press*, May 21, 2018.
116 Rector, "Accumulating Risk," 285–86. Bunyan Bryant, a founder of environmental justice scholarship and activism, blames environmentalists for failing to establish a relationship with African Americans until they were needed as allies against the incinerator. Bryant and Hockman, *Michigan*, 140.
117 Calculations based on the adjoining communities: Augusta Township, Milan City, Milan Township, and York Township, *1990 Census of Population: General Population Characteristics: Michigan* (Washington, DC: U.S. Government Printing Office).
118 Hal Grano, "Area Toxic Dump Fought," *Agenda*, October 1989, accessed June 29, 2020, https://aadl.org/node/246489.
119 Kim Kozlowski, "Fill Cleanup Intentions Questioned," *Ypsilanti Press*, September 16, 1992, Box 7, MCATS Collection, BHL.
120 "Debate Continues on Proposed Toxic Dump Site in Township," *Saline Reporter*, June 14, 1989, accessed June 30, 2020, digmichnews.cmich.edu; John Blair, "Local 898 Retiree Honored," *Raw Facts*, 28, 1 (March/April 1998), Box 7, MCATS Collection.
121 MCATS Newsletter, January 1992, Box 1, Folder: "General Information, 1989–1996," MCATS Collection.
122 Karl Leif Bates, "Safety Concerns Raised Over Planned Incinerator, Landfill," *Ann Arbor News*, April 19, 1992 in Box 1, Folder: "Flyers and Mailings, 1989–1995," MCATS Collection.
123 "Toxics Alert," Box 1, Folder "Organizational Info . . . 1989–19967," MCATS Collection.
124 Pete MacKay, "Voters Approve Envotech Fight Millage," *Milan News*, August 12, 1992, Box 7, MCATS Collection.
125 "You Can Help Our Crucial Cause," *Saline Reporter*, August 12, 1992, accessed June 29, 2020, digmichnews.cmich.edu.
126 "Augusta Clean Air Classic 10K Run," Box 1, Folder "MCATS ORG Materials . . . 1991–1992," MCATS Collection.
127 John Blair, "Local 898 Retiree Honored," *Raw Facts* 28, no. 1 (March–April 1998), Box 7, MCATS Collection; MCATS Newsletter, undated, Box 1, Folder: "MCATS ORG Materials . . . 1991–1992," MCATS Collection.
128 Brandon Ward, "The Promise of Jobs: Blackmail and Environmental Justice in Flint, Michigan, 1991–1995," *Environmental Justice* 6, no. 5 (October 2013): 163–68, https://doi.org/10.1089/env.2013.0030; Richard Kazis and Richard L. Grossman, *Fear at Work: Job Blackmail, Labor, and the Environment* (New York: Pilgrim Press, 1982); Rector, "The Spirit of Black Lake."
129 MCATS Fact Sheet No. 3, March 16, 1993, Box 1, Folder: "Flyers and Meetings, 1989–1995," MCATS Collection.
130 Branim to Engler, October 13, 1992, Box 1, Folder: "Letter Writing Information, 1991–1992," MCATS Collection.

131 Renning to Engler, October 14, 1992, Box 1, Folder: "Letter Writing Information, 1991–1992," MCATS Collection.
132 Bobicz to Engler, October 13, 1992, Box 1, Folder: "Letter Writing Information, 1991–1992," MCATS Collection.
133 Lindsey to Engler, undated, Box 1, Folder: "Letter Writing Information, 1991–1992," MCATS Collection.
134 *Decisions of the United States Environmental Protection Agency: May 1995 to March 1997*, Vol. VI (Washington, DC: Environmental Protection Agency, undated), 260–301.
135 *Decisions of the United States Environmental Protection Agency: May 1995 to March 1997*, 272.
136 *Decisions of the United States Environmental Protection Agency: May 1995 to March 1997*, 271.
137 *Decisions of the United States Environmental Protection Agency: May 1995 to March 1997*, 282.
138 Phrase borrowed from Sylvia Hood Washington, *Packing Them In: An Archaeology of Environmental Racism in Chicago, 1865–1954* (Lanham, Md: Lexington Books, 1994); Julie Sze, *Noxious New York: The Racial Politics of Urban Health and Environmental Justice* (Cambridge, MA: Massachusetts Institute of Technology Press, 2007), 5–6.

EPILOGUE

Age of crises

Two famous artistic depictions of industry in Detroit represent starkly different ways of viewing the industrial city. The photographs of the massive Ford River Rouge plant by Charles Sheeler and the murals by Diego Rivera at the Detroit Institute of Arts reflect the contrasting views. Sheeler's photographs, captured in 1927, showed the might of the new Ford plant in the style of American modernism. Depicting the sharp angles of criss-crossed conveyors and forcing our perspective toward the sky in photographs of the towering smokestacks, the images represent the industrial sublime. The photographs show a factory testing the limits of nature, and indeed seem to suggest the contrast of machines versus nature. Though reflecting the height of American ingenuity and optimism in industrial prowess, the photographs are remarkably devoid of the workers running the behemoth. Removed from the contexts of the natural world and labor, the images are paeans to technological progress, a sanitization of the exploitation of labor and environment central to the manufacturing process.[1]

Contrast the Sheeler photographs with the Diego Rivera murals in the courtyard of the Detroit Institute of Arts – 27 panels painted six years after the Sheeler photographs and commissioned by Edsel Ford. Completed during the Great Depression, Rivera showed a very different side of Detroit industry. Rivera portrayed the industrial ecology of automobile manufacturing, from the harvesting of natural resources to the workers' bulging muscular power as labor inputs, from the pollution emanating from the factory to the finished products. In Rivera's murals, industry cannot be separated from its environmental and social contexts. Rivera's depictions are lively with workers as the central actors in the process, representing his interest in creating artwork that contributed, as he put it, "to the aesthetic nourishment of the working class, in the form of clarifying expression of the things that class must understand in its struggle for a classless society."[2] While Rivera was widely criticized for the murals, coming as they were during a period of accelerating

Epilogue **141**

FIGURE 7.1 Conveyors at Ford River Rouge complex, with smokestacks in the background.
Source: Charles Sheeler, 1927. Call Number HAER MI-325-1, Historic American Buildings Survey Collection, Library of Congress Prints and Photographs Division.

FIGURE 7.2 North Wall from Diego Rivera Murals.
Source: Detroit Institute of Arts, USA. Gift of Edsel B. Ford/Bridgeman Images.

142 Epilogue

labor-management conflict, Edsel Ford defended the paintings. Rivera's "social realism" was not so welcomed in New York, as his benefactor, the Rockefeller Center, pulled the plug on his mural after he depicted the unmistakable portrait of Vladimir Lenin.[3] After World War II, in Detroit, Rivera's murals survived a dangerous period of McCarthyism, but remain an enduring example of viewing Detroit's industry within the contexts of the working class and the natural world.

★★★★★

Writing for the book you are now reading began – and ended – in the thick of two metropolitan crises. The first was the grave state of the city's finances by 2010. As I embarked on research in 2010 as a PhD student, Detroit was the subject of significant media attention as the Great Recession compounded decades of declining tax revenue to push the city to the brink of insolvency. In November 2011, Detroit claimed a cash shortfall approaching $150 million.[4] Just over one year later, Michigan Governor Dan Snyder appointed an emergency manager for Detroit, Kevyn Orr, who navigated the city into declaring bankruptcy in November 2013. At $18 billion, it was the largest municipal bankruptcy in the U. S. history. The same Detroit Institute of Arts that housed the Diego Rivera murals faced the agonizing threat from creditors, which demanded the liquidation of the museum's collections. Only a "Grand Bargain" of private foundation support, state funding, private donations, and the promise to pay $816 million over 20 years to one of the largest creditors, the city's pensioners, could save the museum's collections.[5]

Meanwhile, national media obsessed over the crisis in Detroit, particularly as it manifested in the built and natural environment, producing numerous documentaries, art exhibits, photographic collections, magazine features, books, and news stories providing an "autopsy" of Detroit. Residents lamented the way media hovered like vultures over dying prey, resenting that *Time* and *Dateline* and other major outlets show only the abandoned factories, crumbling homes, and vacant fields (or what some residents called "misery porn").[6] Stories abounded of the supposed return of "nature" to the abandoned neighborhoods of Detroit, as photographs captured trees growing through abandoned houses, former residential neighborhoods looking more like forests, and numerous accounts of the return of coyotes, beavers, lake sturgeon, and bald eagles to the area.[7] What had once been a thriving industrial city, the narratives suggested, had "returned" to nature. Nature had supposedly reclaimed a failed civilization. The racial implications were hard to miss, playing into the hands of the former Detroiters who claimed that African American leadership and majority black population had caused the city's descent into a "wasteland."[8] The national obsession with Detroit's decline, though masquerading as concern, exploited the misery of residents and turned it into a voyeuristic object of fascination and pity, rather than a living city of 700,000 stories.

While national media and popular representations of Detroit rendered African Americans invisible, black Detroiters worked tirelessly to make a livable city, just as they had always done. As geographer Kimberley Kinder argues in *DIY Detroit:*

Epilogue **143**

Making Do in a City without Services, in a city that often fails to provide adequate emergency response, slow-plowing, trash collection, and other essential city services, residents have organized and supplied much of their own labor to keep their neighborhoods viable.[9] The built environment remains a contested terrain for ensuring that people can remain in their homes, against the backdrop of a continuing urban crisis. Kinder asserts that their struggle to survive the city should not be seen in romantic terms, for the vast majority of Detroiters would gladly exchange it for functioning city services. The onus has historically fallen unequally on black residents to "make do" in the city. From the Africans and African Americans who first arrived in Detroit as slaves, to those who struggled to live in and improve their segregated neighborhoods after the Great Migration, to the residents in the 1970s who built gardens on vacant lots, to the environmental justice activists today working for a safe and healthy environment where Detroiters can "work, live, and play," there is a continuity of struggle that defines the city.

A second metropolitan crisis emerged as I finished writing the book. The COVID-19 pandemic, caused by a novel strain of coronavirus, swept across the United States in the Spring of 2020, but familiar patterns of metropolitan inequality were evident in the mortality rates across the Detroit region. In the City of Detroit, now a nearly 79% African-American city, black residents faced poorer outcomes from COVID-19 disease compared with the whiter and wealthier suburbs of Detroit. Officials warned that comorbidities like high blood pressure, diabetes, asthma, and obesity worsened the disease outcomes, conditions which were often associated with poverty.[10] One public health researcher connected the historical patterns of residential segregation and racial capitalism in Detroit to the high mortality rates of African Americans, as "residents in deprived neighborhoods have less access to green spaces and healthy, affordable foods."[11] A Brooking Institution report published in early 2021 found that black Detroiters were significantly more likely to die from the virus than were white residents of the metropolitan area.[12] Though precise statistics were rapidly evolving during the pandemic, the patterns did not surprise researchers, who pointed out the "structural differences in the economy," which meant African Americans were less able to practice social distancing, due to employment in healthcare and other essential jobs. Working-class white residents of the industrial communities similarly faced higher mortality risk due to air pollution-related respiratory diseases like asthma. It is too soon to write the history of the COVID-19 pandemic, but early indicators show that the patterns of metropolitan inequality had deadly consequences for the residents who remained tied to the environmentally disadvantaged sections of the region. The patterns of environmental inequality established and transformed over a century continued to manifest in devastating metropolitan disparities.

★★★★

Detroit is a living city. That might seem obvious enough, but the people who live in Detroit, nearly 80% of whom are black, have often been rendered invisible in

144 Epilogue

popular depictions of the city. While much of the nation has focused on the shuttered factories, Detroit's bankruptcy, and the creeping abandonment from downtown to the residential neighborhoods, the voices of those who remain have too often been obscured. As Diego Rivera's murals centered the workers who made industrial capitalism possible, it is also critical to assert the significance of ordinary Detroiters who labored mightily to make their homes, neighborhoods, and region livable and sustainable against the backdrop of overwhelming crises.

Notes

1 Karen Lucic, *Charles Sheeler and the Cult of the Machine* (Cambridge, MA: Harvard University Press, 1991). The contrast between Sheeler and Rivera was also described by Thomas J. Sugrue, *The Origins of the Urban Crisis: Race and Inequality in Postwar Detroit* (Princeton, NJ: Princeton University Press, 1996), 17.
2 Diego Rivera, *Portrait of America: With an Explanatory Text by Bertram D. Wolfe* (New York: J. J. Little and Ives Company, 1934).
3 Raymie E. McKerrow, "Visions of Society in Discourse and Art: The Failed Rhetoric of Social Realism," *Communications Quarterly* 41 (Summer 1993): 355–66; Pete Hamill, *Diego Rivera* (New York: Harry N. Abrams, 1999), 164–66.
4 "Detroit's Mayor Says Budget Gap May Require Emergency Manager," *New York Times*, November 3, 2011.
5 "Grand Bargain," *Encyclopedia of Detroit*, Detroit Historical Society, accessed July 29, 2020, https://detroithistorical.org/learn/encyclopedia-of-detroit/grand-bargain.
6 *Detroit Lives*, directed by Johnny Knoxville (New York: VBS Films, 2010).
7 See, for instance, Mark Binelli, *Detroit City Is the Place to Be: The Afterlife of an American Metropolis* (New York: Picador, 2013), 9, 39–41. "Detroit's Dumps are Slowly being Reclaimed by Nature," *Smithsonian*, September 12, 2014, accessed August 6, 2020, www.smithsonianmag.com/smart-news/detroits-dumps-are-slowly-being-reclaimed-nature-180952676/.
8 Rebecca J. Kinney, *Beautiful Wasteland: The Rise of Detroit as America's Postindustrial Frontier* (Minneapolis, MN: University of Minnesota Press, 2016), 1–37, 150–52.
9 Kimberley Kinder, *DIY Detroit: Making Do in a City Without Services* (Minneapolis, MN: University of Minnesota Press, 2016).
10 Benjamin Wallace-Wells, "Inequality Intensifies the Coronavirus Crisis in Detroit," *New Yorker*, April 7, 2020, accessed August 7, 2020, www.newyorker.com/news/news-desk/the-coronavirus-and-inequality-meet-in-detroit.
11 Whitney N. Laster Pirtle, "Racial Capitalism: A Fundamental Cause of Novel Coronavirus (COVID-19) Pandemic Inequities in the United States," *Health Education & Behavior* 47, no. 4 (August 2020): 504–8, https://doi.org/10.1177/1090198120922942.
12 Rashawn Ray, Jane Fran Morgan, Lydia Wileden, Samantha Elizondo, and Destiny Wiley-Yancy, *Examining and Addressing COVID-19 Racial Disparities in Detroit*, accessed March 29, 2021, www.brookings.edu/wp-content/uploads/2021/02/Detroit_Covid_report_final.pdf.

INDEX

Note: Page numbers in italics indicate a figure or map on the corresponding page. Page numbers followed by "n" indicate a note.

Abbott, Carl 40
AFL-CIO *see* American Federation of Labor-Congress of Industrial Organizations (AFL-CIO)
African Americans xix; in Detroit xviii; during COVID-19 pandemic 143; discriminatory laws against 12; efforts to resist urban decay 15; lack of recreational opportunities for 6; neglecting 32, 34; population in Detroit 4, 8–9, *9*; residential segregation 3–4, 9, 11, 14; restrictive covenants case 10; Revolutionary Union Movements 77; segregation and poverty trapped xx; struggles for fair housing 11; under-reporting of health complaints 55; unemployment rates 128; in urban renewal projects xx; vectors of diseases 3; vision for urban environment 91; *see also* black environmentalism
Agent Orange 59
air pollution 83; Dearborn 76; Detroit-Windsor Air Pollution Study 54–55; in Donora, Pennsylvania 54; environmental survey 83; incinerator and 129
Alinsky, Saul 94
Alston, Dana xxiii
American Federation of Labor-Congress of Industrial Organizations (AFL-CIO) 60, 120

American Public Health Association 17
AMY (Augusta, Milan, York) coalition 131, 132
Ann Arbor 114, 127
anti-incinerator 133
anti-pollution activism 49–50
Anti-Pollution Committee 63
anti-pollution laws 50
Arkona Road Landfill 130–131
Arsenal of Democracy xix, xxiii, 4, 6, 34
Atomic Energy Commission 123
atomic radiation 123
Audubon Society 129

Baby-Boomers 48
Bacon, David 117
Beautification Council 41–42
Belle Isle, racial violence in 5–6, 11, 30, 97–98
Black Bottom 1, 3, 19, 103
black community *see* African Americans
black environmentalism 85; in Detroit 91, 102–108; Earth Day 100–102; freeway to rebellion 91–94; rat infestations 96–97; recreation and wreck-creation 97–100; West Central Organization 94–100
Black Lake conference 81–82
blue-collar workers 27, 49, 80
Blum, Barbara 127

146 Index

Blum, Elizabeth 124
boating 60–61
Braun, Laurence 63
Brewster Housing project 11
Bridges, Nathan 106
Brodhead, William 121
Brough, Michael 112, 116
Brower, David 64, 80
Bruno, Vincent 75
Bullard, Robert xxiii
Bulldozer in the Countryside, The (Rome) 39
Bush, James 126

C-56 & C-59 chemicals 123
capital flight xix
Carey, E.B. 6
Carpenter, Robert 35, 36, 37
Carson, Rachel 25, 48, 59, 123
Carter, Edward 98
Cavanagh, Jerome 95–96
central city, underdevelopment of xviii
CERCLA *see* Comprehensive
 Environmental Response, Compensation,
 and Liability Act (CERCLA)
Chemical Control Corporation 124–125
chemical wasteland 123
children, in recreation 107
CHPC *see* Citizens' Housing and Planning
 Council (CHPC)
Chrysler xxiv, 84
Chrysler Freeway 19
Cialdella, Joseph 14
Citizens Advisory Committee 41
Citizens' Clearinghouse for Hazardous
 Waste 124
Citizens' Housing and Planning Council
 (CHPC) 29
Citizens Opposed to Super Sewer (COSS)
 114–115, 118
City Care conference 124, 125–127, 133
City Plan Commission 37–38
Clean Air Act 81, 129
Cleveland Plains-Dealer, The 79
Clinton, Bill 132
Clinton River valley 35
Coalition of Labor Union Women 84
Commoner, Barry 80, 112
Comprehensive Environmental Response,
 Compensation, and Liability Act
 (CERCLA) 125
Conservation Committee 15–16
corporate welfare programs 70
COSS *see* Citizens Opposed to Super
 Sewer (COSS)

Council of Social Agencies 7
Couzens, James 28
COVID-19 pandemic 143
Craig, Roger 75, 76
Crittendon, Willie 97
Cuyahoga River, Cleveland 79, 124

Danger–Men at Work see *To Your Industrial
 Health!* (radio program)
DAPL *see* Downriver Anti-Pollution
 League (DAPL)
DARPC *see* Detroit Area Regional
 Planning Commission (DARPC)
Darrow, Clarence 10
DART *see* Deprived Areas Recreation
 Team (DART)
DDT pesticide *see* dichloro-diphenyl-
 trichloroethane (DDT) pesticide
Dearborn, air pollution in 74–76, *75*
deindustrialization xix, 91, 102, 113, 123
Dempsey, Dave 124
Deprived Areas Recreation Team (DART)
 73–74
Detroit xvi; 1943 riots 5–6; abandoned
 102–108; air pollution 56; towards
 black protest 19–20; bulldozing
 13–15; Committee for Neighborhood
 Conservation 15; COVID-19
 pandemic 143; demolishing diseases
 6–8; downriver 56–57; dynamic
 region 29–31; environmental decline
 (1945–1952) 48–50; environmental
 inequalities 8–13, 55; from factories to
 communities 53–56; fishes or factories
 56–61; gardening programs 107; healthy
 landscapes for family (1947–1955)
 50–53; inner-city neighborhoods 19,
 41, 92, 97, 120, 126; massive duck and
 fish kills 57–58, 62; Motor City 19;
 neighborhood conservation 15–19;
 organizing for environment (1958–1962)
 61–64; population after World War
 II 29; rebellion in 73; river pollution
 56–61; sickness in 2–3; tuberculosis in 3;
 urbanization of 36; urban renewal plans
 13, 15, *16*; wartime environments 3–6;
 and Wayne County 39
Detroit Area Regional Planning
 Commission (DARPC) 35
Detroit Audubon Society v. City of Detroit 129
Detroit Common Council 54, 92
Detroit Edison electric plant 58
Detroit Free Press xviii, xxiii, 24; *Free
 Press* 63

Detroit Housing Commission 9
Detroit Metropolitan Area Regional Planning Commission (DRPC) 32
Detroit Metro Water Department 114
Detroit Sportsmen's Congress 49–50
Detroit Urban League (DUL) 13–15, 17–18, 38, 93
Detroit Water and Sewerage Department (DWSD) 39
Detroit-Windsor Air Pollution Study 54
Dewey, Scott 89n75, 89n85
dichloro-diphenyl-trichloroethane (DDT) pesticide 64, 123
Dinosaur National Monument 64
DIY Detroit 106, 142–143
Dodge Revolutionary Union Movement newspaper 77
Donora disaster 54–55
Douglas project 11
Douglass, Bruce 11
Dow Chemical Company 59
Downriver Anti-Pollution League (DAPL) 78–79, 82–83
drained wetlands xxi
DRPC *see* Detroit Metropolitan Area Regional Planning Commission (DRPC)
DUL *see* Detroit Urban League (DUL)
Dunmore, Albert J. 98
DWSD *see* Detroit Water and Sewerage Department (DWSD)

Eagan, Lloyd 49
Earth Day xvi–xviii, 48, 80–83, 100–102
East Michigan Environmental Action Council 127
East Side Concerned Citizens 104
ecology 101–102
Ecorse 49, 78–79
Edsel B. Ford Expressway 19
Edward J. Jeffries Freeway 91–92
Edwards, George 31
EIS *see* Environmental Impact Statement (EIS)
Enabling Act of 1939 121
environmental abuse, corporate xix
Environmental Action 81
environmental activism xvi, xviii, 49, 101
environmental awareness 48
environmental blackmail xvi, xx, 84
environmental crisis xvii, 69
environmental decline 48–50
Environmental Defense Fund 129
environmental degradation 63

environmental discrimination xxiii
environmental health: indicators of 120; inequalities of air pollution 55; risks 6–7, 14, 51, 54, 102; slum clearance 6–7
Environmental Impact Statement (EIS) 115, 122, 128
environmental inequalities xviii, 8–13, 55, 74, 143
Environmental Inequalities (Hurley) xxiii
environmentalism; social-justice perspective of 82; in United States xxi; urban and industrial roots of xxi; *see also* black environmentalism; metropolitan environmentalism; working-class environmentalism
environmental justice xxv
environmental organizations 107–108
Environmental Protection Agency (1970) 83
Environmental Protection and Maintenance Department (EPMD) 106
environmental quest, for living 24–42; balancing region 37–38; breathing room 34–37; dynamic region 29–31; greener living during Great Depression 28–29; growing pains 39–40; postwar dreams 31–34; toward "pure" Michigan 40–42; suburbs region 27
environmental racism xxiii
environmental regulation 49
environmental survey, of downriver project 82–83
Environmental Teach-In xvi, *xvii*, 80–83, 101
Envotech, Arkona Road Landfill 130–131
EPA 114–115, 132
EPMD *see* Environmental Protection and Maintenance Department (EPMD)
Esch, Marvin 115
Evergreen Alliance 127, 128–129

families, healthy landscapes for 50–53
Federal-Aid Highway Act of 1944 92
Federal Emergency Relief Administration (FERA) 28
Federal Housing Act (1949) 13
Federal Housing Administration (FHA) 10
Federal Water Pollution Control Act (1972) 81, 83
Federal Water Quality Act of 1965 123
FERA *see* Federal Emergency Relief Administration (FERA)
FHA *see* Federal Housing Administration (FHA)

148 Index

Fine, Lisa 57
Fine, Sidney 72
Fisher, A.C. 58
food deserts 106
Ford, Edsel 140, 142
Ford Company xxiv, 76
Fredrick, William G. 55
Free Press 63
freeways 91–94
Friends of the Native Landscape 25–26

Gable, William 38
garbage heaps 8
gardening programs xxii, 107
Garreau, Joel 27
Gazlay, Gene 118, 122
GDRRF *see* Greater Detroit Resource
    Recovery Facility (GDRRF)
General Motors xxiv, 128, 131
Gibbs, Lois 124
Gillette, Genevieve 24–26, *26*, 40, 48;
    supporting development of HCMA 30;
    in Westacres 28–29
Gioielli, Robert xxvin9, 94, 125
GM Hamtramck-Detroit Assembly Plant 128
Goetz, Fred 61
Gomon, Josephine Fellows 1, *2*
Goodman brothers 96–97
Gorsuch, Anne 125
Grand River 24–25
Gratiot Redevelopment Project *see*
    Lafayette Gardens
Great Depression xix, 28–29, 140
Greater Detroit Resource Recovery
    Facility (GDRRF) 128
Great Lakes Steel 58, 62
Great Recession xxiii, 142
Great Society program 69
Greenbelts 28–29, 38
Green Islands 41, 74
greenlining phenomenon 126
Grosse Pointe 90

Hair (musicals) xvi
Hamtramck 27
Hare, Nathan 102
Hart, Phil 80
Hastings-Oakland Expressway *see* Chrysler
    Freeway
Hatcher, Richard 103
hate strike, at Packard plant 4
Hayes, Denis 80
HCMA *see* Huron-Clinton Metropolitan
    Authority (HCMA)

Hendershot, Burrell 59
Highland Park 27
highway project 19, 41, 91–92
Hobart Street incident 90, 94
Hoffmaster, P.J. 26
Hogan, Audrey 100
Home Owners' Loan Corporation 10
Hookendrooper, Dotty 52
Hooker Chemical Company 123–124
Hoskin, Samuel P. 12
House Bill 3781 93
Housing Act of 1949 32
Housing and Urban Development (HUD)
    105–106
Howell, Charles 100
Howie, Tom 121
HUD *see* Housing and Urban
    Development (HUD)
Humphrey, Cliff 101
hunting 61
Hurley, Andrew xxiii, xxviiin15
Huron-Clinton Metropolitan Authority
    (HCMA) 26, 30–31, 34–35; metroparks
    116–118, *119*; regionalism concept 121
Huron River 35, 113–114

Improved Housing *see* Conservation
    Committee
industrial capitalism 82, 144
industrial chemicals 123
industrial pollution xvi, 49–50, 80
industrial safety hazards 51
Interstate Highway System 19
Ivory, Marcellius 84
Izaak Walton League xxi

Jeffries Freeway Action Body (JFAB) 93
Jeffries project 11
Jensen, Jens 25
JFAB *see* Jeffries Freeway Action Body
    (JFAB)
Johnson, Lady Bird 41, 70
Johnson, Lyndon 40, 64, 69, 96, 98, 123
Johnson, Tom 97
Jones, Clifford 8
Jordan, Vernon 126

Kachman, Nicholas 129–130
Keast, William 99
Keep America Beautiful campaign 106
Keep Detroit Beautiful campaign 78, 106
Kennedy, John F. 64
Kerner Report 1968 98
Kinder, Kimberley 106, 142–143

Index 149

Knight, Charleen 119
Knox, Robert 95–96

Lafayette Gardens 14–15
Laidlaw, David 121
Laier, Donald 118
Lake Erie 113–114, 115
League of Women Voters 56
leisure time 100
Lenin, Vladimir 142
Leopold, Aldo 25
Levin, Carl 121
Liebert, Hillel 79
Lightfoot, Gordon 80
Lincoln Park 79
Local 600 activism 75, 76–77
local sovereignty 113
Lodge, John C. 19; Lodge Freeway 18
Lombardi (Father) 76
Los Angeles, tuberculosis in 3
Love Canal poisonings 124

Macomb Nature Association 59
Madar, Olga 70–71, 73, 78–79, 83–84, 120
Maher (Judge) 9
Man's Living Environment (conference) 81
MAPCC *see* Michigan Air Pollution
    Control Commission (MAPCC)
Marshall, Thurgood 10
Mastin, Phil 116
Maybury Sanatorium 3
MCATS *see* Michigan Citizens Against
    Toxic Substances (MCATS)
McGhee, Orsel 10
McGuire, D.E. 58
McGurty, Eileen 124
McLaughlin, Malcolm 96
MCRC *see* Mill Creek Research Council
    (MCRC)
Mercer Brick Company 75
mercury, in fish 123
metroparks xxi, 24, *30*, 35, 116–118, *119*
metropolitan environmentalism xviii,
    112; city care 125–127; parks and
    conflicts 116–122; Super Sewer system
    113–116; toxic backyards 130–133;
    toxic metropolis 127–130; toxic nation
    122–125
Michigan Air Pollution Control
    Commission (MAPCC) 129
Michigan Chronicle 6, 8, 9, 11, 13, 14, 102,
    106
Michigan Citizens Against Toxic Substances
    (MCATS) 127, 130–132

Michigan Conservation magazine 61
Michigan Environmental Policy Act 115
Michigan legislature 30
Michigan Natural Resources Council 99
Michigan United Conservation Clubs
    (MUCC) 49; against anti-pollution
    56–61; raising environmental
    consciousness 50
Michigan Water Resources Commission
    114
Milan Middle School 132
Mill Creek Metropark 59, 117, 119, 122
Mill Creek Research Council (MCRC)
    117–118, 122
Milliken, William xvi, 99, 127
Monguagon Creek 49
Montrie, Chad xxii, 78
Morrow, Donald 105
Moses, Robert 35
MUCC *see* Michigan United Conservation
    Clubs (MUCC)
Mumford, Lewis 29, 40
Muskie, Edmund 80

NAACP 6, 91
Nader, Ralph xvii, 101, 128
National Environmental Policy Act
    (NEPA) 81, 83, 112, 115, 133
National Institute of Occupational Safety
    and Health 123
National Wildlife Foundation 56
neighborhood conservation xxii, 15–19,
    105
Neighborhood Legal Service organization
    97
Nelson, Gaylord xvi, 80, 81
NEPA *see* National Environmental Policy
    Act (NEPA)
New Federalism 104
New Orleans, rat infestations in 6
Nichols, John 103
NIMBY environmentalism *see* Not-In-My-
    Backyard (NIMBY) environmentalism
Nixon, Richard 81
noise pollution 51
Norton, James 7
Not-In-My-Backyard (NIMBY)
    environmentalism 112–113
nuclear annihilation 61

Oakland County 28
Occupational Health and Safety Act in
    1970 123
Office of Censorship 4

150 Index

oil pollution: in Detroit River 57–58, 62;
   Santa Barbara spill 79–80
Okie, William Thomas 25
Olmstead, Frederick Law 5
open spaces 37, 78, 117
organized violence 11
Orr, Kevyn 142
outdoor recreation 48

Packing Them In (Washington) xxiii
Palchlopek, Michael W. 98
Paradise Valley 3, 19
Patrick, William T. 74
PCB *see* polychlorinated biphenyl (PCB)
Pearson, Harold 54
People of Color Environmental Leadership
   Summit xxiii
Peterson, Sarah Jo 32
Philips, Norman 99
phosphate detergents, banning 113–114
P.J. Hoffmaster State Park 42
Pointe Mouilleé Wildlife Refuge 58
pollution 51; abatement 1, 76; air 54–55,
   76, 83, 129; industrial 49–50, 80; noise
   51; oil 57–58, 62, 79–80
Pollution Action League 77–78
polychlorinated biphenyl (PCB) 123, 124
poor housing 11–12, 15
Pope, Betty 7
Price, William L. 18, 19
public health 6–8, 14
public housing 4, 11

racial inequalities 10
racial segregation 1
racial violence, at Belle Isle 30
Rat Extermination and Control Bill 96
rat infestations 6, 96–97
Ravitz, Mel 92
Reagan, Ronald 127
recreational inequalities, within states 99
recreational provision 36–37
Rector, Josiah 85, 128, 130
redlining 10
regionalism 121
re-housing plans 18
Resettlement Administration 28
residential segregation 3–4, 9, 11, 14
restrictive covenants, racially 10
Reuther, Roy 55–56
Reuther, Walter xvi, 4, 33–34, *33*, 71, 84;
   and UAW leadership 77–78, 82; critique
   of industrial capitalism 81; about Earth
   Day 81–82; environmental teach-in

80; red-baiting crusade 103; support to
   Great Society 69–70
Richards, Glenn 8
Ripple (Red) xvii, 101
Rivera, Diego 140, *141*, 142, 144
river pollution 58
River Rouge 75, *75*, 78–79, 98, 140, *141*
Rockefeller, Laurance 41
Rome, Adam 39, 80
Romney, George 93, 96
Roosevelt, Eleanor 1, *2*, 8
Roosevelt, Franklin 28
Roosevelt, Theodore 69
Rouge Factory 75–76
Rouge River 58
Royal Oak 90

sanitation services 8, 41, 98–99
Santa Barbara oil spill 79–80, 124
Save Our Streams (Van Coevering) 49–50
Scheele, Leonard 8
Schofield, Samuel 12
SEMCOG *see* Southeast Michigan Council
   of Governments (SEMCOG)
sewage systems xxi, 39, 59, 62, 114 *see also*
   Super Sewer system
Sheeler, Charles 140
Shelley v. Kraemer case 10–11
Siegel Management Company 97
Sierra Club xx, xxi, 64, 125, 127, 129
"silent" health threats 51
Silent Spring (Carson) 48, 59, 64, 123
slow violence/slow disaster 46n88
slum clearance xxii, 1, 3, 13; in Black
   Bottom 14, 128; and DUL 15, 93;
   Housing Act of 1949 33; and public
   health 6–8; for removing black people
   91
Smith, Mildred 90
smoke regulations 53–54
Snyder, Dan 142
Sojourner Truth housing project 4
Solidarity (UAW's periodical) 61, 63–64
Southeast Michigan xviii, 27, 39
Southeast Michigan Council of
   Governments (SEMCOG) 114, 122
Speck, Edward 49
sporting lands 50
sportsmen, in Detroit 59–60
Stacey, Charles 54
Stanecki, Jerry 125
Starling, Juanita 96–97
State Water Resources Commission 57–58
Steel Labor 72

Steering Committee 79
Stein, Murray 71
Sterling, Morton 78
Stokes, Carl 79, 103
Stradling, David 79, 103
Stradling, Richard 79, 103
substandard housing 6, 14
suburban sprawl 27, 39, 59–60, 115, 122
suburbs, overdevelopment of xviii
Superfund 125
Super Sewer system 113–116
sustainability xxiv–xxv
Sweet, Ossian 10
synthetic insecticides 59

Tanner, Howard 122
Thomas, Danny 98
Thomas, June Manning 14–15, 96, 128
Thomas, R.J. 32
toxic hazards 123
Toxic Substances Control Act (TSCA) 124, 126
toxic waste landfill 130
Toxic Wastes and Race xxiii
To Your Industrial Health! (radio program) 47–48, 51–53
transportation revolution (1956) 19
Truman, Harry 13, 33, *33*
TSCA *see* Toxic Substances Control Act (TSCA)
tuberculosis 2–3, 7

U.S. Census Bureau 6
UAW *see* United Auto Workers (UAW)
UAW-CIO Health Institute 53
Udall, Stewart 71
UEC *see* Urban Environment Conference (UEC)
union environmentalism xxii
Union Oil Company 79–80
United Action for Clear Water conference 71
United Auto Workers (UAW) xxii, xxiii, xxiv, 127; 1967 uprising 72–74; environmental teach-in to Earth Day 80–83; environmental transformed agenda 83–85; factories shifted to war preparation 4, 32; Health and Safety Department 53; Health Institute 51; Local 600 76; natural resources policy 77; Olga Madar and 70–72; Pollution Action Line 78; radio program 47–48; raising environmental consciousness 50; Recreation Department 118–120;

responsibility in environmental matters 63–64; shop-floor environmentalism 74–77; *Solidarity* periodical 61, 63–64; *War on Pollution* 69, 77–80
United Church of Christ xxiii
United Community Services 7
United Nations Symposium of the Environment at Onaway 82
United States Public Health Service 56
United Steel Workers (USW) 72
urban crisis xx–xxi, xxiv, 27, 38, 40; UAW and 69–85; black environmentalism, 90–108
urban environment 73–74
urban environmental activism xxii
Urban Environment Conference (UEC) 125
Urban League 91, 125
urban planning 1, 6–8, 38
urban renewal plans xvii, 15–16, *17*, 19, 90, 100–101
urban resilience 38
urban revitalization 99
USW *see* United Steel Workers (USW)
utopianism 32

Van Coevering, Jack 48–50; against oil pollution 58–62; *Save Our Streams* 49–50
vest-pocket parks 74

Wagner-Ellender-Taft Bill 11–13
war mobilization 31
War on Poverty programs 72–73
Warren County 124
wartime mobilization 3–6
Washington, Sylvia Hood xxiii
Washington Post 69
waste-to-energy incinerator 128–133
water pollution 56–57
Water Resources Commission 50, 56–57
Wayne County 30–31, 39, 120
Wayne State University 73, 99, 100–101
WCO *see* West Central Organization (WCO)
Westacres 28–29
West Central Organization (WCO) 94–95; living with rats 96–97; recreation and wreck-creation 97–100
white people xviii, 10; abandonment of city 103–104; conflicts against black people 5–7, 97–98; COVID-19 pandemic 143; escaping unhealthful conditions 3; housing project 9–10; toxic battle 130

152 Index

Who Killed Lake Erie? (NBC documentary) 114
Whyte, William 61
Wiesner, Robert 76
Williams, Mary 73
Williams, Robert 4
Williams, Roy Lee 93
Windsor, Canada 54
women, environmental health risks in 52
Wonder, Stevie xvii

Woodcock, Leonard 82, 84–85
working class: communities xxii; conservationism 58, 60; environmentalism 48, 85
workplace toxic hazards 123
World War II xix, 33
Wright, Frank Lloyd 25
Wyandotte 79

Young, Coleman 17, 102–105, 128–129, 133

Printed in the United States
by Baker & Taylor Publisher Services